BUSTING THE BRASS CEILING

BUSTING THE BRASS CEILING

How a Heroic Female Cop Changed the Face of Policing

Fanchon Blake and Linden Gross

INTEGRATED MEDIA
NEW YORK

All rights reserved, including without limitation the right to reproduce this book or any portion thereof in any form or by any means, whether electronic or mechanical, now known or hereinafter invented, without the express written permission of the publisher.

This work is a memoir. It reflects the author's present recollections of her experiences over a period of years. Some names and identifying characteristics have been changed in order to protect the identity of certain individuals. Any resulting resemblance to persons living or dead is entirely coincidental and unintentional.

Copyright © 2020 by Linden Gross

ISBN: 978-1-5040-9672-0

This edition published in 2024 by Open Road Integrated Media, Inc.
180 Maiden Lane
New York, NY 10038
www.openroadmedia.com

Dedicated to female police officers everywhere.

FOREWORD

by Joseph Wambaugh

Fanchon Blake has been a hero of mine for many years. Her contribution to the equality of women and other minorities is immeasurable. During her twenty-five years on the force, sex discrimination limited Fanchon's career. Despite her dedication, her talent, and her tenacity, she was not allowed to even try to promote beyond the rank of sergeant. The LAPD simply didn't allow women to hold higher positions.

Although many of her female colleagues didn't dare speak out, Fanchon refused to join what she would call the silent force. She complained to her superiors, to the LAPD brass, to the city council, and to the police commission. She paid a price for speaking her mind. The department punished her attempts to challenge the status quo by banishing her to less than desirable posts. Still, she continued to fight the LAPD's blatant sexual discrimination and to push for parity. Eventually, Fanchon realized that she would never be able to change the LAPD's anti-female culture from within. So she sued.

She single-handedly initiated one of the country's landmark Title VII cases. "You stood a combat line and had little, if any, support from others," reads a letter written to Fanchon by LAPD veteran Robert F. Rock, who briefly held the position of interim LAPD chief of police.

Fanchon's actions, seen by many as a betrayal of the LAPD's codes of silence and loyalty, did not go unpunished. Retaliatory intimidation tactics against the whistleblower extended past the silent treatment from fellow officers to active harassment. Despite being afraid for her safety, she did not falter. Fanchon and her attorneys waged a tough battle against not just one daunting foe but two—the LAPD and the City of Los Angeles. And in 1980, after seven long years, they prevailed.

Her case would make history not just for women, but for minorities as well, because the U.S. Justice Department had filed its own employment discrimination lawsuit on behalf of non-whites being discriminated against on the LAPD, and then consolidated its case with Fanchon's. When the Supreme Court let the Ninth Circuit Court of Appeals ruling stand, the LAPD was forced to agree to a historic consent decree. They would increase the number of sworn female officers on the force to 20 percent. And they would increase the number of minorities on the force to a ratio commensurate with minority representation in the Los Angeles workforce. In addition, both women and minorities would be allowed equal rights for career opportunity and advancement.

"This tough ex-cop and former Army major is the reason why there are now female lieutenants and captains on the Los Angeles Police Department—and why there may eventually be female commanders, deputy chiefs, and possibly even a woman chief of police," reads a 1990 *Los Angeles Times* article, one of dozens written about this trailblazer. Part of that prediction has already come true. Since Fanchon's case was finally settled forty years ago, the number of sworn female officers in the department has climbed to more than 18,000 which represents just over 18 percent of the force as compared to a national average of about 12 percent. Women account for 20 percent of the LAPD's captains. And five women now hold positions of LAPD commander or above, including Beatrice Girmala, assistant chief of police, and Regina Scott, the first Black female on the department to achieve the rank of deputy chief.

Fanchon is also the reason that, in 2020, a full 70 percent of the LAPD's sworn officers are non-white.

The class action that Fanchon spearheaded helped end institutionalized sexual and racial discrimination practices not just in the LAPD, but law in enforcement in general. Because of the precedent it set in civil rights law, Fanchon's crusade for women's rights has impacted—and improved—workplaces across the country. We owe her our respect and our gratitude.

BUSTING THE BRASS CEILING

"They've moved out of the society that would have protected them, and into the dark forest, into the world of fire, of original experience. Original experience has not been interpreted for you, and so you've got to work out your life for yourself. Either you can take it, or you can't. You don't have to go far off the interpreted path to find yourself in very difficult situations. The courage to face the trials and to bring a whole new body of possibilities into the field of interpreted experience for other people to experience—that is the hero's deed."

—Joseph Campbell, *The Power of Myth*

PROLOGUE

I loved being a cop on the streets, even in the 1940s, when women were not supposed to be doing things like that. I loved being an investigator. I aspired to be the first female chief of police on the Los Angeles Police Department (LAPD), just as I had aspired to be the first female general in the Army. But during my twenty-five-year career on the department, neither my female colleagues nor I could ever reach our potential.

The name Fanchon means freedom. All my life, I have struggled to achieve that. So in 1973, after my efforts, along with those of others, to engender change within the department had repeatedly failed, I finally sued.

Claiming equal opportunity rights does not make me a man-hater. I held high admiration for many of the male police officers with whom I worked. Claiming all my rights, however, did make me controversial.

The LAPD, like so much of the rest of the world in those days, practiced wholehearted discrimination against women. It was an accepted way of life, a world view. Changing it was inconceivable. The United States Constitution had awarded women voting rights. The Civil Rights Act had declared that I was equal to men. But in the LAPD, policewomen weren't allowed to promote past the rank of sergeant, which curtailed not only our professional advancement and pay scale, but also our pensions. For many years, we had to wear skirts and high heels, and carry our guns and handcuffs in our purses. We were considered weak and incapable of apprehending criminals. Worse, the department held our male counterparts accountable for our safety, which they understandably resented. By the early '50s, we had been barred from regular police patrol assignments and relegated to safe assignments such as administration, community relations, or tasks related to females and juveniles. Being excluded from street patrol, a requirement for promotion, squashed any potential advancement.

Every time I rebelled at restrictions the LAPD placed on my career, I was labeled a troublemaker. It did not take a genius to understand that the real roadblock to changing the status of females on LAPD lay in the deeply ingrained attitudes of most male officers. Still influenced by the Victorian age that had long since passed, they perceived women as inferior to men—unable to make decisions or care for themselves as cops. No real he-man would tolerate a female giving him orders. Besides, most everyone "knew" that maintaining law and order required the kind of physical strength and intimidation that only a man could provide.

Ironically, in 1991, the Independent Commission on the Los Angeles Police Department, known as the Christopher Commission and formed in response to the Rodney King beating, would find that manifesting feminine behaviors and avoiding masculine ones caused female officers to outperform their male counterparts. The report indicated that women were rarely cited for using more force than necessary, in large part because female officers are "more communicative, more skillful at de-escalating potentially violent situations, and less confrontational ... Many officers, both male and female, believe female officers are less personally challenged by defiant subjects and feel less need to deal with defiance with immediate force or confrontational language."

Because there was "persuasive evidence that most female officers use a style of policing that minimizes the use of excessive force and inappropriate confrontations," the Commission concluded, "the continued existence of discrimination against female officers can deprive the department of specific skills and thereby contribute to the problem of excessive force." Their recommendation: Feminize the force.

A 2005 study titled "Women Police: The Use of Force by and Against Female Officers" reaffirmed those assertions. "The findings suggest that female officers and same-gender female-female officer pairs generally use less force in police-citizen encounters than do their male counterparts. The influence of officer gender remained significant even after considering other potentially perplexing factors including gender differences in the need to use high levels of force and bias associated with extreme scores for a small group of male officers. There was no evidence to support the proposition that citizens used less force against female officers compared to male officers. Overall, the findings support the original assertions that women and men perform policing duties differently and that hiring more women as police officers may help to reduce excessive force in some police departments."

Unfortunately, police training has emphasized the opposite. Police officers have been overly desensitized to killing during training, which builds an unreal fear base. Day in and day out for one solid year of probation, they've heard, "If you do that, you'll get wasted." Add to this equation the notion that the male must constantly prove himself to be a man according to the standards set by the men around him and a culture that demands a code of silence, and you wind up with a toxic mix.

"Police work is not about physical altercations . . . [or] about shooting people," my friend Joseph Wambaugh, a fourteen-year veteran of the LAPD and bestselling author of police and crime books, told an interviewer in 1991. He stipulated that we need women police chiefs and police forces of "50 percent women or more" because "female cops can go a long way toward helping to mitigate the super-aggressive, paramilitary macho myth of the gung-ho cop and introducing the sobering element of maturity in police work."

A 1992 *Time* magazine article agreed with that premise:

> *The growing presence of women may help burnish the tarnished image of police officers, improve community relations, and foster a more flexible, and less violent, approach to keeping the peace.*

The heart of social oppression is power and control through the use of accepted discrimination. It's an underlying, ugly practice that fosters hate and violence. We've still got a lot of work to do on that front. Still, we've come a long way.

When I was on the department, the LAPD could not fathom the potential of Title VII of the Civil Rights Act of 1964 (as amended by the Equal Employment Act of 1972) or begin to envision the traumatic social change destined to unfold from its enactment. To a woman, myself included, the department's female officers were cowed by fear and dared not confront the chief of police about higher promotions and better assignments for women. But I would come to know firsthand that as long as people refuse to honor guaranteed rights and as long as aggrieved people refuse to act, discrimination persists.

When we are denied our civil rights and freedoms, and we

raise no hand to stop the denial, we are guilty of deserting human dignity. Freedom is based on courage. Only by challenging that power and control can democracy deliver a reality of the people, by the people, and for the people. Fortunately, change, however long it takes, cannot be stopped.

PART I

1

ENOUGH!

The words CONFIDENTIAL SURVEY caught my attention. I picked up the paper and read: *A Survey to Justify Why Men Do Not Want to Work with Policewomen.* I loved the LAPD. But I sure didn't love the way they treated the women on the force. Were things about to get worse?

I looked around the LAPD squad room, where I worked as a detective investigating forgery, but no one was paying attention to me. I gazed again at the paper I held. It was from the chief's office, complete with an authenticated signature. For years, I had protested the fact that no new women officers were being hired, and that a substantial number of female sworn officers had already been reassigned to desk jobs. Now it seemed that management was setting up a justification to eliminate women from the job altogether.

Surely, the chief had more brains than to try to circulate something as bizarre as this survey, but nobody else would dare take that kind of action without his knowledge. I couldn't let this go unchallenged. I would have to flush it out into the open, which meant confronting the chief. I couldn't do that alone. He would crucify me.

I convinced the president of the Los Angeles Policewomen's Association to ask the chief to explain the blatantly anti-female survey to his female officers. Surprisingly, he agreed to meet with us on January 13, 1971.

"It's been brought to my attention that the men do not want to work with women," he announced after taking the stage in the police auditorium in front of about one hundred of us. "The survey confirms this allegation."

The fact that he didn't deny the survey seemed to confirm what we had suspected all along. He'd had a hand in the survey from the beginning.

"As you know," he continued, "I'm in the process of re-evaluating the entire structure of the police department."

He proceeded to explain that he planned to reduce the number of women officers from some one hundred eighty down to no more than twelve. Perhaps female reserve officers could be used for those situations where the handling of a female required a woman to be present, he hypothesized.

My God! I could feel my blood pressure rise. I gripped the arms of my seat and tightened my lips to keep from saying anything.

He whispered a few words to Deputy Chief Dale Speck, who stood beside him, and then turned back to us. "And, ladies, if you have questions, I'll answer what I can."

I could feel the shared anger as I heard the women mutter.

"The bastard!"

"How dare he?"

"What can we do?"

I could also sense how scared they were to challenge the chief. Unable to stand it any longer, I rose to be recognized. "Chief Davis," I said.

He peered out from under his hand, shading his eyes. "Fanchon. That you, Fanchon?"

"Yes, sir."

"I was a little nervous," he said. "I thought you'd never speak up." He and Speck laughed.

"Sir, I find it difficult to believe what I've heard from you today. Do you mean to tell me and the rest of these women who have been screened, trained, and worked as police officers that we're not qualified? There's Sergeant Leola Vess with her master's degree in psychology. Sergeant Marie Thomas with her law degree. Sergeant Jerry Lambert with her bio-scientific degree. Sergeant Marjorie Cramer who speaks, reads, and writes seven foreign languages fluently. That's just to name a few. Myself with a major's military commission. All the women have graduated from the police academy. And you're standing here, telling us that we can't be assigned to police responsibilities?"

He nodded. "I knew you'd get my meaning. I believe street detail is beneath the dignity of a woman. You have no business playing cops like the men."

"That's your opinion, sir. Every corporation in this city would gladly recruit this caliber of women to work for them. We're one hundred and eighty educated, intelligent women capable of far more than we've been allowed to demonstrate." I sat down.

"The idea of a woman becoming a lieutenant is ridiculous," he countered. "You know you can't handle the pressures of the job." He stepped away from the podium to the edge of the stage. "You know what I mean. You have your little monthlies and go through the change of life."

Our little monthlies! Was he kidding? He had actually just said out loud that a woman's period was reason enough to deny her advancement?

Davis' insulting comments shocked the other policewomen as much as me. He had become so cocksure of himself since the city council had passed his recent reorganization ordinance that he couldn't resist boasting about his intentions to phase most of us off the department. He clearly felt there wasn't a damned thing I or anybody could do to stop him.

Not since marching in unison with a battalion of WACs (Women's Army Corps) at Fort Des Moines in the '40s had I felt more in step with my fellow female officers. The department's refusal to let us promote had been as irrational as it was infuriating. And now this.

I stared at the chief and clenched my teeth. I wouldn't let him get away with eliminating women from the job just because of our sex.

You don't know it, Chief, I thought, *but war has just been declared between us. I'll not be your pawn. A queen checkmates a king.*

He had already established his position, but by raising a stink, I could take his chessmen. I would appear at every commission and council hearing I could when the subject of policewomen was on their agendas. He would come to know I was not afraid to fight.

Determination is fine, but strategy wins the war. I figured if I were going to step into the waters, I would stand a better chance if I found highly positioned women to back me. I knew just who I needed to approach. Through my work in the bunco-forgery division, I had gotten the opportunity to deal with Judge Joan Dempsey Klein, an appeals judge who would become California's senior presiding justice, in court. A woman judge on our side would add clout to my mission.

Judge Klein was as smart as she was down to earth. "Just a minute," she had once remarked when a policeman was on the stand. "Are you wearing a black shoe and a brown shoe?" That just tickled me. I figured she would take my call, and I was right.

"I have a matter to discuss with you," I said. "I'd like an appointment."

"Fine," she answered. "Let's go to lunch."

Over burgers at the Hamburger Hamlet, I explained the pattern of discrimination that the women on the LAPD, myself included, had been subjected to. As a pioneer in the legal arena and one of the few women on the bench, she, too, had battled to push her way into a male-dominated profession. Along the way, she had met, in her words, a huge headwind of opposition. So she understood all too well what we women on the LAPD were up against. She didn't mince words.

"Sue the bastards, Fanchon," she said. "You women have been waiting years for the chief to bestow rank. It will never happen. They have no intention of elevating women. You'll have to fight for equality or accept what you've always been given—token positions."

That was assuming we stayed on the force at all since the chief wanted to get rid of us. Someone had to have enough guts to take this fight to the courts. I wondered whether that someone would be me.

2

JUMPING INTO POLICE WORK

I knew nothing about the Los Angeles Police Department in 1947 when I began the civil service written, oral, physical agility, and physical examinations, each designed to weed out candidates. At age twenty-six, after a successful five-year Army career, which included serving in World War II and being promoted to captain, I had left to get married. The happy union—my second—lasted just six months.

I could have been sucked into that vortex of self-pity, but that's just not the type of person I am. Instead, I sat up in bed one morning, threw the covers off, and bounced out of bed as I recounted my blessings. How lucky that I had my sister Jean's love, support, and hospitality. My high school diploma would be worth something. And surely the rank of captain wouldn't be ignored. Change my attitude, and I would change my life. I would take what I had accomplished and find a job.

Eventually, I relocated to Los Angeles after landing a temporary three-month contract as a county deputy sheriff overseeing women inmates in one of the local jails. But I wanted fieldwork, and the LAPD was offering downtown beat assignments and higher pay. Besides, being a cop just felt right to me. In middle school, I was a hall guard. I joined the Army after high school and became a captain. It was as if this kind of work was in my blood.

All the LAPD had to do was show me how to perform. I stood up straight and grinned. *We'll clean up Main Street,* I thought. *I can take care of myself.* I felt my formed muscle underneath my shirt sleeve. *If I have to, I can fight dirty.*

I could already see myself in LAPD blues, having passed the written examination, when I learned the physical agility test to be held at the police academy required scaling a six-foot wall. Not even in the WAC officer's class did I have to do more than twenty mandatory push-ups. But this was the vaunted LAPD pre-hire physical agility test, which would dramatically cut the list of female applicants.

I knew I would do well in the shooting portion of the trial. When I was eight and living in California's isolated Tehachapi Mountains, my dad had taught me to shoot so I could protect myself from snakes. Oh, yes, I could accurately hit my prey. But I was less confident about the rest of the test.

I needed to practice. So I headed out to the police academy in Elysian Park. I wasn't prepared for the scenic view as I drove under the filigreed black-iron police academy sign. The early morning sun rose through the eucalyptus treetops that hugged the sloping ravine. Then I saw the six-foot wall standing by itself on the athletic field across the road from the academy building. I froze. I wasn't about to find out if I could get over it in plain view, especially since I hadn't engaged in that type of physical activity since climbing live oak trees as a seven-year-old.

I returned well after hours a few days later, determined to learn how to get over that wall. No luck. For the next three weeks, I spent many moonlit hours trying to figure out the technique of running, jumping, and vaulting over the wall. Night after night, I went home battered and bruised, but I persisted. Then, just forty-eight hours before the scheduled test, having watched how the men used leverage, I found the rhythm and coordination that put me over that infernal wall. It was a miracle how easy it was. After several more flyovers, I landed on my feet. I couldn't control the victory yell that erupted. I was ready.

It wasn't easy waiting my turn as I watched one woman after another struggle to pull their hanging bodies over the top and fail. "On your mark," the timer barked. "Get ready, go." My gym shoes dug into the dirt path as I ran. I timed my lead. My feet slammed the wall waist-high, as my hands grabbed the top. I used my momentum to swing my big butt, which felt like it weighed a hundred pounds, up and over. I had beaten the wall, the one significant elimination for most failed applicants! I landed in a crouch and took off through a maze of flat tires, pumping my knees and hoping I wouldn't fall on my rear end. Thankfully, running the tires, which hadn't shown up until today, proved less challenging than mastering the technique of vaulting the wall. I completed the test at a full-speed run around the oval field. A thumbs-up from the male officer sent my spirits soaring. Now I just had to get through my orals, having already passed the written portion.

To help prepare for the oral and written exams, at the first of the year I had enrolled in the University of Southern California's criminal law class on penal code. On the last day of the semester, I raced to class, anxious to learn how I had fared on the final test. At five o'clock, the downtown, second-floor classroom felt like a sauna. As the only woman, I chose to sit in the rear behind twenty male police officers. Our instructor from the

Los Angeles Police Department leaned against the blackboard with his hands in his pockets. When he pushed away from the wall, his tweed jacket flapped open, showing his .38 detective special and the badge on his belt. *Where would I wear a gun?* I wondered. Under my armpits, I would run into trouble with a thirty-eight-inch bust. Around my waist, it would be bulky in women's clothing.

He looked around the room at each of us. When his black eyes reached mine, I looked away. "The final exam was a surprise, gentlemen. The lady in this class takes the honors."

My hands flew to my mouth—he was talking about me.

Every head turned to stare. "Excuse me, gentlemen," the handsome instructor said. "I need to have a word with Fanchon. It'll only take a few seconds."

After a whole semester, I had finally caught his attention, but I couldn't imagine what he wanted to talk to me about. He bent over until his lips were close to my ear. A whiff of sweet-smelling aftershave sent a thrill up my back.

"Would you mind leaving early?" he whispered, his voice raspy as usual.

That thrill in my back vanished as I shut my notebook and reached for my purse. He touched my arm and moved to look directly into my eyes. "I'm not used to a woman in my class," he said. "On the last day of a semester, I tell off-color jokes. It helps the men loosen up, especially if they're disappointed."

He straightened and turned from me. I gathered my belongings and was pulling the door shut when I heard, "There goes another Dickless Tracy." The men roared with laughter. What a bastard! Angry but undaunted, I tucked away the put-down for future ammunition and focused on qualifying to become a cadet at the police academy. I knew I would have to place in the upper 10 percent to qualify.

When the letter with the city seal arrived several weeks after my oral exam, I poured a scotch and soda, sat on the couch, and tore it open. I whooped when I saw the words *You are directed to report to the police academy on May 17th, 1948, at 8:00 a.m.* Thank God.

I had struggled to make this happen. Three months of experience as a county jailer had convinced me I didn't want to be a turnkey on the thirteenth floor of the women's jail at the Hall of Justice. Recently divorced, I was emotionally depleted, broke, and terrified that I couldn't take care of myself. With this call to report to the Los Angeles Police Academy, I could change my life.

On May 17, 1948, two days after my 27th birthday, the bright morning with blue skies matched my optimism. I strode up the winding road in Elysian Park, passed male trustees from the city jail cleaning the street gutters, and entered the police academy through the brick gates. The grounds spread out on both sides of the arroyo nestled in a pocket of the foothills. Despite my high heels, I swung my shoulders as I walked, a habit I had retained from marching in the Army. I turned right to pass the small-arms firing range with its black silhouetted targets held at the ready, passed under the tree-covered walkway that bordered the Olympic-size swimming pool, and joined other women candidates gathered in the shade of the gymnasium. Across the road on the elevated oval athletic field, male recruits in gray sweats did push-ups. Further to the east and out of sight, I heard the rapid-fire of another combat range.

Waiting with the other candidates, I caught my first glimpse of Sergeant Mary Galton as she hurried from the gymnasium. Despite the heat, she wore a small, white hat over her short blonde hair. She moved with ease in her blue and white seersucker suit. Her white-gloved hand clasped a clipboard to her bosom. She stopped next to me and didn't smile as she waited for quiet. Her flushed face couldn't hide the aging lines of an older woman. "Ladies, quiet, please!" Her high-pitched voice made me flinch. If she had been in the Army, she would have been required to drop down an octave. "There'll be no more talking," she said. "Listen to directions. Ask questions."

"How can I ask questions if I can't talk?" I blurted.

Her steel-blue eyes cut through me. My blood iced. She held her gaze, and then her eyes swept my body from head to toe. "Your name?" she snapped, her pencil poised to write.

From years of military discipline, I snapped to attention, rendered a stiff military salute, and bellowed, "Prichard, ma'am" (my married name at the time). My military response startled me, as well as the other candidates.

In a loud voice, she said, "Smart alecks are washed out. Do as you're told."

I lowered my voice. "Yes, ma'am." Red-faced, I silently vowed I would mind my tongue.

She escorted us to the corner classroom, over the Revolver Club offices on the second floor of the vast gymnasium, where we were seated alphabetically. Galton adjusted her glasses, wrote her name on the blackboard, and waited for us to quiet.

"I'm your six-week academy supervisor. Take the badge on your desk and pin it over your heart. Wear it every day. If you lose it, you'll be washed out."

The oblong shield covered the palm of my hand and felt surprisingly heavy. At the top of this emblem of power, in blue letters, the word *Policewoman*, made a crescent over the image of City Hall embossed in gold. The number eighty-six at the bottom, slang for being kicked out, made me smile.

"You're the second class of women to receive academy training," Sergeant Galton said. "You're making history as the first class to be trained on the gun range. You'll be the first to graduate in full dress uniform and walk a beat." She paused. "It won't be easy, ladies. What you do and how you perform will be closely monitored. The men will be watching you. And, I might add, they'll be waiting for you to fail.

"Buy your handcuffs and revolvers downstairs. I'll tell you where to purchase your uniforms. The police credit union will advance you a loan of $350 to cover your initial costs. And ladies, bad debts are cause for immediate termination even after your twelve months of probation."

Everything she said ended with the threat of being sacked. Without a word, just a nod, Galton picked up her papers from the rostrum and left. Just then, the male recruits thundered up the stairs, running double-time past our classroom, and the same lieutenant who had taught the preparatory class I had taken before my exams stepped through the door. I hadn't realized he taught here.

He looked at his notes. "You, you," he shouted as he pointed to two women in the front row. "Take your belongings and report to Sergeant Galton in her office."

A tall, lithe woman with a mannish haircut and a smaller woman next to her eased from their chairs. They bumped into each other and hurried out the door. The lieutenant followed them with his eyes and then turned to face us. "They didn't last long," he said. "That's the last of those queer bitches!"

I was aghast. Those women hadn't done anything wrong. Besides, how did the department know those women were gay? Was *I* tainted because I had been in the military?

The lieutenant hooked his thumbs in his pockets and smiled. "Some of you will be gone by graduation," he said. "Half of you will be terminated by the end of the year. Face it, ladies. You broads will never be the cops that men are."

I could barely breathe; my internal pressure gauge was sitting on red. How dare he talk to us like that? At 5'9" with a robust and healthy body, I could hold my own on the LAPD or the street. I wanted to explode, but I didn't dare open my mouth, or I would be the next wash-out. Galton had done me a favor by disciplining me in front of the other cadets. I would not get a second chance if I made a mistake. But he sure wasn't making it easy for me to keep quiet.

"It's a man's world, ladies," he continued as he leaned on the lectern and pointed his finger at us. "You dames are more trouble than you're worth. You belong at home."

Almost five decades later, a secretive, all-male "club" within the LAPD, formed in the 1980s but still operating under the same bias, would be exposed. The mission of Men Against Women (MAW) as it was known to some or White Anglo Saxon Police (WASP) as it was known to others: To harass and drive from the force women officers and other minority group officers, and to intimidate male officers who fraternized with their non-white male counterparts.

While I had no way of knowing how entrenched this bigoted attitude was on the LAPD, the lieutenant had made it clear that we women weren't exactly welcome here. I looked away. I knew he was trying to bait us, but I wasn't biting.

3

DOING A MAN'S JOB

Despite the negative reception, I knew I could withstand the pressure and hack it no matter what anyone thought. I could be tough. I had survived the raw wilderness of the Tehachapi Mountains during the Depression and lived in the Eastside of Los Angeles. No one intimidated me. I would hold onto my badge no matter what.

I couldn't wait to perform all the duties of a police officer. I had no love for indoor tasks, a sentiment that would be reinforced after working in the Lincoln Heights Jail, located across the Los Angeles River, during a subsequent part of this probationary period. *The more police action I can become involved in, the happier I'll be*, I thought.

When Sergeant Leola Vess appeared in the roll call room of Georgia Street juvenile division, ten teams of uniformed policewomen put out their cigarettes and waited for her to begin. Tall and slim with short, dark hair, bright lipstick, and matching nail polish, Vess wore a gray sharkskin suit and complementary small veiled hat. A square, black police purse hung from her shoulder, her gloves tucked under the flap. Her high heels tapped lightly on the bare wooden floors as she moved to the front. She picked up the clipboard and waited for total attention, then called each name and flashed a smile of approval as she inspected our grooming. Next, she named the beat patrol and partner assignments.

Vess had been the first woman ever promoted to sergeant in the LAPD, and I studied her every move. Her quiet, no-nonsense talk projected a professional polish I envied. "Before you leave for your beats," she said, "the lieutenant who oversees street patrol has ordered you to keep your guns holstered. I'm to remind you that you're not out there to clean up Main Street. You're to concentrate on missing juveniles and curfew violators. No headlines, ladies. Stay out of trouble."

Vess's admonition cooled my exuberance. Her orders were clear. Female teams were to refrain from becoming involved with adult arrests. I resented the LAPD's limitations on my scope of duty merely because I was a woman. I would also quickly come to resent how we were treated—not on the street, but in the department. While some of the male officers were gentlemen, most made it clear they didn't want women muscling in on their turf. It not only got raunchy, but it also got nasty.

Even so, I was in heaven. I was a cop walking a beat. I was young and idealistic, and I was saving the City of Los Angeles. At least that's what I thought at the time.

I had drawn Mickey Dunbar as my partner. A smaller woman than I, with brown hair that curled around her hat, she was an ex-WAVE (a World War II-era division of the U.S. Navy) from the East Coast. We had been assigned a beat on Main, between First and Ninth Streets, in downtown Los Angeles. Although our duties were usually limited to flushing out missing juveniles in a bus station or hauling a teenage curfew violator out of one of the seedy, all-night theaters in that neighborhood, few nights passed without some action.

Between five and ten o'clock at night, Sixth and Main Street's bustling transportation terminals spewed passengers from streetcars and buses. As they waited to make cross-town connections, they shared the sidewalks with derelicts. I would watch the homeless, with bottles of cheap wine in brown, crumpled bags clutched to their chests, find refuge in grimy alley corners behind the burlesque theater.

Garish neon signs lit the outsides of bars and peep shows with their bawdy posters of naked women, while the foul air from inside wafted to the street. The residue of vomit, urine, and semen was never cleaned off the floors in these places, so I dreaded having to enter in response to a police call. While I couldn't see the accumulated slime in the darkness, I would feel my pumps slipping in it.

Aside from the heat, there was nothing special going on the evening Dunbar and I stopped for our coffee break at an open hot dog stand next to an alley. My brass buttons and my badge were the only items not affected by the steamy temperatures. Everything else was wet, wrinkled, or melting. Sweat seeped from under my hat. My white shirt and black tie wilted beneath my navy blue uniform jacket. My blue serge skirt felt so hot that I wanted to hike it up past my knees. It didn't help that my police purse containing eight pounds of gun, ammo, and handcuffs dug into my shoulder.

My partner and I eased onto wooden stools and kicked off our high heels at the open counter. Dunbar's exhaustion showed on her heart-shaped face. She lit a cigarette, inhaled a long, relaxing drag, closed her eyes, and slowly exhaled. I could never inhale without choking, so I blew smoke rings instead. As we sipped our coffee, the noise of the street quieted. Only the voice of a newspaper vendor roaring, "Extra! Extra! Getcha red-hot news" could be heard.

"Feels great to sit," Dunbar said. "I'll be glad when tonight ends. My feet hurt. God, look at them. Swollen. I wonder who dreamed up walking a beat in high heels."

"Remember to be ladies first and cops second," I parroted. "It's stupid. Who cares if we're ladies if we get the job done?"

I finished my coffee and applied fresh lipstick. "You ready to go?" I asked. It was time to get back to the beat. Suddenly I realized how silent the street had become. Even the newspaper vendor had stopped yelling. I sensed something was about to happen. I turned to my partner. "Mickey—"

Simultaneously, we heard the report of gunfire and a bullet ricochet off the brick wall over our heads. We threw ourselves down on the gritty sidewalk. The fry cook yelled, "Oh my God!" and disappeared behind the stand.

Footsteps pounded toward us as I tried to get into my policewoman's purse. During the fall, however, I had smashed the clasp on the flap, so I couldn't pull my gun free.

I could see Dunbar's legs in front of me. "You okay, Dunbar?" I asked and was mightily relieved when I saw her legs move.

"I'm scared, Prichard."

I gave up on the purse and flipped back onto my stomach. A rough-looking bearded man gasping for breath stormed out of the dark alley. As he cut around us, a small gun in hand, I clawed the cement to move toward him and kicked my leg out. Restricted by my standard-issue, navy blue skirt and required girdle, I missed tripping him. He bolted into a bar two doors away.

Dunbar staggered to her feet. "What the hell ya trying to do?" she screamed. "Get us killed?"

"Calm down," I said, surprised she thought I would put us at risk. "If I'd caught his ankle, I'd have bashed his head in with my purse. We would have nailed him cold."

I was shaken but also humiliated. We were on probation, but we were cops, and people were counting on us to protect them. I spotted a Gamewell box. In the days before cell phones or even police radios, we used the Gamewell phones, installed on nearly every block in downtown L.A., to communicate with headquarters.

Before I got to the Gamewell, an undercover agent whom we all called Jake burst from the dark alley.

"Where is that son-of-a-bitch?" he yelled, waving his .38 revolver.

I pointed, and he ran into the bar.

I yanked the flap of my purse. It broke loose, and I pulled out my gun and started for the bar. Dunbar grabbed my arm. "For God's sake, Prichard. We can't go in there."

I shook off her hand. "Jake's by himself. He needs help."

Before I could move, screeching sirens came from every direction. Three squad cars, red lights flashing, skidded to a halt in front of the bar. Plainclothes cops broke cover and came running with their badges hung on their shirts and their weapons drawn. Five shots exploded inside the bar.

"Watch it!" I shouted as Dunbar and I ducked into a recessed storefront. "We could get creamed by our own troops."

The men dropped to the ground, sheltering themselves behind parked cars. Police cars blocked traffic as people began to crowd around. Suddenly, the suspect reeled, glassy-eyed, out of the entrance of the bar. He stopped, fell backward, and smacked his head on the sidewalk. His arms flopped, his body jerked, and he lay quiet. Blood oozed from his black hair into a dark pool.

Oh, my God! I thought. *What could have been worth dying like that?*

Next, Jake staggered out of the bar, still clasping his revolver.

Blood soaked the shoulder of his plaid shirt, and his left arm hung limp. He weaved, straddle-legged, a few steps down the sidewalk and then fainted. An enormous, Black street person grabbed him as he fell and gently lowered him to the ground.

Dunbar tugged at my sleeve. "Prichard, I feel sick."

"Take a couple of deep breaths; it will pass. I don't feel so hot, either. We'll ring in as soon as the street clears; the lieutenant will want to know. I feel awful that we couldn't do anything."

"Yeah," she said. "And Sergeant Vess won't be happy with us. Look at our uniforms." She brushed at her skirt again. "We'd better get them cleaned up before she sees us."

"We'd better get our facts down," I said. "They'll want a written report before we go home. And, Dunbar, you can leave out that I finally freed my weapon."

I felt useless standing on the sidelines as the ambulance arrived. I watched as Jake was lifted onto a stretcher. He had lost a lot of blood; in his pallor, he looked almost dead. As for the suspect, the medics covered his body with a sheet.

In the crowd behind me, I heard someone say, "Goddamn cops! Wasted another one." The words cut through me. At our June graduation only months before, I had shot five bullets through the heart of the target silhouette. If I had been able to use my gun this time, maybe things would have turned out differently. But as it was, one man was dead, and a cop was seriously wounded.

Despite being conspicuous in our uniforms, the policemen on the scene ignored Dunbar and me. I was a cop, but, I realized with a jolt, I might as well have been one of the crowd.

At roll call the following evening, the lieutenant complimented us on taking care of ourselves and not becoming involved. I couldn't get over the quandary the shooting had helped crystallize. I had chosen to dedicate my life—my energy, my intelligence, my passion, and, most of all, my spirit—to a career I hoped would find me giving my best to help people in the worst moments of their lives. But because I was a woman, I wasn't allowed to do my job.

Walking the beat settled into a routine that was occasionally spiked by special assignments with male detectives. That was right where I wanted to be—in the middle of the action. I had no desire to be assigned to police desk work. I wanted to be a sleuth. The only problem was that aside from one policewoman chemist who was an expert on the intoxication field test, the choices for women officers largely boiled down to juveniles, jail, and desk work. The military had been a more level playing field than this.

I knew early on that the policewomen who fared the best were the ones who kept their mouths shut, did their jobs—even if that meant being stuck at a typewriter for eight hours—and went home. But I wasn't about to be that passive. Undaunted by overwhelming odds against promotion for women, I was determined to try for sergeant. I wouldn't be eligible until the summer of 1952, which meant I had four years to prepare for the written and oral examinations. My research indicated that most captains and those of higher rank in the LAPD were educated in police administration, a subject foreign to me. Aware that I would need more schooling to qualify for advancement, I signed up for the next available class.

In preparation for the first day, I purchased the text and studied the first chapter. References to budget and management concepts immediately challenged me. Already feeling insecure, I made my way to the classroom, which was filled with men. I slid into an empty seat in the front row and opened my notebook. Our instructor stood to make his opening remarks. He reminded me of my dad. His intense dark eyes stared at me.

"What are you doing in my class?" he asked with not a trace of a smile.

Embarrassed, I looked around. Was he talking to me? The men whispered. When I pointed to myself, questioningly, the lieutenant nodded.

"This is police administration, isn't it, sir?" I asked, thinking I was in the wrong class.

No one made a sound. After staring at me, his voice finally boomed, "Who okayed your admission to my class?"

I sat straighter and replied, "My money was accepted, sir."

"It's my policy, miss, to interview all new students before registration. You don't belong here."

I sprang out of my chair. "Sir, there was no mention of your policy when I enrolled."

He walked to the blackboard and wrote his name, his back to me. "I suggest, miss, that it would be to your advantage to drop this class."

"I was told there were openings. I'd like to stay."

The room grew so quiet that I could hear myself breathing. I tensed as the lieutenant returned to his desk and sat down. He fiddled with a pencil for a moment and then threw it down on the desk and stood up. "If you insist on staying, young lady, I don't see how you can be graded higher than an F!"

Face flushed and hands shaking, I picked up my books, took a deep breath, and squared my shoulders. I had to clench my jaw to keep my eyes dry, especially when the men began to stamp their feet in unison as I walked the ten or fifteen steps to the door. As the door slammed shut behind me, I heard them jeering. I was furious.

It was no use fighting to stay. I had to accept the humiliation. The instructor held so much influence in the department, all he needed to do was put out the word that I was a troublemaker, and I would never pass another oral. I couldn't even talk about what happened since that would brand me as emotional.

There had to be another way. In the meantime, however, my career at the LAPD wasn't exactly progressing as planned. Instead of the action I craved, I had been assigned to work vacation relief back at the Lincoln Heights Jail—a thankless, unchallenging job. Off duty, I became active with Police Post 381 of the American Legion, hoping to establish friendships with some of the men who were also military vets.

In July, I left for two weeks of military reserve training with the Women's Army Corps Center at Fort Lee, Virginia. I returned with a promotion to the 399th Military Police Battalion as an administrative officer. I was in high spirits.

Militarily, I outranked a majority of the LAPD male reservists. On the job, however, I was kept humble. After my stint at the Lincoln Heights Jail, I moved to the juvenile desk at Georgia Street Receiving Hospital, which lacked air-conditioning despite temperatures often rising into the high eighties. Since there was no centralized police station, most of the officers who worked downtown L.A. were located on the third floor of the brick building, one of the first built in the area. Our street-level office, however, sat right next to the covered ambulance drive-thru, so emergency sirens shrieked twenty-four hours a day as people in the city called for medical help.

In the middle of a siren blast, I answered the phone and was directed to report immediately to our watch commander. As I approached his office, I hoped this meant I was needed on a field assignment. Anything would be better than working that stifling hot desk.

We shook hands and sat. He cleared his throat as he fumbled with papers. "I see, Prichard, that you have completed probation."

I nodded.

He bent over to tie his shoe. "I understand that you have signed up with the active Army Reserves."

"Yes, sir. I signed up the same time as ninety-nine other policemen did." The lieutenant was so busy avoiding eye contact that I began to feel uncomfortable. Why was he interested in my military service, especially since, by law, he would have to honor it?

He raised his head. "You understand, of course, that when an employee is gone, it causes deployment problems?"

"No, sir! That is not my responsibility, sir. Volunteer military duty is covered by federal law. What I know is that when an employee is gone for any reason, the divisional commander resolves the absence." I was indignant, and it showed. "Do you have any complaints, sir, about my police work?"

"No, no, no, Prichard. You're doing fine. Do you plan to remain in the Army Reserves?"

His sudden question seemed inappropriate, but I answered, "Yes, sir." I watched him stiffen and realized he certainly wasn't going to talk to me about working another detail.

"I'd like to ask you, Prichard, about the women in the military. Are you aware of their reputation for homosexuality?"

There it was, that shadow that had caused me sleepless nights. Because I had served in the military, my sexuality was being questioned. At the time, I didn't recognize my proclivity toward homosexuality. I had dated only men, two of whom I had married. It would take me years to come to terms with my sexuality, which I buried more successfully than some and would question yet again years later. Still, instinctively, I knew

I had to be cautious. I had already witnessed how ruthless the men could be to those women they judged to be queer.

I would later figure out that the system itself was rigged against officers deemed to be lesbians. Even those who passed the written exam in the upper 90 percent got failed on the oral. The administration just used the system against them, which was the way it was designed. Standard operating procedure. They only elevated the ones they wanted.

As I thought about the two women candidates terminated at the academy, I recalled an interview I'd had with Sergeant Sydney Ball while still on probation. I had known I could be fired for almost any reason. So I felt anxious even before knocking on Sergeant Ball's door. I tucked in my shirt, cinched up my black belt, and made sure the oversize jail keys were securely fastened to my waist. I was ready.

Her small office at the south end of the fifth floor, equipped with a sink, a mirror, screened-off commode, and a rack to hang clothes, had no windows. Two straight-backed chairs with a small table in between sat close to the wall. The dim light made the area feel shabby. Sergeant Ball stood 5'2", and I towered over her. I wondered how she had qualified for the LAPD. Her singsong voice commanded, "Sit down, my dear. This won't take long." She didn't look at me. Instead, she opened a compact and applied powder as she spoke. "You'll be on the next transfer. I must write your final probation report and need to discuss your walk."

"My walk?" I asked. "What's the matter with my walk?"

Not lowering the compact, she looked into its mirror and exclaimed, "Oh, my dear! You do know that you stride like a man?"

I couldn't believe what I had just heard. My walk. Good God. Was that all she could find to criticize? How could I help how

I walked? Maybe I could take smaller steps. "Am I going to be washed out for the way I walk?"

She lowered the compact to look at me. "We women have to be so careful, Prichard. You know how cruel men are. They're much worse than women."

"Sergeant, I don't understand. What do the men have to do with my walk?"

She looked back into the compact and traced one eyebrow with her finger. "I'm required to discuss with you any adverse comments. Homosexuality."

I cut her off. "What does my walk have to do with that?" I took a small notebook and pencil from my shirt pocket and began to write. I needed to get the facts concerning this interview on paper. I noted that so far, there had been no accusation.

Ball snapped shut her compact. She stood up and smoothed her skirt, then leaned toward me, trying to see what I had written. Her voice was sharp as she asked, "What are you doing, Prichard?"

"I thought it might be wise to document this conversation."

"That will be all, Prichard. Return to your duties."

I had received no further comments about my gait, but the encounter had been so unnerving that I had actually tried to walk differently.

Now, as I sat in his office, the watch commander was using the same tactic as Ball had—the inference of homosexuality. At this point, I still hadn't figured out that merely being a qualified, divorced woman with Army experience—the only woman on the department with that background—would make me a target for all those ugly, queer rumors. I just knew I was being dogged by a perception that at the time was patently untrue. But hell's fuzzy! I sure wasn't about to go to bed with any of those men who didn't accept me just to prove my heterosexuality.

My pulse raced as apprehension built.

"Lieutenant, I would appreciate it if you would turn around and face me," I said. "I do not want any misunderstanding between us."

He returned to his desk and sat down.

With my hands clasped in my lap, I leaned forward. "I'm aware, Lieutenant, of rumors about queers in the military," I said uneasily. "To tell you the truth, sir, I don't have a clue what they're all about. I do know that I'm tired of departmental innuendo and of being singled out for interviews on the subject under one pretext or another. So I'm going to ask you straight out. Are you implying that because I'm a captain in the Army Reserves, I'm suspected of being queer?"

He sputtered, "Oh no, no, no. Not you. But the department is concerned that your affiliation with the military will affect the policewomen's good name."

I sat on the edge of my chair, fighting to understand. "That, sir, is ugly! My affiliation with the military reflects only honorable service without a blemish on my reputation."

He blushed and stammered again. "You know how people talk, Prichard. Management would like to avoid any unpleasantness by having you drop out of the Army Reserves."

Whoa! To hell with management! For starters, as a newly divorced woman who had to support herself, I needed the extra $100 I would receive from Army Reserve training. More importantly, if I let management strong-arm me into quitting, I would lose my self-respect. Nothing was worth that.

I had to make a stand. "Lieutenant, if you have any information about me other than the management's paranoid attitude toward my being a woman associated with the military, I need to know, and right now. I'm proud of my honorable military service. As much as I've been investigated by the LAPD before hiring on, I'm appalled that I'm now expected to resign from the Army Reserves because of a rumor." I glared at him.

"Now, now, Prichard. The higher-ups merely wanted me to ask if you would consider their request. You know what I mean, for the good of the department."

I swallowed hard. I hadn't fully recovered from not being allowed to enroll in a class just because I was a woman. Now, the LAPD didn't approve of women in the military. That wasn't my problem. I had fallen in love with the Army during my first year of service, due in no small part to the fact that I managed to qualify for officer candidate school even though I only had a high school diploma. I had trained five companies of women in a single year. I had made captain by watching the men and following their example. Even though I had to resign to get married, I had remained in the reserves to stay in touch with the Army. I wasn't about to relinquish that now.

"I have no desire to discredit the department or myself, sir. But I do not agree with you that I must resign from the Army Reserves to protect the reputation of LAPD female officers."

He moved to the window. "You won't reconsider your answer?"

"Sir, I don't know what this is all about, but I'd like to ask whether the same request has been made of the ninety-nine men who signed up for the Army Reserves the same day I did."

He whirled around and blustered, "I thought I made it clear. Women have more problems than men."

"Oh, yes. You made it quite clear that if I were a man, we wouldn't be having this interview. Lieutenant, I will gladly resign from the Army Reserve when the same demand is made of the men."

"It's your decision, Prichard. Before you leave, I must remind you, I can't promise how long you will work street patrol."

I fought the urge to slam the door on the way out. Thank goodness I was no longer on probation. But career or no career, I wasn't about to accept another humiliation or the arrogant power of the brass without a challenge. I didn't have to fear the police administration, I realized. If they could have sacked me, I knew I would already be gone. And although I didn't understand then how powerful management could be, they didn't realize how powerful I had become simply by standing firm.

On January 11, 1950, less than a month after the interview about the Army Reserve, I was transferred, without explanation, to work Lincoln Heights Jail full time. No one willingly worked the jail if they wanted to be promoted. The jail was the cemetery for police careers and was frequently used by the administration to discipline officers who had fallen from grace. This was a disaster for my career. I watched the transfer teletype printout roll from the machine and realized I was in trouble. I couldn't talk as I turned to leave. If anybody believed for one moment that I would leave the Army Reserve now or settle for this jail position, they didn't know me.

4

THE CRADLE WILL ROCK

Five months later, the transfer from street patrol still stung, even though the LAPD soon stopped assigning women to street patrol on the pretext that it was too dangerous for them. No woman had been hurt or killed walking beats, and female officers had done a superior job of fulfilling their mandate. Preventing women from walking a beat or going out on patrol not only deprived women of that kind of active duty, it deprived them of many job opportunities that required precisely that kind of experience.

I began to quietly document how the women on the department, starting with myself, were routinely shunted aside. I quickly found that there were very few incentives for women in the LAPD. Qualified policewomen were never given top assignments, and only minimal advancement in rank was possible. In 1945, eight new sergeant positions had been created for women officers. The eight women who filled those positions weren't about to leave since women were banned from promoting above the rank of sergeant. So the rest of us would have to wait until those eight retired or died. Although the institutional limits on women's advancement meant that women officers' talents and training were often wasted, few had challenged the inequity.

In the LAPD, a secret was no longer a secret once shared, so I kept my research to myself and focused on learning how to perform as a police officer since the LAPD wasn't anything like the Army. Despite the long odds, I had no problem sticking tough and waiting for change. I had never been a quitter. By all that was holy, I would stay to rise in rank. Unfortunately, my instincts didn't always coincide with the LAPD way of doing business.

I had settled in and come to enjoy working the women's fifth floor. The busy day watch included booking and processing prisoners and escorting them to and from court. I often felt, "There, but for the grace of God, go I." I would look at the women grouped in different tank holdings separated by bars—misdemeanor or felony crimes—and cringe at the lack of privacy. I could not even imagine the loss of dignity.

About four months after my return to jail duty, I was walking down the middle aisle of the jail one morning and stopped to check on the detainees awaiting arraignment. In the windowless holding tank, lit only by dim overhead lights, women dressed in ratty civilian clothes sat on the bare concrete floor or paced.

"Hey, Officer," an inmate with a cigarette hanging from her mouth yelled. "When do we get the fucking hell out of here for court?" Dirty blond hair covered red-blurry eyes that barely focused on me.

"Watch your mouth, miss!" I responded. "The court officer will be here soon. Enjoy your smoke." I knew the judge would levy time to be served. I felt sorry for her and the rest who had been pulled into jail. Once they sobered up, that nasty behavior almost always dropped away. Unfortunately, after doing short time, they would dive right back into the bottle.

Officer Roberta Reddick, a gorgeous Black policewoman, came up behind me and whispered, "Watch it, Prichard."

"Good grief! What did I do?"

"The sergeants have a tizzy about fraternizing. So have as little conversation as possible with the prisoners, then move on. And don't get soft in the head about their plight in life. Bars separate them from us for real reasons."

I nodded my head and went back to the booking area. Wiry Officer Edna Disney was finishing paperwork for downstairs processing. She scooted around the desk, lit a cigarette, and blew a perfect smoke ring, "Tell me, Prichard. What did you do to come back to us?"

I smiled. "The lieutenant dumped me into the jail because I wouldn't leave the Army Reserve. I'm mad about it, but I'm not going to resign my commission. I don't see how he can get away with this."

"Would you share what you just told me at the Policewomen's Association tonight? There's a meeting downstairs after work tonight to vote for a new board of directors."

It took me a moment to sort out her request. I knew that many other policewomen on the LAPD were unhappy about the limitations imposed on their careers. I also knew that fear of retribution had silenced them. They didn't want to risk losing the assignments they held or their paychecks. For better or worse, however, I wasn't the kind of woman to hold her tongue.

"I'm not afraid to speak the truth," I said. "Sure. I'll talk. Love to."

Disney ran her fingers through her short brown hair. "I have to warn you, Prichard. There are women snitches among us who delight in reporting what we do to the chief's office. If our actions displease him, we are rated down in loyalty."

I knew that speaking out could translate to another shadow over my shoulder and more trouble for me. But that possibility sure wasn't going to silence me. The Los Angeles Policewomen's Association had been started in 1925—just fifteen years after the LAPD's first female officer, Alice Stebbins Wells, had been sworn in, and five years after the Nineteenth Amendment had granted women the right to vote. The four women who had launched the association had fought for and won pay parity with the men. This was no time to fall short of the example they had set.

The association met in the jail's main-floor meeting room. I knew about half of the thirty-five women in attendance. As a new member, I wasn't familiar with the association politics or the undercurrents about a woman's place on the LAPD. But I was in no mood to placate anyone, so I didn't hold back.

I surprised even myself with my intensity and level of frustration. Some younger policewomen in the audience vigorously applauded and hooted for more, while the senior women whispered. From the looks on their faces, I realized that I had done the unthinkable. I had openly challenged the discrimination that held all our careers hostage.

As I sat there, I knew I would hear about my brashness. I had barely completed two years seniority and hadn't earned the respect given the more seasoned officers. So I was downright shocked when Disney stood and nominated me for 1950–51 president of the Los Angeles Policewomen's Association as a write-in candidate. I fussed with my purse, pulled my skirt down, and tried to remain calm. The policewomen from the jail whispered among themselves. I heard someone say, "We haven't a thing to lose. Let's do it."

I did not know that the outgoing president, Sergeant Kay Sheldon, was running for re-election. Sheldon unfolded her tall body from her seat, the tally in her hand. There was no emotion on her face as she announced, "Your next president is Officer Prichard."

I was stunned. I'd never been president of anything in my life. Besides, I was just a rookie. Still, it never occurred to me to refuse the office.

Most of the older women weren't happy. Sergeant Rose Pickerel, hired in the late twenties and the first woman ever to walk a beat in Los Angeles, stopped me as I headed out the door. "Who put you up to this, Prichard?" she asked.

"No one," I said. "I can think for myself."

"I underestimated you. If I ever run for political office, I'd like you for my campaign manager."

I spent the following summer training with the Army Reserve in Fort Ord. I wasn't so happy upon my return to take up my new position at the department's youth program staff offices. I had been a cop for more than two years, but once again, I had been moved to a job that bore little relation to the kind of policing I wanted to do.

The Deputy Auxiliary Police, known as the DAP program, offered activities for youngsters that ranged from organized sports and camping, to excursions to places like Catalina Island and Camp Valcrest, located in the Angeles National Forest. Although there were DAP branches citywide, I was stationed in the central office, located across the street from City Hall on the second floor of the old Central Police Station, where I functioned as an event coordinator. The position was fun and rewarding, especially when I visited various schools to see how I could better help those youngsters who tended to get in trouble with the law. That made me feel like I was a cop again. Still, the job was far from the investigative position I coveted.

I tortured myself over how to remedy the situation. My only hope was to do the best job possible. If I could make exceptional ratings in my job performance, I might be able to turn around my floundering career.

That would take a lot longer than I ever imagined. I was still in my pajamas on a Sunday morning when my doorbell rang. I peeked out the front window and saw a uniformed postman. I opened the door, and he handed me a special delivery letter from Sixth Army Headquarters. Although the letter was dated 14 February 1951, I knew it wasn't a Valentine's greeting from Uncle Sam.

I climbed back into bed, sipped my coffee, and looked at the envelope. I wondered what could be significant enough to warrant such a delivery. Finally, I opened the letter. The words *ACTIVE DUTY* made me gasp. Surely this couldn't mean what I thought it might. I read, "By direction of the President and the Secretary of Defense, examination 19 February 1951, Fort MacArthur."

My God. That was only two days away.

I had no way of knowing that my involuntary recall, which would trigger my departure from the LAPD in just eight weeks, would give me the fieldwork experience the LAPD seemed intent on denying me as well as all the other women on the department. I had no way of knowing that it would teach me firsthand about how to fight for my rights when they had been denied. Still, for whatever reason, I felt that this sudden and unexpected Army recall might just be a godsend.

PART II

5

THE MORE THINGS CHANGE

Why had the Army yanked me out of civilian life on such short notice? Perhaps it had something to do with the fact that I was now a police officer. For the first time in months, I felt as if my luck was changing. I avoided running a red light by hitting the brakes and sliding on the slick streetcar tracks and pulled into the vacant lot at First and Broadway, across the street from the police station.

Overworked police vehicles with broken windows, missing back seats and crunched fenders were parked in every direction. In one of the cars, I spotted a red lantern sitting on the floor of the front seat. While working morning watch patrol, I, too, had stolen one of the red lanterns set out at night by city street maintenance to warn motorists of dangerous road repairs. The city fathers didn't believe that police patrols required heaters in their cars, and I had needed to keep my feet warm.

I entered the Central Police Station's arched stone doorway. The broad, oak banister, worn smooth by thousands of hands, evoked feelings of touching the ghosts of previous generations. The condemned building would soon be gone, along with all the other old structures from First to Sixth Streets, and I wanted to remember my part in its life. But that was the past, and I definitely needed to focus on the immediate future, no matter how uncertain.

During a sleepless night, I had considered not opting for the military. But that would have also entailed resigning my Army officer's commission, and I just could not give up what I had worked so hard to achieve. My absence would delay the possibility of promotion at the LAPD, but while on military leave of absence, my job was protected by federal and state law. The time of military service would not be deducted from my LAPD pension. By obeying the Army, I would preserve—and hopefully advance—both careers.

I entered the small squad room on the second floor and moved toward the watch commander's glass-enclosed corner office. I had walked in a police officer, I realized, and would walk out an active Army captain headed for another military tour of duty. I waited for Lieutenant Koenig, my immediate supervisor, to complete a telephone conversation while the rest of the staff, curious about why I needed to see the lieutenant alone, peered in at us. I respected Koenig and felt comfortable working for him, so I had to stifle a twinge of regret at the thought of leaving. When his conversation was over, he indicated for me to sit down.

"You're not going to like what I have to say," he said. "The citywide schedule for summer camp must be completed a month earlier than we thought. I want—"

I interrupted. "Excuse me, Lieutenant. Before we talk about the job, I have something else to discuss."

I handed him a copy of my military orders. "These came in the mail—special delivery. I don't know what it's all about."

He read the orders. "I don't understand. Does this mean you're back in the Army?" He handed back the papers.

"I think so, sir. I must report to Fort MacArthur in San Pedro for a physical on Wednesday."

"The least you could have done, Fanchon, was to give us advance notice. You know, it takes time to fill a vacancy."

My voice tightened. "I'm telling you, sir, as soon as I could. I didn't know until yesterday, Sunday. You weren't at work."

"You mean to tell me you're being recalled to active duty for, let's see... my God, three years, without your prior knowledge?"

"I'm shocked, Lieutenant. Nobody contacted me. I haven't had time to investigate why this has happened."

"When do you leave?"

"I don't know. If I pass the physical exam, I imagine orders will be cut within a few weeks."

He frowned and waved his hand in dismissal. I returned to my desk and phoned around the Army Reserve, trying to find someone who could tell me about this recall. Not a single source was willing to enlighten me. Was this some kind of super-secret operation?

Once it became known on the department that I was being recalled to the Army, the tone of my life there changed abruptly. I wasn't quite an outsider, but I was being ignored and even prevented from participating in work plans. I might just as well have stayed home. I spent my time finishing up at the schools I had been working with and relinquishing the responsibility of my assignments as well as the offices I held with the Policewomen's Association and the American Legion. But I knew in my heart I would be back. I would have unfinished business with the LAPD until my badge read "Detective Sergeant."

After thirty-four topsy-turvy months, most of which I spent heading up a criminal investigation in Japan, I returned to the LAPD. During my time away, I had earned the rank of major and been certified as an investigator, a particular distinction since only five women in the United States had been chosen for this role. Surely, since I was no longer a rookie and had training as well as field and leadership experience that exceeded many of the male officers', they would give me a chance to work a bona fide police assignment. The most prestigious and powerful positions for my current rank were in the detective's bureau. Now qualified, that was where I hoped to be assigned.

As much as I deserved the promotion, I knew it would be a slog. But I was ready for the fight. In the last months of my involuntary recall, I had been set up by Army intelligence to take the fall for the very incidents I had been brought back to investigate. The Army brass certainly hadn't expected me to rebel or do whatever I had to in order to prove my innocence. I guess they didn't know me. And the LAPD had no way of knowing that I had come back much better prepared to fight for myself and challenge the department's discrimination than I had been when I left.

Despite the training and experience I had received, I feared my Army accomplishments as a criminal investigator would not be acknowledged, and that I would simply be assigned to the DAP youth program or the fifth floor of the women's jail at Lincoln Heights. As I entered the police department personnel office, the captain behind the desk frowned and motioned for me to join him. Through the window, I could see the pot-bellied trucks pouring concrete into forms for the new freeway system.

When California had been admitted to the Union in 1850, the City of Los Angeles was home to 1,610 people, with a bar on every corner and 400 gambling halls. There were no paved roads, and the City did little to make life livable for humans or horses. A hundred years later, the physical look of Los Angeles was now changing daily, with ribbons of concrete strips slowly rolling out a wide road system in all directions from the main interchange south of Elysian Park. Across Los Angeles Street from City Hall, a new police building that would centralize under a single roof the police department, which had been scattered throughout downtown and the Eastside, now rose toward completion.

I handed over copies of my military orders returning me to civilian status along with a short resume of my investigative accomplishments. The captain quickly scanned the file.

"The only opening right now is on the fifth floor of Lincoln Heights Jail," he said. "Take it or resign."

Jail matron. They were offering custodial duty again. Nothing had changed. I had graduated from the Army criminal investigation school, qualified for top-secret military clearance, and received an assignment as the Assistant Chief of the Sixth Army Criminal Investigation Division (CID). But all my accomplishments in the Army didn't mean a thing with the LAPD. It was as if the more qualified I became, the more trouble I represented.

When I spoke, I managed to sound calm. "Captain, I'd like my Army documents placed in my 201 file. In the Army, I acquired valuable investigative training both in school and during fieldwork. Surely the department could use my talents to better advantage than the jail."

"What you did in the military has nothing to do with the Los Angeles Police Department."

"Doesn't my three years of field experience in investigation qualify me for consideration for detectives?"

"Things have changed since you were recalled," he said. "Only sergeants are assigned to the bureau. Report to the captain at the jail on Monday. You'll need a uniform. You can pick up your badge, buttons, hat piece, and ID card on your way out." His phone rang, and he turned away, dismissing me with a wave. The interview was over.

I couldn't push for anything better. Take it or resign. That's what the captain had said. The department still condemned my involvement with the military and would refuse to consider me for any police work until I resigned my commission. They could go plumb to hell. I had worked my hardest to rise in the ranks and become a commanding officer in the Army. I had never been to college, so that Army diploma was like gold in my book. No way would I consider resigning my commission.

Full of rebellion, I left his office. I couldn't do a damn thing, and he knew it. I was halfway to retirement and couldn't blow it right now. I didn't have to like it, but I could take whatever they could dish out. I could bide my time. Nothing stayed the same, and in the meantime, I could improve my chances for a promotion.

Returning to jail duty did nothing to stimulate my morale or my pride about being a policewoman, and working the morning shift, which started at midnight and ended at 8 a.m., challenged my health. My feet were already ruined from walking street patrol in high heels; walking the concrete floors in the jail just added to my misery. I fretted about the indoor confinement and wondered whether I would spend the rest of my career there.

I should have had more faith. Two months later, I was transferred out of the jail position. The orders came, and I was expected to jump. I was informed that I would now be the female coordinator of the DAPS in San Pedro. I didn't particularly want to go back to the Deputy Auxiliary Police. Still, it would get me out of the jail and move me closer to recapturing the faded dream of police work, even if it did involve doing activities with hundreds of teens.

For the next several years, marriage to Shannon Dexter

Blake, a Phil Silvers lookalike whom I met on a blind date, and the birth of our son Kelly Clinton two years later, preempted much of my work focus. Returning to my job three months after Kelly's birth in 1958, however, left me less than thrilled since I found myself working that fifth floor again. My feet hadn't healed from surgery before Blake Junior had been born and working on concrete floors in the jail made them swell. By the end of watch, I could barely drive home. Eventually, I paid $200 to have custom police pumps made that wouldn't cripple me.

I wanted out almost as badly as the criminals I guarded. Looking for advice about where to find a new assignment, I spoke with Deputy Chief Richard Simon. It happened that he was looking for a female replacement in the public information division (PID). That sounded good to me, especially since the stability of a daytime shift would help now that I was a new mother. He wrote the blessed order for my transfer then and there, ensuring my escape from the Lincoln Heights Jail.

When the transfer list came out, I sallied into the PID and smiled when I saw a lieutenant I knew from when I had walked a beat sitting at his desk next to the captain's office. He bent over his paperwork. I waited until he looked up.

"What brings you here?" he asked.

"You mean you haven't been told?"

"Told what?"

"Deputy Chief Simon transferred me in. It will be on the teletype transfer today."

"Are you sure?"

That didn't sound good. *How could he not know I would be starting today?*

While that all quickly worked itself out, I wasn't sure how happy I was about my new assignment. Ironically, my duties included giving tours to groups of forty or less. My poor feet.

How would I tolerate walking through six floors of the jail as well as all the various divisions and bureaus including scientific investigation, administration, fingerprint classification, records, and identification?

My stay at public information would not be happy. Up to this point in my life, I had suffered subtle discrimination. But after taking a position with the PID, the discrimination became flagrant and undeniable. Captain Ray Plant and Lieutenant William Wagner refused to accept me. No matter how well I performed, no matter how many letters of commendation I received from the public, they never acknowledged my work or gave me any encouragement.

In addition, it soon became obvious that my efforts to speak up on behalf of the department's policewomen weren't appreciated either. After I had been in the public information division for six months, I received the worst efficiency rating of my career to that point.

"Of course you know any 50-percent rating requires that I explain it to you," said Lieutenant Wagner, who would wind up being promoted to deputy chief a few years later. "There's nothing personal about this."

Famous last words. It was definitely personal. And I wouldn't be able to do a thing to change it.

"Sign here," he said, pushing the paperwork across his desk.

I scanned the page. I couldn't believe I had four 50-percent ratings. I clenched my jaw and fought back the desire to tell him to go to hell. Only one rating, the one for physical fitness, came anywhere near the truth. "What's this about initiative?" I asked. He wouldn't look at me. "I've never been short on taking charge. How have I qualified for such a rating?"

He stood up. "You come to work every day, but you haven't grasped the essence of your assignment."

"I don't accept that as a reasonable explanation," I said. "And here's another. 'The force to carry out with energy and resolution that which is believed to be reasonable, right, or duty.' You rated me down by 50 percent on that item. How have I failed? Even though you haven't given me a chance, I've always carried out my assignments with energy and resolution."

He put his hands in his pockets and walked to the window. With his back to me, he said, "You haven't measured up."

"That's the first I've heard about it. On this one, 'common sense.' I want to know the specifics. On what have you based your findings?"

I could see he had not expected my questions. He squirmed in his chair. "Ratings are only an administrative tool," he said. "You'll probably do better next time."

"I did better this time! Don't you think it would be more honorable to tell me that I'm not wanted in this division?" I shot back.

"Ratings don't mean a thing," Wagner said. "All you have to do is sign."

I stepped back from his desk. "I don't believe it. You're making it impossible for me to get a transfer or a promotion. No captain in his right mind would want to accept anyone with a rating as odious as this one. These are terrible percentages and I have no way to rebut their falsity."

"That's my judgment of your performance."

"If you were so dissatisfied with my work, why didn't you say something before this?"

"I've completed my interview with you," he said. "You're required by departmental rules to sign this. At once."

I bent over his desk and picked up the pen. My hand shook as I wrote my name. "I hope you sleep well tonight, Lieutenant," I said. "I've signed this pack of lies only because you ordered me to."

I'm sure my division heads had figured that this efficiency rating would destroy my chances for a decent promotion or transfer and would drive me from the department. Instead, the treatment fanned the flame of rebellion in my heart even further. Even if it took years, I resolved, I would change the second-class citizenship foisted on LAPD women.

I took my copy, straightened, and headed for the business office division (BOD) located at the main entrance of the police building. I had heard that thirteen new slots for policewomen, five at BOD, would replace veteran policemen for the first time in the history of the department. I wanted to be one of those more than ever.

Captain Robbie Robertson met me at the door of his small office. His captain's bars flashed from his collars, and he had enough white service stripes on his left uniform sleeve to signal that he could retire.

"Robbie," I sputtered. "I'm so angry I could chew bullets, spit them out, and hit a target at ten feet. Look at this!" I handed him a copy of my rating.

He took it and motioned for me to be seated. After he had read it, he looked up. "They're wrong," he said. "Dead wrong. I've watched you conduct tours."

"I appreciate your support," I said. "Would that rating negate my applying for one of your new spots?"

"Hell no, Fanchon. You'd be my first choice."

"But what about that rating?"

"Not good, but not fatal. Put alongside your others, and it would be obvious that it's biased."

"Then, would there be a job for me here?"

"Hang in there. You'll be transferred next month. Here," Robbie said, handing me the rating. "Keep this and consult it at least four times a year. Let it be a reminder to not wait until they rate you. Check with your supervisor so you won't be surprised. If you've done something that displeases your supervisor, clear it up before it becomes a problem."

A month later, as I watched the teletype machine at detective headquarters, I saw my name appear, followed by "Trfd fr PID to BOD." My morale soared. I chuckled as I thought about leaving PID the same way I had arrived—without their approval.

6

PROMOTION TO DESK JOCKEY?

My anger over the efficiency rating made me ready to challenge every manager. If my performance rating dropped, I wanted to know immediately. My assertiveness paid off when I was assigned the job of desk officer. On the first of April, 1960, Diane Harber, Lomie Rich, Patricia Renfew, Nancy Lukes, and I posed for a *Times* photographer, happy and grateful to be the new women desk officers, especially since these assignments had traditionally been given to males.

Over the next few years, I performed well and felt comfortable working the day shift on the West L.A. desk of the old, two-story brick building. Our wooden U-shaped counter faced east on Purdue Street, and on scrutiny, the ceilings, walls, and molding bore witness to careless policemen practicing quick-draw and leaving tell-tale bullet holes.

Telephone calls and taking reports from citizens who paraded in after fender benders and the like kept us busy. Life became interesting when actresses like Natalie Wood dropped by to file minor insurance reports, or a three-year-old went for a 5 a.m. stroll before his parents awoke, or a person with Alzheimer's turned up lost, befuddled, and belligerent. Otherwise, working the business office proved less than challenging, although it did allow me to improve the horrible rating from my days at PID. During lulls, I kept my nose in the department's big blue book of regulations. I had but one drive—to be promoted to sergeant. I would take every opportunity to further that goal.

Everything changed when the Watts riots broke out in August 1965. By the time the anarchy in Watts ended six days later, thirty-four people had been killed, more than a thousand had been injured, and over $40 million worth of property had been destroyed. The anger inflamed by cries of police brutality being ignored has not abated in the decades following the Watts riots. And it won't as long as suspects feel the police department is unfair, and scared officers respond with antagonism and use unnecessary force to keep a suspect under control.

As I continued to work year after year to garner the upper 10 percent ratings needed for promotion, I witnessed deteriorating race relations among officers on the LAPD in the aftermath of the Watts riot. The discrimination, however, was not just reserved for Black policemen. Women, too, effectively became segregated from the rest of the department.

Of course, the mistreatment of females on the LAPD was nothing new. As president of the Los Angeles Policewomen's Association, this time from 1963 through 1965, I had gathered even more evidence about the inequitable working conditions for policewomen. I had also documented the fact that no new women officers were being hired. I continued to speak out about what I found, and life on the department continued to have its unpleasant moments. But that wasn't going to stop me.

My experience on the LAPD had been challenging and disjointed almost from the start. My involuntary recall, ongoing training for the reserves, and maternity leave hadn't helped much on that front. But I finally made sergeant in 1967.

"Lieutenant!" I exclaimed. "It's happened. The chief's office just called. They want me downtown on the sixth floor by two this afternoon for the oath of office."

My lieutenant stood immediately and grabbed my hand. "Congratulations. I'll call in a field unit to replace you. And Blake," he added. "I'll miss you. Now don't waste time, or you'll be late for your promotion."

I flew into the locker room, stripped off my uniform, and slid a black, sleeveless dress over my head. I ran a comb through my hair and applied fresh lipstick and powder. Then I emptied my locker into a cardboard box, stopped for a moment at the police desk, and mentally said goodbye to the small, cramped area I had worked in for the past seven years. Bidding adieu to my long-held resentment as well, I smiled, and headed for my car. After a challenging nineteen years of bouncing around the department, I was going to be promoted to sergeant, and my life at the LAPD would change.

As I drove east on Santa Monica Freeway and headed for police headquarters downtown, I knew I had finally beaten the odds. I turned the radio to jivey music, rolled the window down, and let the hot breeze whip through my hair. Maybe now I could try for lieutenant. Ha! They would have to open that up to women at some point.

In the meantime, Inspector Vernon Kerr, who had a lot of power on the department even though he was about to retire, had promised he would get me into the detective bureau, provided I kept silent about the help he provided. I never questioned Kerr about the need for secrecy; I just kept my part of the bargain. After I was sworn into office, how I got there would be history anyway. I didn't intend to louse this up.

I made my way from the stifling July heat into the air-cooled building and the elevator. At the sixth floor, I stepped into the quiet corridor. A sudden pain shot through my chest and down my left arm. During my annual police physical that past February, the doctor had discovered a slight heart murmur. The heart condition was controlled by medication, and an occasional ache hadn't forced me into disability retirement. But this episode left me gasping for air. I leaned against the wall and closed my eyes to keep from fainting.

When the sharp pain slowly released, I managed to cautiously make my way into the small conference room next to the chief's office. The room buzzed with more than thirty men and women about to be promoted. My head throbbed as I wiped the sweat from my neck. A cold blast from the air conditioner made me feel a bit better. I swallowed a headache pill and sat still on my chair, afraid to move. The discomfort, for which I would later be given nitroglycerin, lingered, then ebbed away. I concentrated on trying to relax. I was sure not going to allow this to interfere with receiving my new rank.

Scattered among the males about to become sergeants were a dozen or so women who were also being promoted. What a big day! The department had finally opened up sergeant ratings for more than one or two of us. A uniformed male sergeant about to become a lieutenant sat next to me. I smiled at him as he stretched his arms across the backs of the seats. He flipped his blond hair to one side. "I hear you dames had to be bonused for this promotion," he said.

The gall of him. Bonused indeed. I had worked my tail off for this promotion. So had the other women being advanced because of their on-the-job achievements. I wouldn't let him spoil the occasion. I turned full-face toward him. "What do you mean?"

He flushed but continued. "You know what I mean. Your scores were too low for promotion, so they raised them."

"Is that so?" I snapped. "Where did you get your facts?"

"Everybody's talking about it," he said. "You dames aren't smart enough to make it on your own."

The other men in the room shifted in their seats. The women fell silent. I had passed the written by only two-hundredths of a point, but a high oral had given me an overall score of 82.2 percent. Passing was 70 percent.

"I don't even know you, Sergeant, but I believe you're full of hot air," I said. "Had Civil Service bonused my examination, they would have to post that information along with how they computed the scores. I received no such notification."

The women snickered, and his face reddened. I didn't relent. "You could be brilliant if you opened your mind as wide as your mouth."

Luckily for him, Tom Reddin, who had been appointed chief in February 1967 and would be remembered as one of the first progressive leaders in law enforcement, strode to the front of the room right then and faced us with a nod and a smile. After his opening remarks, Chief Reddin called my name. I stepped to the front, and he took both of my hands into his. "It's a pleasure to promote you to sergeant," he said. "Congratulations, Fanchon. You're now assigned to the fraud desk in the detective bureau."

I stepped back. "It's no joke?" I asked. "I'm assigned to forgery?"

"It's true," he said with a laugh.

"Thank you, sir."

He handed me the badge and the certificate of office. I trailed my finger across the curved top of the badge over the letters that spelled out SERGEANT. For nineteen years, this promotion had proved so elusive that it now seemed like more of a dream than reality. Then I caught the number "69" at the bottom of the badge. Wouldn't you know I had been given that number, then still known as a violation of the California Penal Code? The men, bless them, would tease me unmercifully.

Surprisingly, my promotion didn't go over well at home, in part because the accompanying raise meant that I would be making more money than my husband. Monday morning, however, I put aside my personal problems and made my way down the hall to bunco-forgery. At the door, I could hear the men inside laughing and talking as they readied for the 7:30 a.m. roll call. I stepped into the squad room. Lieutenant Ryan Shift came toward me when he saw me and waited for me to speak. "I hope I'm in the right place," I said. "This is forgery, isn't it?"

He nodded.

I stuck out my hand. "I'm Blake. Sergeant Blake, reporting for duty."

Shift looked at me sharply but ignored my hand. "I haven't," he stuttered. "I mean, I don't know. The transfer sheet doesn't come in until this afternoon."

In the softly lit squad room, the men stopped talking. My first day on a new division. This didn't feel good. I stood waiting for a welcome, but the men's faces did not radiate smiles.

"I wouldn't be here if I hadn't been told to report," I said.

Shift's hands moved to the telephone. "I'll have to call personnel," he said. "The captain is on vacation. He won't be back until next Monday."

I nodded, acutely aware that once again, I wasn't wanted.

I had hoped for a major change in assignments once I passed the sergeant's exam, but that wasn't to be, I realized, as I was led to the reception desk. I had time to observe the politics of my new division and to think about how to challenge this assignment as I waited for the captain's return from vacation. It was déjà vu all over again, but this time the unprecedented promotions of women to the rank of sergeant had shaken up the standard pecking order. Lieutenant Shift obviously couldn't imagine installing me on an equal level with the other sergeants in the division, so he was storing me on a shelf just above the civilian secretary, at the very bottom of the departmental hierarchy.

I hadn't fought for my promotion to sergeant only to become a glorified desk officer. The reception desk should have been assigned to one of the officers below the rank of sergeant. I learned to my amazement that the men had rebelled against the desk assignment, deeming it beneath them, and had been allowed to get away with it.

I would wind up doing desk duty for a lot longer than I ever anticipated. The desk sat in front of our office's main entrance, with a view through the glass partition into the crowded squad room. Aching to be assigned to felony investigations with the men, I would try not to look, focusing instead on the telephone console. I needed to fight for an assignment as a forgery investigator, I realized, if I didn't want to be stuck being a receptionist as long as I worked in the division. If I could keep my mouth shut, not alienate the men, watch what happened and learn as much as possible, I'd get that chance and I'd be ready.

7

DOING MY JOB AT LAST

Getting along with the men, at least those who weren't openly anti-women-on-the-force, came fairly easily. I liked many of them and it showed. It always had. Take the day I met my friend Joe Gunn, who would go on to become an LAPD police commander, a producer on Dragnet and, in 1998, the Los Angeles Police Commission's executive director. We were in a crowded elevator in Parker Center. It being Christmas, he had hung mistletoe near his desk and was trying to hustle a young secretary into visiting his office so he could lay one on her. I couldn't help myself. Shouldering my way through the elevator, I yelled, "I don't need any damn mistletoe to kiss a young, good-looking officer." Then I pinned him against the wall and planted a big smooch on him. "Merry Christmas, honey!" I shouted before plunging back into the elevator and returning to work.

I may have felt comfortable among most of the LAPD's rank and file, but my lack of advancement remained a sore spot and put me at odds with the brass. I had always been ambitious. I aspired to nothing less than eventually being chief of police. Even now that I had gotten a foot on the ladder and been promoted, at least in name, I hadn't managed to ascend the ranks on the actual work front. It was time to take this up with my captain.

"Excuse me, sir. I'm sorry to bother you, but I'm upset."

The captain's head snapped up, and he threw his pencil onto his paperwork.

"What is it, Blake?" he asked, massaging his neck as he nodded for me to sit.

I closed the door and remained standing. I knew I might be treading on dangerous ground, but it was time to argue for that team assignment I had been waiting for.

He leaned forward. "I've been meaning to tell you, Blake," he said. "You're doing an outstanding job. I'm very pleased with you on the desk."

That was supposed to make me feel grateful when all I wanted was a fair chance.

"Thanks for the compliment," I said. "But to put it bluntly, sir, I detest working the desk. It's especially difficult when I know there are also three policemen junior to me in rank who have been assigned to teams. I'm sitting at that desk as a sergeant with expertise. How would you feel, sir, if you were me?"

I watched his eyes dart away as he drew in a deep breath. "You have a point," he said.

"I need to know now if you'll consider me for investigations."

He picked up a divisional roster and scanned it. "We're setting up a new organization of the teams that will split the misdemeanor checks away from the felonies. The project needs another investigator. How would you like to work misdemeanor checks?"

"You mean, just like that, I'll be assigned to a team?"

He stood up. "It will take a couple of weeks. I'll need to find a new desk officer."

I reached for his hand and pumped it vigorously, having no idea that none of the men had wanted this detail since it entailed so much work. He did not smile. "Blake," he said. "Say nothing of this until I announce it at roll call. I need to iron out the details."

"Yes, sir." I could barely keep from turning a cartwheel and yelling, "Yahoo." Instead, I popped a nitro pill under my tongue. Once the ache in my chest calmed down, I could think. I had been stupid to assume he would automatically change my assignment without me asking. I wouldn't be afraid to speak up for myself again. I had earned my seat in the detective bureau, and somebody else could be the desk officer.

Time no longer dragged. Since walking a beat, I had never been happier on the Los Angeles Police Department. All I had wanted as a woman were the same considerations enjoyed by the men. I worked as hard, if not harder, than they. Given the opportunity and training, I functioned above average. I had believed that if I produced results, I would be given prestigious felony investigative assignments. That's what I had thought then, even though it had taken months just to make it to misdemeanor investigations. Still, this was progress.

After waiting so long for a chance to prove myself, I didn't waste any time. I became immersed in the game of matching wits with the criminal mindset. Of all the crimes, forgery, bunco (persuading someone to purchase worthless property), and embezzlement are usually committed by a higher criminal mentality. Already thinking ahead, I decided to become a forgery expert and worked at home to study some of the more complicated cases that had been solved, a number of which had been masterminded by engravers and printers. By comparison to the sleuthing that would be required for felony check investigations, however, misdemeanor checks simply required laborious work to build a solid case that would garner legal arrest warrants.

At the end of the summer of 1969, bunco-forgery moved into new quarters on the north side of Parker Center, and I acquired a new partner. I had worked with Sergeant Dorothy Pathe at the jail when she was on probation and couldn't have picked anyone I would have liked to work with more.

Dottie, a tall, stately woman who was a walking advertisement for policewomen, approached my desk one Monday morning. She held out her hand. "Hi, Fanchon," she said. "Who do I see to report for duty?"

"I've been waiting for you, Dottie. You're my new partner. You report first to the lieutenant, right over there." I pointed out Lieutenant Shift, who sat at the first desk facing the rows of investigators at tables.

"Good-looking guy. He looks too young to be a lieutenant," she said, and then stepped to his desk. I envied her dark, wavy hair, her trim figure, her youth that radiated energy from every movement, and her pure feminine appeal. Immediately, I wanted to drop the weight I had never lost since my son's birth and to get rid of the dowdiness I felt as I pushed fifty.

Dottie and I became close as partners, sharing confidences about our lives at home as well as on the job. We trusted each other, and both believed in delivering an honest day's work. It took everything we had to stay ahead of the seventy-five to two hundred and fifty new misdemeanor crime reports inundating our desks every day.

Our efforts, however, didn't seem to matter in terms of being accepted by our fellow officers in the division. Then it got worse.

It's difficult to pick a particular date when I began to feel that the attitudes of many of the men had started to sour. By and large, I'd had a blast with my fellow officers over the years. By May 1969, however, I had begun to pick up asides from some of the men, as well as rumors that the department planned to cut the pay of its female officers. The undercurrents were subtle and initially seemed like an extension of the supposedly good-natured, but ongoing, battle of the sexes. Gradually, however, the comments became increasingly negative and increasingly disparaging.

I particularly remember the day Dottie, ever the regal lady in a smashing blue-silk suit, stood behind her chair, looking over the pile of cases covering our desks. "Think we can scoot to the academy and make our monthly shoot?" she asked.

"Of course, Dottie. God, how I hate shooting since my eyes have changed. It's dreadful. If I focus on the sights with my glasses on, I can't see the target."

"We may have to shoot several times to qualify," she said with a laugh. "If it gets too tough, I'll ask Willie Gough to help us."

I slung my black police purse on my shoulder, and we headed for the door. "You mean, Willie would shoot next to me on the firing line and send a couple of his rounds into my target so I could pass?"

"That's the general idea."

"No way. I know some of the men do that, but I'm not that desperate. I brought an extra pair of reading glasses just to see the sights on my snubnosed special. Once I focus on the sights, all I have to do is point the weapon at the target. Trigger squeeze is the trick to accurate shooting."

"Think you could hit a suspect without your magnifiers on?"

"If I couldn't, I'd de-ball him," I joked.

Lieutenant Shift called to us from his desk. "Hold up, you two. And gentlemen, your attention please." He stood facing the squad room. Dottie and I didn't move. "This is an official announcement. Chief Reddin will resign as of the fifth of May to run for mayor."

It took a moment for the information to penetrate, and then it hit me. "Wouldn't ya know it?" I said to Dottie in a low voice. "We lost a friend of the policewomen. God only knows who'll end up chief."

She turned toward the door. "Yeah. Nothing we can do about it, and we do have to qualify. Let's go."

Sergeant Ty Dalton blocked our way as he stood in the doorway. "Did ya hear that? We're going to have a new chief. Maybe now they'll pick someone who's a real cop. Maybe now we'll have a leader who won't be afraid to keep you broads under control."

I tried to pass him, but his hands flew up against each side of the doorjamb.

"Move it, Dalton. We're leaving," I said.

He didn't budge. "You broads are a pain in the ass!" he spouted.

Bias toward women on the LAPD wasn't new to me or any of the other women—present or past—on the force.

"Tomorrow's the big day," an officer in the 1920s had said to Marguerite Curley, who walked a beat armed with only her police badge.

"For what?" the six-foot, muscular female cop asked.

"Doesn't surprise me that you haven't heard as it doesn't involve you."

"What do you mean it doesn't involve me?"

"Simple," the officer said. "You ladies won't be getting a raise, that's all."

Marguerite reacted by reaching across the desk, grabbing his biceps and half-lifting him out of his chair. Then, in the company of most of the other seventeen women on the force, she launched a counterattack.

I was about to do the same. Unlike Marguerite, and even

though I stood close enough to count his whiskers, I didn't grab Dalton. Instead, I stared at him before exclaiming, "I don't need any man to protect me, Dalton. Put your arms down. I'm about to bust you right in the balls." He turned red and quickly stepped aside. Dottie and I shared a laugh as we left.

Once on the firing line of the combat range, I couldn't calm down about Dalton.

Just focus on the task at hand, I told myself. I could see the sights of my two-inch, snubnosed revolver through the reading glasses, but at twenty-five yards, the half-torso silhouette target was a big blur of black. When the timed target turned, I grabbed my weapon from the waist-high bench we stood behind, quickly aligned my sights, pointed at the center of the black, and squeezed off five rapid-fire shots before the target turned away. Then I reloaded, fired, benched my weapon, reloaded the final round, and fired the last five shots.

Sure that I hadn't qualified because I couldn't clearly see the target, I slowly reloaded my weapon and slipped it back inside the gun holder of my purse. "Come on, Dottie," I said. "Let's clean our .38s at home. I don't think I made it."

"No sweat. We'll come back tomorrow, and the next day, and the next after that until you qualify. Think how you'd feel if you couldn't protect your life or mine."

"I've thought about it. With a single exception, I haven't had to pull my piece on the job. I guess I'm not destined for a medal of valor award. But one of these days, Dottie, we're bound to pop into a bank when a holdup is in progress. I've wondered just what I'd do under those circumstances."

We were quiet, and then Dottie said, "Wouldn't hurt if we talked about it and had a plan. There's a bank holdup every day. What do you think you'd do?"

"Look for cover and hit the floor. But from now on, when we stop at a bank to pick up account information, my hand will be in my purse on my weapon ready to draw."

The range master stepped from his glassed observation booth and handed us our ticket stubs. When I held mine at arm's length, I couldn't believe my eyes. I had shot a perfect score. "Dottie! Look at this! I've never done this before, and I'll probably never do it again."

She studied my ticket stub, which I still have to this day. "Maybe I should try your new glasses," she said. "You sure put them all in the black and neatly grouped. None of the guys could do better. What did you do differently than just the glasses?"

"Tell you the truth, Dottie. I was so upset over Dalton, I visualized his face out there. It worked like a charm."

She laughed. "When we get back to the office, why don't you casually stroll over to Dalton and show him today's qualification?"

"It would be a pleasure. I'd enjoy watching him squirm. You'd think he'd have enough sense to cool it with us. I read somewhere that women don't have to be trained to shoot. Angry but deadly cool, most women involved in homicide never miss the first shot."

We both laughed and headed back to our car.

"With Reddin gone, we don't have the backing of a single man on this department. If anything happens to us because of his resignation, I'm going to get active in the Policewomen's Association again," I said. "It's the only organization that gives us a direct channel to the chief. But we're so damned scared to use it, it's pathetic. It's no wonder women can't advance."

Any organization in a democracy must be free to pursue life without fear. That was clearly not the case at the LAPD. And that was unacceptable.

"But if we make the men mad at us, we'll never manage to get ahead."

"The guys are always throwing it in our faces that the women sit back and let the men run the show. We haven't one woman on this department who'll even try to be elected to the Academy Revolver Club, the Police Relief Association, the Credit Union, or the Police Protective League."

"Do you think the men would vote for a woman?"

"If they thought she had enough clout to get better benefits for them, they would back her. What we've got to do is find someone willing to give the time to do it."

"How about you, Fanchon?"

I knew that until one of us stepped out to be heard, nothing would change for the women officers. Remaining silent would ring our death knell. So what the hell, why not me?

"I could start by being a delegate to the Protective League. Shift asked this morning for someone to volunteer as the divisional representative. I'd only have to attend one meeting a month. That shouldn't interfere with home or job."

"As long as it doesn't get you into trouble. In the meantime, let's hit up the captain for assignment to the felony teams. Are you with me?"

"Of course. They keep bringing in new men to fill the felony vacancies, so we'd better have Shift make us an appointment with the captain. I wonder what excuses he'll give us."

8

CLIMATE CHILLS

Sixty investigators waited restlessly in the squad room for Lieutenant Shift's return from detective headquarters to announce the name of our new chief. I caught the grin on the lieutenant's boyish face as he strode into the room past Dottie and me to his desk. He waved a copy of a teletype and waited for quiet.

"Listen up, troops," Shift said. "Today, August 29, 1969, Edward M. Davis was appointed the chief of police of the Los Angeles Police Department."

Spontaneous yells from the men split my ears. Sergeant Dalton, two rows of tables from me, waved his fist in the air and yelled, "Did you hear that? We got us a red-blooded man for chief."

Damn it! Why did we have to draw the most reactionary male on the job for chief? I didn't trust Davis. I knew he had established clout at his oral board by brilliantly presenting a new plan to update the organization of the police department. He had done his political homework and had been selected unanimously by Mayor Yorty, the police commission, and the city council.

"Fanchon, what are you thinking?" Dottie asked.

"It's no secret that Davis has plotted to become chief since he was a sergeant at juvenile. I'm not surprised, but I can't shake this awful feeling. Davis doesn't give a damn about women. In all his efforts to make it better for the men, he hasn't lifted a finger to help us."

She stood by my desk and leaned closer. "Maybe you're right and maybe not," she said. "We can't do much except buckle down and hope for the best."

"I can't change that he's our chief, and he'll have my support," I said. "Meanwhile, maybe we can convince the captain to give us a chance in felony investigations."

"How can we accomplish that?"

I sat straight. "We could work to increase the number of arrest warrants. Try to up them from ten to fifty a month."

"We'll have to raise our production of cases to take to the city attorney for arrest warrants."

"That means we need more bank info, more handwriting samples, more paperwork, more witnesses for court," I said. "If we don't do the footwork for the men, those cases we transfer to them will die in the files."

Our decision to work harder turned our attention away from Davis. Convinced that the higher clearance of crime reports would capture the captain's attention and allow us to work felonies, we concentrated on our misdemeanor checks. Each morning we made up our day's work. We plotted court time and stops at the city attorney's office and banks. We located witnesses, served warrants for arrests, booked suspects, filed our never-ending river of incoming misdemeanor check reports, and transferred cases we worked into felony filings.

One day, Shift picked up a sheaf of papers from his desk and walked toward us. He towered over us as he thumbed the packets in his hand. "Here, you two." He tossed them on our desks. "Need these back by Friday for Deputy Chief Wagner."

Hearing his name made me uncomfortable. When I had worked for Wagner in public information, he would have fired me if he could have justified it.

Shift waited while Dottie and I scanned the forms. It didn't take me long to know this was a questionnaire about our assignment. We would need help justifying our existence as misdemeanor investigators, or we would be surveyed right out of bunco-forgery.

"Lieutenant, haven't you been helping the men with this? Is there some kind of formula to follow?"

Shift frowned. "Come on, Blake. Don't make a federal case out of this. I haven't time to work with the two of you. Just do it." He started to leave.

"But, assignment analysis isn't something to just dash off. What we submit must be done professionally. Can you give us some guidance?"

"Ladies, just do it. It's no big deal," he said as he sidled away.

"Wait a minute, Lieutenant," I said. "This looks like we could be eliminated from our assignments. Is that true?"

"Yes. Why all the fuss?"

"That's enough right there to make this important to us. Does this mean that we won't work felony teams?"

He stiffened. "Why bring that up now? Just do what you're told."

"I'll do what I'm told. But I've brought the subject up. When do we get to talk to the captain about working felonies?"

"I'll set up an interview," he snapped.

"Terrific. What about this stuff?" I picked up the packet. "We need the evaluation key to know how our positions are weighted."

He threw up his hands and walked away. I knew it wouldn't do for me to pressure him further.

"That was scary, the way you talked to the lieutenant," Dorothy said.

"I haven't stopped shaking inside. But it's a mess, Dottie. With all the speculation about the men not wanting to work with women, and recently about women officers potentially having to take a pay cut, I don't know who to believe. This could be our death knell if we don't come up with the right information."

She frowned. "I don't know. You pushed the lieutenant pretty hard. Do you think it's that important?"

"Hell, yes. The lieutenant is holding something back. This department hasn't been overhauled in years, and I don't see a crack in the wall for females. If the men continue to get away with not working for women, we'll never be more than sergeants."

"Don't you think you're getting too worked up?"

"No. And I'm going to get more worked up, especially since their wives are suddenly getting into the act. They think we're sleeping with the men. I've had to work with the men. Nobody cared a twit what my husband thought!"

Dottie's deep, satiny laugh filled the air. "If I'd slept with every man I've been accused of being with on the department, I'd be Wonder Woman. You're right. Bring your packet and a notepad. We'll go to the library and see what we can find. Didn't somebody say this is called the Jacob Survey?"

We found a similar study in the Los Angeles City personnel office and worked the rest of the week to put together a paper that would do credit to any administrator. If we were to be sacked, it wouldn't be because of what we submitted.

9

POWER BASE

Rumors about women being eliminated from the department kept me on edge and unable to concentrate on crime reports. I put my head down on my desktop of two hundred and fifty new misdemeanor crime reports and let the angry tears flow. Sergeant Dalton's latest dig, one of many, had hit its mark.

"The chief is planning to use the Jacob Survey to eliminate all but twelve of you women. See ya," he had announced, running out the door before I could respond.

It was 4 p.m., our quitting time, and all fifty-nine investigators in the elongated bunco-forgery squad room had left for the day.

Fired up by Dalton's remark, I bounced out of my chair and started to pace.

"It'll be a cold day in hell before I'll let Chief Davis or anyone mess with us. Just the thought that I've been closed out of felony investigations after it took nineteen years to make sergeant is enough to make me want to retaliate. But throw over a hundred policewomen off the department . . . he has completely underestimated me."

My ongoing efforts to communicate with the administration's chain of command had resulted in tension that had continued to slowly build against me. That wasn't going to be great for my career. But my career, along with the careers of almost all the LAPD's female officers, would die if I didn't make a significant move.

Had there been any kind of a support system in the LAPD, I might have been able to solicit the women officers for their help and advice along the way. That, however, was not the case. How could I create some kind of power base now? Where could I find backup?

Frustrated, I picked up the Los Angeles City in-house telephone directory, leafed through the pages, and inadvertently flipped it open to the mayor's office. The name Eleanor Chambers, Deputy Mayor, held me motionless. She was a woman and would surely understand. But would I dare call her? I would be taking one hell of a chance. It was definitely against departmental policy to contact anybody in City Hall. If caught, I'd be eighty-sixed right off the LAPD. On the other hand, if it got down and dirty, I could retire on the spot since my twenty years in guaranteed my pension. And I'd never forgive myself if I didn't try.

Taking a deep breath, I picked up the phone and dialed. The deputy mayor's secretary gave me an appointment for the following week.

How about that! I felt better immediately. No, I wouldn't tell Dottie, who had already left for the day, or anyone else. The women would think I flipped, but we sorely needed outside clout. Maybe, just maybe, this could turn our careers around.

On a very hot November Monday, I slipped out of the office, walked across to the Main Street entrance, and mounted the wide concrete steps leading into City Hall. I hadn't used the

Los Angeles Street entrance because I didn't want to be seen by anyone coming or going into the police building. As I passed into the cool, dark passage on the main floor, I stopped a moment outside of the council chambers to wipe perspiration from my face, straighten the seams in my hose, apply fresh lipstick, and cool down. I needed to calm my nerves. This wasn't going to be one of my everyday interviews.

I turned right under the high rotunda, passed between the marbled columns, and found the short, angled stairwell that led to the Hall of Mayors. The guard admitted me to the reception office, and my heels sank into the thick carpet. Oil portraits of former mayors, all men, smiled at me from the walls.

If only Chambers would listen. And then what? Would she be prone to notify the department that I had been brazen enough to enlist her help? Or would she keep my confidence?

The secretary, a mature, well-dressed woman, held the door open and beckoned me to follow. She pointed to an office on the west side of the inner hall. "The deputy mayor awaits you. Go in and be seated."

Sure, just go right in. I was in forbidden territory and could be ending my police career. When I stepped through the door, Eleanor Chambers sat lost in her executive chair, her back toward me. She was talking on the phone and waved a freckled hand with flashing rings at me. High, arched windows stood ajar behind her desk, which overlooked the inside of the city council chambers on the main floor, giving her the ability to eavesdrop on council business from her office any time she wanted.

I strained to hear the voices of the city councilors as Chambers finished her call, oblivious that down the line I would wind up taking my complaints to them directly, often in the company of other policewomen. When Chambers hung up the phone, she wheeled her big chair around to face me. I hadn't expected her to be so old. Her double chin hung loose. Her hair was waved back into a bun with wispy strands playing around her neck. Her black eyes flashed behind horn-rimmed glasses. When she stood, she offered her hand. "Sergeant Blake," she said. "I'm delighted to meet you."

I accepted her firm grip and immediately felt comfortable.

"Do be seated while I close the windows. The council can get noisy." She returned to her chair, sat back, and folded her hands in her lap. "Now, my dear, we can talk. What brings you to me? Your contact has me extremely curious."

"Yes, ma'am." I felt awkward, fighting for an opening that wouldn't make me sound like a teenager.

"Call me Ellie," she said. "Everybody does. Deputy mayor is a mouthful. Mrs. Chambers is too formal. Haven't made up my mind about Ms. as yet." Her strong voice filled the room.

I nodded, tongue-tied. My law enforcement journey stretched behind me—the challenge for women like me to be seen as persons, and men's unwillingness to yield power or control over us. We all sat on that human volcano that eventually had to erupt because management refused to acknowledge or deal with this sub-rosa battle of the sexes.

Suddenly my voice boomed. "To tell the truth, Mrs. Chambers, I mean Ellie . . . I'm petrified!"

I was about to do something that police officers just don't do. I was about to break the code of silence.

She pulled her chair closer.

"I didn't mean to yell," I said, my face now on fire.

"It must be important for you to be here, Sergeant. Let's get right to it."

I had to level with her and fast. "I'm not here with departmental sanction. I'm in deep trouble if they find out."

She reached over and patted my hand. "I can assure you, my dear, nobody will know. If you're questioned, you have my permission to tell them I called you."

"This is more difficult than I thought."

"Can you relax, Sergeant? What's this all about?"

"The time has come for me to trust someone, and it might as well be you. This is about the careers of L.A.'s policewomen. I've tried to work through the system on the job. They won't let me or any of the other women promote beyond sergeant. So assignments are not exactly the best."

She sat straight, her hands clutching the arms of the chair and leaned forward. "You mean to tell me there's discrimination on the Los Angeles Police Department?"

"They won't even let us take the lieutenant's exam."

"Have you tried?"

I nodded. "But there's more to it than that. The men can't stand that we make the same money they do. There's a movement among them to make us accept less than they're paid. This is idiotic. Our pay has been equal since 1925."

She shot out of her chair, startling me. "Not good. Not good at all."

I didn't know what to expect, but I knew I had won her attention and decided to push ahead. "You know, don't you, that there's a big reorganization slated for the police department?"

"Yes. That's one of the reasons why the mayor chose Davis for chief. He presented a detailed plan that both the mayor and the city council liked." She went back to her desk chair. "What you've told me about the women will shock the mayor. Davis wouldn't be the chief today had Mayor Sam Yorty had any inkling that Davis wouldn't support the women. This is distressing. The mayor is going to be very disappointed in his chief."

After a pause, she continued. "I can't abide mistreatment of people. Sergeant, I want you to know I worked for Franklin Roosevelt. I helped run the Work Program Administration (WPA) during the depression. That experience has made me a fighter for equality for everyone. What do you want me to do to help the policewomen?"

My God! She had worked for Roosevelt. I'd hit pay dirt. "I don't know where to start, but I believe that we must get the attention of the police administrators before the new ordinance is drawn up by the city council. Before it's too late."

"How many women are on the department now?" she asked.

"Approximately one hundred and eighty."

She put her hand on my shoulder and gently squeezed. "I'm grateful you had the courage to call. Trust me, Sergeant. The wheels will start turning."

She hit her intercom switch. "Bring me the entertainment folder."

I stood rooted before her as she fired questions.

"Sergeant. Do the policewomen have an organization?"

"Yes, ma'am."

"Who's your president?"

"Joan Simpson. She's assigned to the complaint board in communications."

The secretary came in, gave her the folder, and left. Chambers flipped it open and studied it for a few moments. "What do you think about the mayor demanding that the administrators come to a party for all the policewomen? We'll hold it upstairs in City Hall's Tower Room. We'll make it a night for the mayor to meet the women on the force."

The wheels hadn't just started turning; they were burning rubber.

"Well, Sergeant. I'm waiting."

"I'm speechless. Just like that, you can achieve a miracle for us. Where have I been that I haven't met you before now?"

"I've been here all the time." She picked up her calendar book and checked for an opening. "It'll have to be in a couple of weeks, before the holidays. Contact Simpson and tell her to call me as soon as possible. I want you to keep me informed and to help coordinate this event. Here's my direct telephone number. You won't have to go through the secretary. Any questions?"

"How do we pay for this?"

"It's coming out of the mayor's entertainment fund. I'll put you in touch with the staff that sets up the festivities. This will be a command performance by the mayor and a must for the chief and his staff plus all of the policewomen. Do you understand, Sergeant?"

"Yes, ma'am."

She rose and escorted me to the door. "This will definitely get the chief's attention. He's not to fool around with the City's policewomen."

The event created quite a stir on the LAPD. Suddenly, the policewomen had moved from the shadows to center attraction. To my amazement, the men complained that they had been left out.

That November evening, Simpson, Chambers, and I entered the small elevator on the twenty-second floor, rode the short ride to the top of City Hall, and stepped out. Chambers put her arms around our shoulders and drew us close to her. "This is the beginning of a new career for our policewomen," she said.

Simpson and I smiled. We both knew that the arms of the mayor's office did more than surround us. That vast, square cavern of a room reflected the opulence of power. With thirty-foot windows, draped in dark-red velvet with golden tiebacks on all four sides, we could see the city lights from every direction.

I pulled away from the view and turned to Ellie. "Look what you've accomplished for us."

"Yes, my dears. We'll have waiters from Chinatown serving the appetizers and drinks. This occasion calls for the best."

Chambers and Simpson positioned themselves at the elevator door to greet the guests, while I arranged the agenda at the podium. I watched the room fill, amused that the top brass from the department milled about, cocktails clutched in hand, with glazed expressions of disbelief.

Mayor Sam Yorty, dubbed the Maverick Mayor because of his independence in politics, arrived accompanied by Chief Davis dressed in a civilian suit. Mayor since '61, Yorty walked with cocksureness as he moved through the crowd toward Chambers. Ignoring the podium, he faced the gathering. "I want to talk to each of you before you leave tonight," the mayor said before turning to the chief. "You've been holding out on me, Ed. I had no idea we were gifted with so many beautiful women officers."

Davis didn't show a trace of a smile, nor did he say a word. He must have been wondering how all this had happened. He would be surprised and probably angry if he knew I had made a single telephone call, which had set all this in motion. That thought made me drain my cocktail in one swallow.

Chambers flashed a thumbs-up at me behind the mayor's back. I raised my glass in recognition. What a night for us. The two-hour cocktail party accomplished what Chambers had intended, sending a not-so-subtle message to the department that the women were not to be taken lightly. I could see a good number of the female officers present talking to the men, and from the expressions on the listeners' faces, I knew they were not letting this opportunity to further the cause of equality slip away. I had no way of knowing that this gathering of policewomen in the tower room would become a tradition.

* * *

My efforts to create a power base took another leap when Officer Shilah Johnson, then president of the Policewomen's Association, called sometime later. "I'm referring the chief's request to you. None of the other women have the balls to volunteer, including me."

"Whoa! What on earth are you talking about, Shilah?" I held the phone and waited.

"Well. Chief Davis wants one of us from the association to ask Russell to vote for our officer pay raise."

"Are you serious? Did I hear you right?" Talk about irony, after all the department speculation regarding women not being included in the pay raises.

"Will you do it?"

"Hell, yes! I've wanted to meet her, and the chief just gave his permission. This is a sanctioned opportunity. He may not be happy that I drew the straw of action. Are you sure you want me?"

She was quiet and then found her voice. "Yes. I won't tell them it's you until you report your results to me. I trust you."

"Hang up, Shilah. I've got a call to make, and right now."

As a detective sergeant working forgery, I had managed to go as far as a woman could go on the LAPD. While I hadn't as yet realized that one woman might have the power to change the status quo, I was increasingly ready to rebel, and Pat Russell might just be able to help.

It didn't take me five minutes to contact Russell's office and set up an interview. Even at such short notice, I lucked out. She was available the next morning at 7 a.m. sharp in her office. This time, unlike my secretive trip to meet Chambers, I walked proudly across from the police building to the Los Angeles Street entrance of City Hall, hoping the rank could see me.

The high, alabaster-white building hadn't awakened for the day's activity as I made my way past the guard to Russell's office on the main floor. Seeing the frosted glass door that stood ajar with her name and title emblazoned in bold type, I suddenly had second thoughts. Years of "don't rock the boat" crept into my mind. But as I opened the door, I felt this was a good thing I was about to do. "Go, girl," I whispered.

"Councilman Russell?" I finally sang out.

Pat Russell, who had recently been elected to the city council in a precedent-setting special election when one of the councilmen had retired, surprised me when she appeared in a flowered print dress more suited to a homemaker than a politician. Her short dark hair hugged her face like a cap, accentuating her intense brown eyes and dainty earrings. She moved with the grace and assurance of a ballerina. In fact, she was a mountain climber and took pride in staying in shape.

"Sergeant Blake."

She held out a tanned hand devoid of jewelry. Her grip was firm and quick. I nodded. "Councilman, you keep early hours."

"Pay no attention to the word *Councilman*. As you can see, I'm very much a woman. Just call me Pat," she said with a laugh.

She moved quickly, alive with energy, as she led me to a couch.

"Have a seat, Sergeant. I'm sorry I haven't much time this morning. Now, what's the problem? I can't imagine why a police sergeant would want to see me."

What could I say that would be appropriate? The more I worried about it, the more flustered I felt. I sat up even straighter than usual and leaned forward. "To tell the truth, Pat, I'm not sure how to start."

"I'm sure it can't be too serious. Just tell me what you came to say."

"Chief Davis would appreciate it if you would vote for the police pay raise." Oh, balls! There! It was out. To cover my embarrassment, I kept talking. "The chief's office is a bit nervous that the raise won't pass the vote of the city council. I think they sent me because they don't know how to approach a woman on the council and fear alienating you."

"I know," she said softly. "The men on the council still get flustered every time they address me in the chamber. I can't speak for them, but I can give you my vote without hesitation. You can relay my message that I've studied the facts and shall vote *yea*."

As she started to rise, I touched her arm to remain seated. "Let me thank you on behalf of all the officers on the job. Before I go, may I have another fifteen minutes of your time?"

She settled back. "Of course, Sergeant."

I needed to find out if she would be receptive to our problems as women officers. My gambit might create an awkward situation, but it was worth a try. I had to act or lose the present opportunity, and who knows when I would have another chance to try to enlist council support.

My intuition was dancing a jig, alternately telling me to proceed with caution and to go for it. Once I opened my mouth, I would be stepping deeper into the world of politics, whether I wanted to or not. I took a breath and jumped.

"I want you to know, Pat, I'm not a chronic complainer. But, I also want you to be aware of the battle we policewomen are waging to further promotions and assignments. The impasse on the department is deadly. I would like to make another appointment with you to inform you about what is happening to us on the job."

She sat still and didn't say a word. Maybe I had pushed too hard. Should I say something about my contact with Deputy

Mayor Eleanor Chambers? I decided I didn't know Pat well enough, so I said nothing further. The silence was ominous. I would have bolted if I could have done so gracefully. She picked up her appointment book. "That sounds serious to me, Sergeant. I'd like to know more. In the meantime, I'll have my staff research the facts about the policewomen. How about lunch next Tuesday?"

"That would be splendid, Pat," I said, as relieved by her response as I was pleased. "Where would you like to meet?"

She strolled with me to the door. "I like to walk as much as possible. Meet me here at 11:30, and we'll hike the few blocks to Olvera Street for tacos."

"Thank you for this morning. I'll be looking forward to lunch."

Outside her office, I let out a whoop in the quiet hall. Now, maybe she could help us, too. With Pat in the council and Ellie in the mayor's office, I had established a cornerstone of the support I needed—especially if they joined forces. I didn't dare take anyone into my confidence about what I had done. I didn't want a ripple of this potentially powerful alliance I was orchestrating to get back to the department.

I hurried back to my office, trying not to contemplate the price I might have to pay if I got caught by the men. They would make my life hell. Even so, I was determined—no matter the risks—to force the problems of the LAPD's female officers out into the open for debate before I retired. Somehow, the stranglehold on our careers had to be broken. Sixty years of stagnation had to come to an end.

10

BIAS IN BLOOM

Captain Rock Bookman, commander of the bunco-forgery division, stopped at Shift's desk. I watched him square his shoulders and button his twill jacket over his protruding belly. He had once been a handsome, trim, and tall rookie directing traffic. He did the unpredictable then by issuing a ticket to a freight-train engineer for holding up vehicles at a busy intersection. The brassiness of that ticket had earned Bookman a promotion to captain.

Shift stood and faced the squad room. "Listen up, troops. The captain has an announcement."

Bookman's veined hand nervously stroked his graying hair. "The word is out, gentlemen. And you too, girls." I winced. "The Jacob Career Plan goes to the council the first of next month." He scanned the room. "It's important that you understand the massive proposed change and how it would affect the entire department. It's a new concept for career advancement."

Would the department finally act to improve the careers of the women, too? Hopefully, the chief had felt forced to include us whether he wanted to or not.

"Here's the plan." Bookman paced back and forth. "A police

officer starting out will have two ways to advance through the ranks. Each rank has a three-step pay scale. Detectives are re-titled Sergeant/Investigators I, II, and III. You'll all be grandfathered into Investigator II and," he paused again, "you'll receive a pay raise of more than $100 per month."

The fifty-eight men whistled, stamped their feet, applauded, and yelled. I sat back in my chair. So far, women hadn't been left out. The raise would help all of us catch up since pay increases had been withheld over the past five years.

"There's more, gentlemen." He grinned. "Each team will be assigned, with one person designated team captain at Investigator III pay scale, equal to Lieutenant I."

I didn't move. Those selected as team captains would receive more than a $200 increase in pay. My heart pumped faster, thinking that my experience as an investigator in the Army would finally pay off. Surely I would be appointed team captain and elevated to a III position.

Bookman set his jaw as he paced. "The hardest part of this phase-in is that I'm responsible for the pre-selection process in this division. Half of you cannot be selected." He faced Dottie and me. "Since the number of the III positions is limited, I've chosen to exclude the women. There isn't a woman on the Los Angeles Police Department qualified to handle a III position."

The men whistled and broke out in raucous laughter as I sprang to my feet. Dottie froze, and the room hushed. I stared at Bookman, my face white with rage. I couldn't stop shaking. "Captain Bookman, that's one hell of a statement. What do you base your opinion on?"

"You're female. I don't need anything else."

I stood my ground. If Bookman had more to throw at me, I might as well get it over with. The men hooted as Dottie whispered, "For God's sake, Fanchon!"

I remained standing ramrod straight as I waited for silence. "Captain. I'm appalled. That was a dirty, lowdown blow, sir. Are we such a threat to the male ego that you're afraid to acknowledge how qualified we are? I'm proud of my promotion to major, my agent investigative credentials, and two years as assistant chief of Sixth Army criminal investigators while on involuntary recall to active duty. Add that to my twenty-two years on the LAPD." I sat down.

The undercurrents in the squad room had enough energy to detonate an atomic bomb. Bookman lit a cigarette, his hand shaking. I had to stop confronting or risk a transfer.

"We'll discuss this later, Blake." His face flushed. "For those of you who will not make the first selection without examination, there'll be tests posted as soon as a pool gets set up throughout the department. Shift will give you your new assignments and the names of those I've selected for a III position at roll call tomorrow morning. The new pay scale becomes effective January 1st, 1971."

The hot Santa Ana wind scorching our city on that June day wasn't any hotter than the emotional wind blowing through me. Dottie and I had been pushed aside again. It didn't matter that we had cleared a massive caseload or that our efficiency ratings were in the upper 10 percent. The men avoided eye contact when I scanned their faces. The select few who curried favor with the three lieutenants and the captain sat with Mona Lisa smiles. And those who knew they wouldn't make it tried to hide their disappointment. If I hadn't been so upset, I might have felt sorry for them.

The captain motioned for Dottie and me to follow him into his office. He paused to face the men. "Hold your questions until we know more details. Shift, I want you to come in, too. Bring your notes."

Dottie and I slid into our chairs. Shift followed. After closing the Venetian blinds to shut out the squad room, he squeezed into a chair next to Bookman. Looking through the plate glass window behind them, I spotted the San Gabriel Mountains off in the distance. How I yearned to stand on top of those peaks, free of the undercurrent in that cramped office.

"Captain," I said. "I don't know what this is all about, but I do know I'm tired of the unfairness I'm subjected to just because I was born female. What you said about leaving us out of the IIIs selection upset me."

"At another moment, Fanchon, you and I will talk. Right now, I must complete the changes I have to make. I want to clear up your requests to work felony cases." He leaned back and extended his legs across the top of his desk. He lit a cigarette and blew smoke toward the ceiling.

He wanted to talk to us now about working felony cases? He must have known for some time about the selections of III he had to make. No wonder he kept putting us off. He didn't want to talk to us about working felony checks until he had made his announcement that morning.

"Ladies, your request presents a problem." He blew a ring of smoke upwards.

"Captain, I believe what is at issue here is whether Dottie and I are qualified to work felonies. We both know how to handle felony checks even though we concentrate on misdemeanors. Half of our cases have developed into felonies, which are transferred to the men with most of the work needed to seek warrants already done."

"All we want is a chance," Dottie said. "You know we can handle the job." She sat still and grasped her chair with both hands, her knees squeezed together.

Bookman crushed his cigarette in the ashtray. "You women are working in a man's world. You knew that when you were hired." He drew his legs off the desk and sat up. "There's bound to be resistance from the men if I assign you to work with them."

"There's nothing in regulations, Captain, that allows a junior officer to challenge your authority. The men can't challenge you any more than we can. If they don't like it, they can transfer out. Dottie and I don't have the same opportunities for transfer that they do or the same considerations for assignments."

"Ladies, what I'm about to say is difficult. I've decided to assign one of you to a felony team by the first of the year."

Bookman looked at Dottie, and once again, I felt the cold I knew so well creep through my body. We all knew it would be Dottie. Shift busied himself with his handful of papers, making notes. Dottie looked away.

"I won't assign both of you," Bookman said. "It would strip the misdemeanor check detail of experience. Question is, which one of you do I assign?" He sat back with a wry smile.

I waited.

"Fanchon, because of your health problems, I'll leave you in misdemeanor checks," Bookman said. "Dottie won't leave your team until the division settles down from the changes."

Using my health hit me where it hurt the most. "My health hasn't affected my work. I'm not on limited duty, sir." I didn't want to hear his excuses for not choosing me. Of course, he wanted Dottie, who was younger and not as militant as I.

I couldn't afford to show my disappointment and be seen as emotional, but it took every ounce of control I could muster to remain stoic.

"I'm sorry, partner," Dottie whispered.

"Not your fault, Dottie."

"You'll be given another partner," Shift said.

"Does that mean I'll be in charge of the team?"

"It depends on whoever is available for that spot, Blake. There are lots of changes taking place. The Jacob Plan will become an ordinance next month. The department has the votes on the city council to pass the Jacob Ordinance, but it won't take effect until January. In the meantime, I must put the new changes into place."

"You haven't answered me about being in charge of my team," I said.

"I think, Blake, you should be the team captain."

"Without a III selection?"

"Yes."

It would have been great to suddenly wake up and discover this had all been a nightmare. But it wasn't.

"Don't you think Blake could have the next felony team assignment after me?" Dottie asked.

"It's okay, Dottie," I said. "I'm damned happy you're making the breakthrough as a woman. I hate losing you as a partner. You've been the very best I've worked with." I hugged her, and some of my bitterness abated. "And Captain," I said, "I'll be waiting for my next chance to be a felony investigator."

I would have liked him to confirm these expectations, but he just stood to shake my hand.

Although so much had already transpired so fast, the day's workload needed my attention. After the end of the watch at 4 p.m., when everybody had gone home, I sat alone in that vast squad room, mulling over what had happened to me on the LAPD. Bookman's put-down, the price I knew I was paying for speaking out against the status quo, had shaken my confidence. But there had to be more to what was going on than I understood. Bookman had dared to humiliate Dottie and me in front of the entire squad as if the two of us were powerless.

Around 6 p.m., I called my husband Shannon to let him know I would be late. Before I left the building, I wanted to research the 1964 Civil Rights Act, which supposedly guaranteed equal employment. So I went to the police library and found it. I hadn't paid attention when this federal law had been enacted. Most of the men on the department labeled it "American Civil Liberties Union [ACLU] fodder," and I had accepted their unfounded pronouncements. But after my session with Bookman, I wanted to know what the act stated.

I read, again and again, the most wonderful words, aside from the Constitution of the United States, to be found:

> SEC. 703. (a) It shall be an unlawful employment practice for an employer—
>
> (1) to fail or refuse to hire or to discharge any individual, or otherwise to discriminate against any individual with respect to his compensation, terms, conditions, or privileges of employment, because of such individual's race, color, religion, sex, or national origin; or
>
> (2) to limit, segregate, or classify his employees or applicants for employment in any way which would deprive or tend to deprive any individual of employment opportunities or otherwise adversely affect his status as an employee, because of such individual's race, color, religion, sex, or national origin.

There it was. The law clearly set forth that it was illegal to discriminate against anyone based on sex. I turned out the library lights and locked the door. As I walked out to my car, I couldn't quite grasp the find I had just made, but it erased what had been an awful day. I now had a way to try to improve my lot and that of the other policewomen on the LAPD.

That following Monday before the June 12th examinations for Investigator III, Sergeant Josephine Stevens called me. She was a sharp woman with more intelligence than most men could tolerate. Since completing her minimum twenty years for retirement, she had become more vocal about discrimination on the department. I respected and admired her. "Have you heard what the rank ordered in connection with Investigator III examinations?" she asked.

"Only that the officers being promoted won't be selected until after the ordinance is passed."

"No, no, no, not that! Haven't you heard that the chief initially barred the women sergeants from taking the examination?"

"You're kidding! He couldn't be that foolish."

"If I weren't on a city phone, I'd swear," she said. "He finally reversed that prohibition, but while he's allowing the women sergeants to take the oral examination for Investigator III and be placed in the pool, he has barred the commanders from selecting us for promotion to a III."

"You mean . . ."

"I mean, Fanchon, the women will have to accept that we won't be allowed to promote to higher rank."

Her robust and throaty voice bounced in my ears. So that was why Bookman had made such an issue about Dottie and me not being considered. The chief didn't want any static to surface from the women. God help the captain who couldn't meet his demands. It was a wonder Bookman hadn't been any harder on me. My outburst in the squad room could have severely compromised me. "Jo, I'm sure it's going to get worse. The chief must think we can't do a thing to stop him. I believe he hates women."

"Hate us or not, my husband—you know he's a lawyer now since he retired—is drafting a letter to the chief. Sergeant Audrey Fletcher and I are signing it, and we want to know if you would too. We'll send a copy to Muriel Morse, general manager of city personnel. Nobody is challenging Jacob for any reason. As it stands now, we may be too late."

I couldn't sign after my exchange with Bookman, no matter how strongly I felt about that letter. By then, I knew full well that the frightening autocracy within the internal administration of the LAPD did not allow for criticism or disapproval among the ranks without swift and lasting reprisal.

I didn't feel great turning her down. "Jo, I've been through hell here in forgery this past week trying to get assigned to felony cases. If I sign your letter now, they'll bounce me back to jail duty. I've done more than my share of time working the women's fifth floor. Do you understand?"

"Sure, I do. They've bounced you in and out of Lincoln Heights as often as they've booked some of our finest women prisoners. But if you change your mind, the letter won't be ready for a few days."

"When I heard that William Wagner had headed the chief's super-secret task force, I wondered what the chief would pull," I said. "It may not be Wagner's fault, but I sure have my suspicions. Do you have any idea what will happen when that letter hits the chief's desk?"

"Got my time in," she said. "I can retire, even though I'd like to stay longer. I just don't choose to keep taking what they dish out to women."

"I admire your courage. Stay in touch, and good luck."

I felt like a traitor when I hung up, but I wasn't willing to jeopardize my assignment. At the end of watch, I headed home and poured a double scotch and soda.

Jo's letter, mailed after August 3rd, created problems for the city council, the civil service commission, and the chief. When I learned that Councilwoman Pat Russell, my newfound friend, had pressed for city council action involving equal promotional opportunities for policewomen, I wanted to lead a band around City Hall. I didn't know until much later that Russell had also accompanied the general manager of personnel for the City of Los Angeles, Muriel Morse, to Davis's office, where all three met in closed session.

After August 3rd, Bookman called Dottie and me into his office. "Here's the latest order from last week dated 31 July 1970." He waved a copy at us. "It states that the women sergeants may take the oral examination for Investigator III but cannot be promoted."

"That's ridiculous, but I'll take the oral in hopes that there will be some light of reason in the future," I said. "The chief sure messed this up."

"Agreed," Bookman nodded. "It doesn't make sense. Maybe if you women hang loose, something will open up. Anyway, when your oral is scheduled, I'll do what I can to help you score high. Shift will notify you when the orals are posted."

He hadn't talked down to me. On the contrary, he had been supportive. So I didn't feel defensive. Finally, he had addressed me as an employee rather than a woman. I sensed his delicate position of trying to be loyal to the chief while having to carry out the chief's unreasonable orders. I probably should not have been surprised when, somehow, my chance to take that oral examination never materialized.

On August 11th, the city council passed Ordinance #140 820, effective January 1, 1971. After the passage of Jacob, I settled down to do my job. I knew it would take time to work out the horrendous goof of denying the women the chance to become Investigator IIIs, which probably wouldn't happen until the major reorganization had been completed.

All remained quiet until one morning in late fall, when I stopped at the scientific investigation division in the police building to pick up evidential handwriting exemplars that matched checks written on bogus accounts. Thumbing through the results, I was pleased that five more warrants could now be filed with the city attorney. I needed to copy the handwriting files and stepped to the other side of the three-foot by three-foot support beam that separated the Xerox machine from my desk. I lifted the platen and discovered a sheet of paper left by the previous user. One look at the title on the page made me want to throw up.

I didn't hear someone coming behind me and jerked when a hand snatched the paper away. I whirled to see Sergeant Betty Finch from the office across the hall. She put her finger to her lips. "Don't say a word, or I'm in deep trouble. Only the men are supposed to see this."

Numb, I watched her hurry out the side door. I repeated under my breath, "Only men are supposed to see this," as I returned to my chair and lit a cigarette to calm down.

Dottie's head popped up across our desks. "What's the matter? Your face is white."

"I just saw a paper I shouldn't have seen. There's a confidential survey being circulated among the men asking them how they like working with policewomen. After all the rumors, this is the real thing. They're trying to justify the elimination of women from the force."

"You're kidding!"

"No mistaking the capital letters. It's one thing not to make waves, Dottie, but this is more than I can stomach. What kind of imbeciles do they take us for? The gall of them sneaking a survey around to the men and believing we wouldn't find out. Maybe that's what's made Dalton so squirrelly. My instincts tell me something's afoot concerning our jobs."

"They can't fire us. We're civil service."

After all this time, she still didn't want to believe we had a problem. How could I make her understand this was serious? "Look what we've been through this year since they started the reorganization of the department," I said. "If they can justify cutting us out of the budget, what can we do to stop it? For all we know, they may have already done it in the new ordinance that the city council just passed. By January 1, 1971, when it becomes effective, we could be walking the streets, and I don't mean on a beat. We sit here, Dottie, like lambs about to be run down the chute to the slaughterhouse without so much as a bleat of protest."

Dottie glided to the door. "Grab your purse. We're being tuned in by male radar ears. Let's head for the cafeteria where we can talk."

"Wait a minute. Let me check my appointments. I don't want to screw up with all the heat coming down on us."

"We haven't taken a coffee break this whole week," she said. "And we haven't left work the last two nights before 6 p.m. Come on. We need to get out of here."

In the seventh-floor restaurant, we paid for our coffee and found a corner table next to a window with no one near. I could feel the ache in my chest, which hadn't surfaced for some time. "Dottie, in spite of how bad I feel right now, I think fate has dealt us a good hand. I stumbled on that survey by luck. It will give us time to mount an attack. Question is, what kind of an offense can be mustered?"

"What do you mean?" she whispered.

"There'll never be a better time for the Policewomen's Association to go into action."

"What about Mrs. Chambers?"

"We have to try to resolve some of our problems ourselves. We can't afford to be running over to her office about everything that happens. I think a letter by our president to the chief telling him that we've heard about the survey would let him know it's no longer confidential."

"You're going to get into trouble, partner."

"Not if I take the time to know what I'm doing. It's crossed my mind that we need to be more political. Nothing else has worked through the years. The association can contact the chief directly, so we need to confront him about the survey and demand that he tell us the truth about our careers."

She sat forward and clutched her coffee mug in both hands. "That's insane." She looked up. "I don't want the chief angry at me. I don't want Bookman to change his mind about me working a felony team. We need the chief working for us, not against us. What if he turns us down?"

"Who knows what he'll do. That's the chance we take. If we do nothing, he may be able to remove us from the department. Right now, he's sure not working for us. That survey, as stupid as it is, isn't for fun and games. We have to believe he's behind it. We have to flush this out where we can understand what's happening. Then, we've got to know what action we can take and who we can trust to help us. Do you have any suggestions?"

"Not so fast," she said. "This could get so ugly that it won't be worth coming to work!"

"It's ugly right now. I can't sit here and do nothing. I'm calling our president. She's new to the position, but sharp."

I marched to the wall-hung telephone by the entrance to the cafeteria and dialed. Shilah agreed to deliver a letter to the chief. Because she hadn't been informed about the controversies surrounding the women, she asked me to write up a draft and send it to her.

I went back to Dottie. "Come on. I have work to do. Shilah has agreed to sign it if I write it."

We walked out of the cafeteria, and Dottie stopped. "Are you sure this is the right thing to do? Shouldn't we call a meeting of the association?"

"That's for the president to decide. For now, best we keep our traps shut. There are plenty of town criers in the squad room, and the men will stick together like a gaggle of geese. Anything they hear about our activities will immediately get to the chief."

Before we entered the elevator, she said, "I'm a coward. I don't want to get mixed up in this. I have to think about my husband, too. He wants to be a lieutenant, and something like this would kill his oral."

"I understand," I said.

Back at my desk, I penned the letter and sent it to Shilah through departmental mail. Within a week, we were given a date to meet with the chief in the police auditorium.

As soon as the holidays ended, the Jacob Ordinance went into effect. That didn't give me much of a feeling of triumph as I approached the police auditorium on January 10, 1971. I hoped that at least Davis would confirm the rumors and give us a basis to talk with him. In my twenty-two years on the department, the chief had never met with the women officers as far as I knew.

The lights flooded the stage used for the lineup of suspects, leaving the rest of the auditorium in semi-darkness. I don't know which woman had thought up the seating, but center and midway back from the stage put us at eye level with the chief. I quickly counted close to one hundred women in attendance.

Chief Edward M. Davis, his thatch of white hair haloed with light, strode down the aisle. Deputy Chief Dale Speck followed. Speck placed a leather satchel in front of the podium on stage while Davis adjusted the mic.

Within seconds, Sergeant Josephine Stevens, whose letter to city officials had really upset the chief, marched uninvited to the stage. She shook Davis's hand, reached down, picked up the pouch, stepped back to the rear curtain and set it down. "Chief, it made me nervous to see your leather case too close to the edge with all that expensive sound equipment inside," she said. "I wouldn't want it to topple onto the floor." Grinning, she returned to her seat.

We laughed as Davis's and Speck's faces colored. I was delighted that Stevens had found the courage to show them that we weren't intimidated by them or the recording device they had clumsily tried to conceal.

Davis stood to the side, an elbow propped on the podium. Eyeing the gathering, he struck a casual stance as Speck stood aside. "You ladies requested this meeting," Davis announced, his voice filling the auditorium. "I'm here to address the questions concerning your career status on the Los Angeles Police Department. Specifically, you wanted information regarding a survey circulating among the men."

He was assured and matter-of-fact as he faced us. "Women are no longer wanted or needed by the LAPD," he announced. "Women don't belong in law enforcement and can't do the job. Besides, the men don't want you here."

We didn't have political clout or money. As I listened to him boast about how he would phase all but twelve of us off the department through attrition and reclassification of our civil service ratings, I realized we were in deep trouble.

II

AGAINST THE TIDE

The squad room buzzed with talk. The telephones rang and rang, and a sullen suspect handcuffed to a chair screamed profanities. Short on tolerance, the suspect's last, "Fuck you!" made me want to bolt.

"I'll be back in half an hour," I told Dottie, as I headed for the stairwell and rapidly climbed five flights to the roof. Once out in the sunshine, away from the constant bombardment in the office, I drew in a deep breath and walked around the perimeter of the Parker Center roof, trying to come to terms with why I was so edgy. I loved police work and all the raunchy dirt that went with it. And with a few notable exceptions, I really liked most of my coworkers.

As vehicles below lined up like ants at the signals, people scurried along the sidewalks, and a siren wailed from some distant spot, I realized the problem was obvious. My trouble was that I couldn't accept being ignored or relegated to lesser assignments just because I was a woman. I resented the fact that my qualifications weren't acknowledged. I worked a hell of a lot harder than most of the men. Why couldn't they accept me?

I knew why. I'd been out of step and in conflict so often because I couldn't accept less. Trying to change that when most of those around me were invested in the status quo was bound to lead to problems. And now the chief was working to eliminate women from the job. Whatever his plans, he had to be stopped, but that would take somebody with more power than I possessed.

With another deep breath of fresh air, I left the roof and returned to the squad room. Through the pall of cigarette smoke, Dottie waved a bulletin at me. "Did you see this?" she asked. "Why not try for Board of Directors of the Police Relief Association?"

"Nobody would nominate me."

"I would. I don't like to get involved, but I want to help make things better. Nominations are open from the floor at today's Police Relief board meeting. I'll call and make reservations for two. That okay with you?"

I nodded. It would mean extra work on top of my assignment to misdemeanor checks, but if I made it, that could be worked out with the captain. I would still be assigned to bunco-forgery and responsible for my investigations, but they would have to give me time to function as a director, just like all members of the board.

If I could get elected to Police Relief, it'd be a miracle. I had to convince the men to vote for me. I had heard allegations of higher-up payoffs under the table in connection with our medical insurance. It was an ugly thought. If true, that needed to be investigated. Most importantly, I could talk to the men about expanding medical benefits.

"Dottie, do you think I might have a chance?"

"If they believe you can get us better benefits and can save a buck in their paychecks, they'll vote for you."

"I don't know, Dottie. It's been a rough year. It's quieted since last May's reception with the mayor and the whole Jacob Plan business, but my husband, Shannon, is scheduled for open heart surgery. This might be too much for me to handle."

"It's no different than the Protective League," she persisted. "You would only have to attend one meeting a month. Besides, all I'm doing is nominating you."

"If I make it without the chief's blessings, it'd be an upset. Do you think they can tolerate a female sergeant?"

"If you're elected, they'll have to adjust." She picked up a handful of bad checks. "The meeting starts at noon. I've got just enough time to complete processing this new bunch."

I could not continue to sit back and let the chief's office handpick men for election without challenge. Here was my chance to elevate myself into the inner circle of the department, but I would have to hustle. With only a month to go before the election, time was short.

My heart raced as I thought about how the chief would react, but Mama's influence in my early years had pointed me toward confrontation. I hadn't understood until right now why in 1926 she had moved us away from Utah. She couldn't tolerate the Mormon Church demanding her total acceptance without question. She had dared to think for herself, and Grandpa Renstrom had disowned her. I hadn't appreciated the hell she must have lived through to break away.

Mama had helped me find the precious gift of thinking for myself, a gift I hadn't surrendered. No wonder I was so different from others, so unable to accept unfairness. No wonder I would challenge and ask questions. She wanted me to have a better life than she did. She wanted me to have the freedom to seek both my faith and my career. Because of Mama, I would never allow any institution or any person to rob me of my power of mind.

That's why I had never stopped fighting for what the City had promised when they hired me. No matter how rough it got, I would stand up for myself—regardless of the consequences.

I sat at my desk, feeling calmer than I had in months. The stack of new reports seemed inconsequential.

A couple of hours later, Dottie and I hurried to the seventh-floor cafeteria and slid into our seats at the U-shaped table where the board directors were already being served their meals. I tried my best not to show how nervous I was.

"Pathe," I whispered, using Dottie's last name as cops so often do. "Look who's sitting at the other end."

"It's Deputy Chief Wagner!"

"He made my life hell when I worked public information."

"As the Jacob task force commander, do you think he's the one who thought up removing women from the force?" she asked.

"No. I think that came directly from the chief. But knowing Wagner, I feel sure he did everything he could to make it happen. It'll be interesting to watch his face when you nominate me. Look at him frown. He's probably wondering why you and I showed up."

I wouldn't let Wagner upset me just because he was a deputy chief. If I wound up being elected to the Police Relief Board, it would be interesting to see how he would relate to me.

At the end of the lunch, Dottie nominated me. I knew those in attendance didn't believe I had a chance.

"The nominations are closed," the secretary said. "The ballots will be mailed Monday, and the results will be posted on December 4th."

Until the election, I spent a solid month making divisional roll calls before I reported to work, and after 4 p.m. for all three watches, days, nights, and mornings. I traveled from San Pedro harbor to north San Fernando Valley and from

Hollenbeck to Venice. Some watch commanders would not let me speak, but I still put flyers on the bulletin boards. The best reception came from the elite motorcycle officers when one of them, sprawled in his seat, yelled, "Lady, you've got balls. Brass balls. Any woman with courage enough to come before all us raunchy men and ask for our votes deserves to be elected. We'll spread the word."

There's always a poor response to mailed ballots, but on December 4th, 1971, I received 879 votes, enough to elect me. "Listen up, troops," Lieutenant Shift said. "There's an unusual announcement." He smiled as he continued, "Sergeant Blake has been elected to the Police Relief Association."

As the men applauded and whistled, I grabbed Dottie and danced her around our desks. Over my shoulder, I could see Dalton, my tormentor, sunk in his seat. After the room calmed down, several of the men came to shake my hand and offer congratulations. I answered a phone call from the chief's office. "Dottie, Davis wants to talk to me."

"Think he'll congratulate you? Maybe he's going to give you some instructions."

"I'll know more after I meet with him. I'm on my way now. Shouldn't take long. Whatever he wants to know, it won't be lengthy. Don't say anything to the men."

When I reported to Davis in the small conference room, his white hair caught the sunlight as he filled his pipe, tamped and lit it, drawing smoke into his mouth. "Tell me, Blake." Smoke drifted upwards. "How many policewomen are on the job?" He swiveled to look directly at me.

He certainly wasn't going to congratulate me. He knew better than I how many policewomen there were. It was a stupid question. "Sir, there aren't as many as when you became chief."

"How many do you think voted for you?"

That was it! He couldn't understand how a woman could collect the votes I received. It had taken more than a handful of policewomen to elect me. "I have no idea, Chief. Maybe half of them." I stood still. He hadn't indicated I could sit down.

"How do you account for the votes you received?" He puffed on his pipe and relit it.

No matter what I said, he wouldn't like it. I couldn't resist. "Why, Chief," I blurted, "obviously, I slept with every police officer in town."

He choked on his smoke, and I could see I had embarrassed him. He must have thought I had pulled some sleazy act to get elected. He couldn't accept that a woman could earn 879 votes fair and square. "You may leave, Blake," he said, dismissing me with a wave of his hand.

I headed out the door. He would not give me his blessing, nor did I expect it. It would be tough, but he was still my chief, and, as a director, I would stretch to remain loyal to him. Today was the first time I had met him one-on-one in that role. I hadn't wanted to embarrass him, but I couldn't resist the opening he had given me. Had my quip turned him into an enemy? I hoped not. I had enough trouble in the department already.

Three months later, on the morning of March 12, 1972, I lost a valuable ally when Deputy Mayor Ellie Chambers died after having been admitted to the hospital for complications from the flu. I hadn't gotten a chance to say goodbye or to thank her for her support. None of the LAPD policewomen had. We couldn't even go to her funeral, since it was private. With a heavy heart, I turned my focus back to my work on the department.

As always, I took my responsibilities seriously. As a newly elected Police Relief director, I began to look into several inequities, starting with our medical insurance, that I felt were negatively impacting our officers. It never occurred to me that management would feel threatened since they controlled much of what went on or that they would not tolerate a perceived challenge from an upstart like me. But despite, or perhaps because of, the work I did on the various committees I'd been placed on, I soon found I had become a target for harassment—required, for example, to justify the time spent on Police Relief matters, including the attendance of board meetings. No other board member was required to justify their time. I was sure the fact that I had been directing some unnerving questions at the men who handled the LAPD's health insurance account had something to do with that.

To counter their assaults against me, I submitted an article to the Protective League paper, which shared my discomfort and fears regarding my troubles as a director of Police Relief. I was engaged in a silent war with the chief of police and had to protect myself.

Meanwhile, I would have to get used to a significant change in my day-to-day job.

"You're losing Dottie today as your partner," Captain Bookman announced not long after I had published the article. He stood by my desk with Lieutenant Shift and a Black sergeant named Hubert Greene. "You'll be working with Sergeant Greene."

"That's wonderful," I said, turning to my new partner. "Sergeant, do you mind working with a woman?"

"No problem," he said. "I think we'll get along just fine."

"I thought," Bookman said with a laugh, "that you two minorities would make a great team."

Startled at the captain's insensitivity toward a Black officer, I watched Greene's body stiffen. Shift snickered and went back to his desk.

"Frankly, Captain," I said, "I don't give a damn what color any of us is. I'm proud to work with Greene."

"I just thought," the captain said, "since you're so fired-up about equal rights, that putting the two of you together would meet the affirmative action requirements for the division."

"Come on, Sergeant," I said as Bookman strutted to his office. "Let's get out of here and head for a cup of coffee. We've got some private conversation due us."

"Hubert," I said, once seated in the cafeteria. "That was raw prejudice we just encountered. As far as I'm concerned, they can go straight to hell."

"I've heard worse in my lifetime," he said. "But I resent that we're together because they think it's a big joke."

"Tell you what," I said. "I'm not willing to give them any satisfaction at our expense. They've probably already dubbed us the Odd Couple."

"On this department," he said, "there'll be plenty said behind our backs."

"I happen to know that the white male investigators are not well thought of by the banks run by Blacks. If those banks would cooperate with you and me, we could move a lot of forgery cases forward to prosecution."

"We can't cause trouble for our men. But I'm for making better relations with the bankers."

"Neither the captain nor Shift addressed who's in charge of our team," I said. "They're cowards. I take a dim view of being subordinate when this has been my job for over two years. I'd like to suggest we take turns being in charge, okay?"

"Splendid," he said. "Besides, you'll have to teach me your routine."

We stood up to leave, shook hands, and went back to work.

12

BETWIXT AND BETWEEN

I got excited when I read the robbery-rapist task force memo. The percentage of crime reports from Wilshire and Hollywood divisions had increased by 75 percent. That fall of 1972, the letter-size reports stacked up in piles on every flat surface in the detective bureau. They set up a volunteer task force for a four-day assignment to walk decoy. I hadn't walked a beat since the '40s, but this was going to be an experience I didn't want to miss. My feet still hurt, but I was willing to suffer to have one more shot at street action before retirement. I wasn't too soft for risky undercover work. I might be a bit overweight, but I could still run like hell, especially with my heels off.

I charged into Captain Jack Morris's office, Captain Bookman having been transferred, and waited until he looked up from his work. "The robbery division is calling for women to help. I'd like to volunteer." I handed him the memo.

He was a quiet man with enormous bags under his pale eyes. He stared at me a moment, took the paper, and read it. "It's a dirty assignment for women," he said. His gaze swept my body. "Forgive me, Sergeant, but you're not exactly the youngest woman on the department."

"I'm fifty-two," I fired back. "But I've got plenty of street energy left. Please, don't write me off. I'd like a chance to work this special detail."

"What about your heart problems?"

"The doctor doesn't indicate that I'm disabled. I can take care of myself. I haven't asked for any considerations because of my heart. I want to work this task force."

"I don't know why any woman would want to." He paused. "See Shift to cover your desk. Permission granted." He handed me the memo and returned to his paperwork. I floated out of his office.

The following Thursday evening, I reported to the night-orientation meeting. Ten women and twenty men assembled in the police auditorium. Detective Buckland, also known as old Iron Jaw, passed out basic car plan maps. "This isn't fun and games," he snapped, his brimmed hat cocked back on his head. His voice echoed through the auditorium. "It's damned serious business. You could get killed. Catching a robbery/rapist/purse snatcher is dangerous. The suspects are hitting fast and early this year, and we believe they may be organized."

He held up a hefty stack of crime reports. "Here's over a hundred filed complaints." He paused. "You women libbers make the same money as the men. On this assignment, you'll earn every dollar. Make yourself look as helpless as possible."

He hunched over, shuffled across the stage, and turned back to face us as he continued talking. "If you walk like you graduated from the police academy, you'll scare 'em off. Hold your purses loosely, like this." He grabbed a purse from the table next to him and held it with his fingers at his side. "Make it easy for them to snatch. If you stay alert, you can hear them coming up behind you. Whatever you do, don't look over your shoulder.

That's a dead giveaway. You must let them grab the purse before you react, or we won't have enough for prosecution."

He removed his hat and wiped his forehead, picked up a shawl, covered his head, and tied it under his chin. "See what I mean? Make yourself look like an old woman. These birds hit on frail females." He removed the shawl. "Be sure you open your purse and flash your phony money. You'll each be given one of these." He held up a one-dollar bill wrapped around a wad with a rubber band. "It brings out the greed in them fast. And I repeat. Ignore your two-man tails. This way, the suspects won't know you're being backed up. Our men are trained street men. They'll be there to back any action you draw, but they can't stay too close, or they'll burn their cover. Stay alert. If you lure a suspect, you're to take whatever action you can to protect yourself until the team can catch up. Any questions?"

"What kind of suspects are we looking for?" asked Cecelia Dominguez, a young Latina policewoman.

"They're Black, between 15 and 25. Most are well built, one hundred and ninety to two hundred and twenty pounds. Their MOs: they tail victims, run up behind, snatch the purse and knock the woman into the bushes, or drag her behind buildings for rape. You'll each be wired with a walkie-talkie. Keep it covered at the top of your stuffed shopping bag and ready to activate. Carry your weapons and handcuffs on your belts."

When I had last walked a beat, I had done it in high heels and a skirted dress uniform. The women currently in the room wore slacks, comfortable loafers or tennis shoes, and three-quarter length coats. They all carried big purses with straps.

I drew the area bounded on the north by the Santa Monica Freeway, east by the Harbor Freeway, west by Crenshaw Boulevard, and South at Vernon Avenue. We left the meeting at 8 p.m. with our male teams in undercover vehicles. My detail dropped off at Vermont Avenue, just south of the Santa Monica Freeway. The men assigned to me disappeared to the opposite side of the street.

I started to walk south toward Vernon Avenue, through the heart of a rundown Black business and residential neighborhood. Boarded-up shop windows, stench from street garbage, and long shadows cast by dim street lights didn't need ghostly music to capture my alertness. I approached a tavern where three men outside stared as I walked by. I stopped a short distance from them, rummaged in my purse, pretended to check my fake wad of money, stuck it back into my purse, and slowly continued on my way. My ears ached from straining to hear movement behind me. As I walked, my gun butt rubbed a sore spot on the bare flesh of my paunchy stomach. I didn't dare look around to see if my two tails were really there; instead, I concentrated on stooping and walking more slowly.

The further south I walked, the darker and dirtier the area became. A dog ran across the street, a car cruised by, and the shadows looked like men. A yellow Cadillac turned out of the alley in front of me, and slowly followed me for a while at a discreet distance. Then it cruised slowly abreast with me. A heavyset Black man with steel-gray hair rolled down the window on the passenger side. "Get in, miss," his froggy voice hissed. "I'll give you a lift."

My stomach turned to mush, and I kept on walking. He wasn't the young dude we were looking for. He stopped. "Miss, did you hear me? I said get in!"

I slipped my hand inside my jacket onto the butt of my gun. "Buzz off, mister. I'm not interested."

He burned rubber as he left. Good! I needed to hook the right suspect.

Son-of-a-gun, that yellow Cadillac must have gone around the block. He pulled up again and opened the door. "I said, miss, get in!"

"Buster. You're asking for it." I slammed his door, bent over, and looked him right in the eyes. I kept my hand on my gun but did not draw. "You're cramping my act."

"Come on, sister. Get in. I wanna talk."

"Don't crowd me, buddy. Leave me alone or I'll blow your damned head off," I exclaimed as I made a movement to pull my weapon.

He hit the gas pedal so hard he left half his tread on the street. I couldn't see the two trained men trailing me. In one more block, I would reach Vernon Avenue, where the pickup car would be waiting for my team. It was 2 a.m., and I was dead tired, more than ready to give up decoying for the night. As I crawled into the pickup car, the two men tailing me ran down the street toward us and climbed in.

Back in the safety of the station, I gulped a cup of hot coffee. The bright overhead lights made me drowsy. A grinning lieutenant slid into the seat next to me. "What's this cat and mouse game you were playing with that big yellow Cadillac?"

I set my cup on the table. "I should know by now. There's nothing secret out on the street. Tell me, Lieutenant, how in the name of heaven did you find that out?"

"I got a call from a snitch checking you out."

"As a matter of fact," I said, "a big yellow Cadillac with a senior, fat Black guy driving tried to pick me up. It's no wonder he was upset. Didn't figure him for the suspects we were looking for, and I wasn't friendly. I finally got my message across to leave me alone. Do you know who he is?"

"Some decoy!" The lieutenant slapped his knee and laughed. "That big man is the pimp of the neighborhood. He's mad, thinking you were trying to muscle in on his territory. He thinks you're a madam!"

"Me? A madam? Come on, Lieutenant. Be serious."

"Have to give you credit, Blake. You're trying, but I don't think you'll catch a rapist. You're too tough. Too much like a cop. Better luck tomorrow night."

"I'm happy to know I didn't turn off a likely suspect. Have you heard if any of the teams have been successful?"

"We finally scored." He wasn't laughing. "Here's the teletype just sent."

I read VICTIM: CECILIA DOMINGUEZ, FEMALE, LATIN, TWENTY-SIX YEARS OLD. SUSPECT: CLYDE FREDERICK JACKSON. WEAPON: BODILY FORCE, SIMULATED GUN, SUSPECT IN CUSTODY.

The suspect had come behind Cecilia, simulated a gun, and forced her into his car by punching her in the stomach. When he entered the driver's side, she hit him on the head with a billy club. Plainclothes officers arrived and took the suspect into custody.

"Lieutenant, is Cece okay?" I didn't feel good about her getting hurt. What if the man in the yellow Cadillac...?

"She's doing fine. Gutsy lady. The hospital will keep her under observation for a few hours. She'll be back to work tomorrow night."

"I think she should have a few days off," I said. "I'm dog tired and didn't have near the trauma Cece did. Thank God she's alright."

My captain had been right; I was in no condition to wrestle suspects out on the street. I didn't want to admit I was fat. Cece was twenty-six years younger than me. A hit on my stomach wouldn't have blacked me out, but I couldn't bounce a medicine ball off my abs. Years ago, I had flown over the six-foot wall at the academy even though my rear end weighed a ton. Now, I wouldn't be able to do more than grab the top of that wall.

I finished my commitment to the task force, disappointed I hadn't scored, but relieved I hadn't been victimized. The following Monday, the third of December, I returned to my desk, grateful to be investigating misdemeanor bad checks.

PART III

13

HELL NO, WE WON'T GO!

"Well, little lady," LAPD Sergeant Ty Dalton announced with a sneer. "Looks like you dames will be seeking new employment."

"The name is Blake, and I'm not your little lady," I snapped.

"Haven't you heard?" He obviously knew something I didn't.

"Heard what?"

"The chief is booting you broads out the door." He stood still, watching me.

"Come on, now, Dalton. You know he can't do that." I knew the chief had planned to reduce our numbers by attrition, but booting us?

"It means he's giving police work back to the men," he said, wagging his finger.

"Don't be an ass, Dalton. And take that damned finger out of my face." I heard my voice rising. "As much as you'd like to see me off the job, I'm not leaving until I decide to go."

"You're not listening," he replied. "The chief is a god-damn genius. This is no rumor. It's before the police commission right now." He squinted as he stepped back.

"What's before the commission?"

"Quiet, everybody. Quiet." He cleared his throat. "Finally, gang, the chief is acting like a man. He's asking the police commission today to raise the minimum requirements for women to the same level as ours. They'll have to be 5'8" and one hundred and forty pounds. And fellas, you know what that means. Most of the policewomen can't qualify."

The air filled with whistles and the floor vibrated from fifty-eight pairs of feet stamping on the black and white checkerboard linoleum floors. Fifty-eight pairs of hands pounded on the rows of long tables where we all worked forgery-bunco cases.

"He'll never get away with it, Dalton."

We stood close. I wouldn't budge. His spit sprayed my face as he bellowed, "Yeah? You can't do anything about it."

"Don't bet your life!" I wiped my face with my hand and stared into his eyes. He backed away, and I sat down, hard, at my desk. At 5'9", I didn't have anything to worry about. But most of the women in the department weren't as tall as I was and would be sacked if this new plan went through. What could I do? I couldn't fight the chief alone. But I sure as hell couldn't ignore his actions. The police commission would do anything the chief asked, and since the commission didn't have to answer to the city council or the mayor, that would be that.

I knew from personal experience that the penalty for speaking out was ridicule and crude jokes. But I couldn't let this go. The next morning, Thursday, February 8, 1973, I left my office and headed for handwriting analysis. In the hallway, I encountered Ken Hansen, a reporter I barely knew. "What luck, Sergeant," he said with a smile. "You're the one I want to talk to, if you can spare a minute."

"What have I done that's of interest to you?"

"Is there somewhere we can talk?"

"Nobody's in the burglary squad room right now, except

their secretary. I don't want to talk in my squad room where we could be overheard."

He sat down at a table across from me and pulled a pad and pencil out of his tweed jacket pocket. "I want to interview you about Chief Davis's new Unisex Plan, which he presented to the police commission yesterday. I understand you keep up on these issues. I'd like to know how the policewomen feel about the chief's plan."

I didn't need Dalton to tell me that *unisex* was a euphemism for no women. The name said it all since the prefix *uni* means one.

"It makes me furious," I exclaimed. "That plan would eliminate all but forty-three women from the force. It's another insidious avenue of discrimination against women on the force."

He wrote his notes in shorthand, taking down everything I said verbatim. "You have your facts right, Sergeant. Not only would it eliminate more than one hundred and twenty policewomen who cannot meet those requirements, but Davis himself also said last month that 96 percent of the female population could not meet the height and weight requirements for job applications. Now, what do you think about that?"

"I believe the chief is blatantly discriminating against women. We have 5'4" female officers who've worked undercover. They've done excellent jobs."

"What about field duty, Sergeant?" Hansen asked. "The chief states that never in his thirty-three years on the department has he heard of any woman walking a beat except for one brief period."

I shot out of my chair, shaking. "The chief is abysmally ignorant if he maintains that we don't have field experience. I walked a beat on Broadway and Main, Spring and Hill Streets, between First and Ninth Streets in downtown Los Angeles from '48 to

'51. I don't call that a brief period. I have broken-down feet from walking it in high heels. They've been operated on twice. I even walked with Helen Cochran Davis, the chief's very own sister-in-law!"

"Can you prove it?"

"Would you like to see my officer's notebooks? I have them at home and can bring them in the morning." I was fit to be tied. "The nerve of Davis," I muttered to myself. "He must think we don't have a brain in our heads." I couldn't imagine why he hadn't thought out the ramifications of his plan. It was ludicrous.

"May I use a phone?" Hansen asked. "I've got to call my editor."

"Help yourself," I said. "Nobody will stop you."

"Can you meet with me in the newspaper report room tomorrow morning?" he asked after he had hung up. "Come early and bring your notebooks."

"No problem."

"The editor would like pictures of those notebooks. Is that okay?"

"You have a date, Hansen. I'll be there and ready."

The next morning, armed with a shoebox full of notebooks showing my juvenile division foot patrols and the arrests I had made, I slipped out of the squad room. Using the stairs to go from the third floor to the first, I stormed into the newspaper room. "Which one of you gentlemen is here to photograph my officer's notebooks?"

The small, oblong room was crammed with worn-out wooden chairs. Their midnight-to-morning copy hung limply from their typewriters, and dirty mugs littered the table along with butt-filled ashtrays. A man typed at a dilapidated table. It had been a long, slow night.

Cal Montney, a *Los Angeles Times* photographer, sat on a chair near the door, holding his camera. Reporter Erwin Baker rose from a lumpy couch; his thick glasses flashed as he extended a pudgy hand. "Thought you wouldn't show. Here." He pushed papers off a chair by the window. "Have a seat."

I nodded, clasped the shoe box close, and sat with my back to the nicotine-stained window. The morning sun warmed my shoulders through missing Venetian blind slats.

"I wouldn't let anybody stop me from keeping this date. I might just as well have stayed here all night. I didn't get much sleep."

"We're no prize packages ourselves. We don't look so hot after twelve hours in this dump." Baker buttoned his wilted collar, pushed his tie into place, and grabbed an armless chair. "Let's see the notebook with the chief's sister-in-law assigned to walk a beat with you."

I flipped the lid, found the notebook he had asked for, and handed it to him. "These are all my notebooks from 1948 to April 1951 when I was recalled into the Army."

"You gonna take on the chief full bore?" Baker asked as he flipped through the pages.

"What do you mean, *full bore*?"

"He said women didn't work the field and walk beats like the men. Here's proof that you did. He's a liar. Don't you want to make it difficult for him?"

These reporters were out for blood. Did I want to make it difficult for the chief? Yes, indeed, but I didn't want to see him ripped apart by the press. They could be brutal. I wanted the chief, who was so against women, to know that his Unisex Plan was terrible. I knew that by changing the physical requirements for women, he could potentially speed up his plan to all but eliminate women from the department. But to make this a personal vendetta between him and me? No, I couldn't do that.

"Mr. Baker, I'm not afraid to confront Davis's arrogance about policewomen. He disturbs me, but I don't know about the word *liar*. That's a mighty strong accusation. What do you want me to do?"

"Grab a handful of those notebooks and fan them out in your hand. The picture will tell the story. Montney, snap that shot! Get some with them fanned across her chest. One of you guys get me an open line to the editor." Baker thumbed through my notebooks, pulled his chair to the typewriter, and inserted fresh paper. He cradled the phone in his neck as he spoke with his editor. "Yes, we have a story. Montney is taking pictures now and can make the deadline for the final night edition."

I stood behind the reporter and pointed to verifiable facts, including adult arrests made and court cases.

"I'll have to run this over to the *Times* for Joan Sweeney." He pulled his copy from the rollers. "Come on, Cal. Sweeney's got most of the story already written. We'll have to hustle before the paper goes to press. Sergeant, good luck. We'll contact you by 4 p.m. this afternoon."

I returned to my desk. It took all my willpower to keep my mouth shut and say nothing to Dalton. The day dragged until I thought I couldn't stand it any longer. I went through a pack of cigarettes and too much coffee before the police reporter called as promised. "Kid, you made the front page. Picture included. Come on down."

I slammed the receiver into its cradle and hurried down the stairwell to the newspaper room. When I burst through the door, an old reporter held up a copy of the *Times*.

"Look at that headline!" I exclaimed. There I was, right under the February 9, 1973 dateline, staring back at myself. The headline read: "Davis 'Unisex' Plan Angers Policewomen." The photo of me with a handful of notebooks spread across my bosom occupied half of the page.

Oh my! Policewomen could no longer be ignored on the LAPD. What a gift! The LAPD higher-ups had been caught in a time warp. Maybe this would help them understand that they could not afford to sleep while the world changed, and that every woman in the department deserved a chance to live up to her potential when it came to serving and protecting the citizens of Los Angeles.

When I read the article, however, the words, *asinine and illogical* and *abysmally ignorant*, correctly quoted, drained the blood from my face. "Wait till the chief sees this!" I muttered. "Nobody calls him ignorant and gets away with it." I looked up at the reporter. "All I wanted to do was get his attention. I know he can't fire me, but he can sure make my life miserable. I'm already on his blacklist. I have no idea what he may do now."

"That's what you said. No retractions." He laughed. "Keep the paper. This one's on the house."

"Thanks. At least everyone has left for the day. But I'm not looking forward to returning to work on Monday."

"You have the press backing you, Sergeant. I don't think you'll hear a word from the chief. But if things get sticky, give us a call."

"I'd better hightail it home before my husband learns about this secondhand," I said.

"Too late, Sergeant. It's already on the radio and TV."

"Thanks for the warning."

I carried my copy of the newspaper back to my office, and I re-read the article. The weekend would somewhat deaden its impact by the time I returned to work on Monday morning, but why had I used such inflammatory words? I knew why. I had used them because that was precisely how I felt.

Up until now, I had been battling on the fringes for my career. With this publicity, the *Los Angeles Times* put me right in the middle of the action. I fingered the medallion hanging from my neck, which my husband Shannon had given to me on Valentine's Day. "You have the right to be yourself here and now," the inscription read. I hoped he meant it. I was being myself and had no intention of retreating just because I had hit the headlines.

At 7:30 sharp, Monday morning, I entered the squad room, which suddenly quieted down, and marched directly to the head of my division.

"Lieutenant," I said. "I had no idea I'd make the front page of the *L.A. Times* on Friday. It was just supposed to be an article."

"Whatever it was supposed to be, you've become a celebrity." Lieutenant Ryan Shift fished for a handful of notes. "Take care of these calls on your own time. I suggest you cool it on the job as much as possible."

"I'll do my best, Lieutenant."

Smiling, I turned and caught Dalton glowering at me from his desk. "It's a good thing you didn't bet your life last week when I told you I wouldn't let Davis push the women off the department," I couldn't resist saying. "This is just the beginning."

His face flushed red into his thinning black hair. Back at my desk, I watched Shift's scowl deepen and wondered what tirade about the publicity might have come down to him through channels. He hadn't embarrassed me in front of the men. I was grateful for that. The detectives clearly did not approve of my actions, and many avoided me. Relations didn't need to deteriorate any further. Little did I know it was going to.

14

MAYBE TODAY WE'LL SCORE

I had promised myself that I would no longer stay silent. I would be heard on this issue. So I requested and was granted time to speak before the Los Angeles Police Commission on Wednesday, February 28, 1973. The five senior males appointed to the police commission through the mayoral office, along with Chief Davis, who would be in attendance, would finally have to hear me out about opening promotions and assignments for LAPD's women officers and not allowing them to be eradicated from the department.

The unspoken message from the chief's office to policewomen was that ignoring the rank's silent code would be met with retaliation. Harassment had been routinely used to keep us in line under male domination. Now, knowing I was about to challenge the chief's plan, the men I worked with started avoiding me.

Unable to quell my lurking anxiety, I scooped up my prepared speech and left the squad room for the Parker Center's first floor. It didn't help to see an overflow crowd at the door of the hearing room, or the TV cameras lined up against the east wall.

I elbowed through the small space to an empty chair in the front row. The low fluorescent lights added to the stuffiness. Despite unbuttoning my blue jacket, sweat rings formed in my armpits. I began to wish I hadn't done this.

From a side door, the commissioners filed in behind their leather chairs and sat down at the conference table. Chief Davis and Deputy Chief Jack Collins entered last, in full dress uniforms with double brass buttons. They sat at the end of the table. There wasn't much space between us. As we stared at each other, I refused to break eye contact.

Police commission President Kohn, a brilliant lawyer and seventeen-year member of the commission, whom I would later count as a friend, gaveled for order. Not more than five feet tall, his executive chair absorbed him.

I knew I didn't possess political clout when it came to the commission's decisions. Hopefully, they would listen to me and question the chief's intentions. I knew that if Davis won his request to up female qualifications from 5'4" to 5'8", it would give him the power to start removing most of the women officers from the LAPD. Indeed, it would later be documented that the 5'6" height requirement that the plan finally landed on excluded 87 percent of adult women and only 20 percent of adult men. The interim 5'7" height requirement excluded 95 percent of all women compared to 35 percent of male applicants.

"We're in special session today to discuss Chief Davis's integrated Unisex Plan for policewomen," Kohn intoned. "Sergeant Blake is testifying against the plan." He smiled and nodded for me to approach the podium.

Suddenly, the full extent of the risk I was running hit me. "A lot of us would like to speak out, but think it's just not wise," a fellow policewoman would admit to a *Los Angeles Times* reporter later that day. Another would add, "We are in a military organization where no way a private can stand up and talk against his commander." I was about to do just that.

My insides were jelly, and my knees wobbled, but I was not about to show fright. As I stepped two paces to the podium in the center of the room, the TV lights turned on, blinding me. I hung on to the lectern.

Trying to feign calm, I stood at the podium, squared my shoulders, and silently prayed that my message would lift the career stranglehold imposed upon the women at the LAPD. This was my moment to make an impact and trigger a miracle.

I had justice—and the law—on my side. My research at the law library had revealed that Title VII of the Civil Rights Act of 1964, which the Equal Employment Act of 1972 had extended to the public sector, made it illegal to discriminate against anyone based on sex as well as race in hiring, promoting, and firing. While that didn't help me feel any less nervous, I knew we women were in this mess in part because we had all been too scared to speak up.

Hang in there, Fanchon, I told myself as I heard the TV cameras click on. *The chief can't hurt you. Come on, tighten the old chin. Stand straight. Don't give him anything. Maybe today we'll score.*

I spread my speech before me, took a deep breath, and heard my voice break as I began. "Mr. President." I swallowed and continued. "Members of the Commission, Chief Davis, and guests." After thanking the commission for the opportunity to speak on behalf of the LAPD women officers, I reviewed how Chief Davis had unfolded his blueprint to eliminate women from the department.

"I have to recall from memory, but essentially he stated that as attrition and resignations occurred, he would fill our positions with male officers. This he has done. He informed us that all our positions would be evaluated and that as many as could be phased out would be. He implied that perhaps any remaining positions for a woman could be handled by reserve policewomen; that when everything leveled off, there would be approximately twelve policewomen's positions left. There have been no new policewomen hired for over three years."

I called for the chief to bring to a close twenty-five years of discrimination and to uphold his sworn oath and enforce the law. That included the Equal Opportunity Employment Act, I reminded him.

"Not only has the Chief of Police ignored the federal law, but he has also defied the order of this council to prepare a pilot program and ascertain if women can perform all the duties of a police officer.

"I have volunteered to accept assignment to a radio car on any watch in any section of this city. Again, I offer you my services. I am not afraid. I know my capabilities and have complete confidence in any assignment required of me. I have never refused to accept any assignment that I have been ordered to perform in my entire career.

"My life is no more precious than a man's, and, if it must be sacrificed in the line of duty, that is part of the contract I agreed to and fully understood when the City accepted me as a police officer. In the course of my career, I have had dangerous assignments. I walked foot patrol on Skid Row from 1948 to 1951, when it was the primary, high-frequency crime area of this city. Last November and December, I walked decoy for robbery, rapist, and purse-snatch suspects at night in this city.

"Each of us who has received a measure of trust in our city service status knows that we cannot protect our honor, dignity, or integrity if we have not the moral courage to stop and question and correct what we know is wrong. Discrimination against the Los Angeles policewomen is both legally and morally wrong."

The chief and deputy chief listened stone-faced as I spoke, then began whispering to each other, sending a "lady beware" feeling through my guts. I wanted to break my disciplined composure and yell, "Hey, this time is our time!"

I looked up at Davis, wondering whether he would order me removed from field investigations following my appearance here today and the comments I had made about him in the *Los Angeles Times* three weeks prior. I knew this appearance wouldn't bode well for me. But I could no longer remain silent.

The chief's steel eyes bored into mine without blinking. His head swiveled on his thick neck even as his fleshy jowls held firm. I blinked. My stomach tightened. The television camera hummed as the silence in the room magnified. I heard whispered comments from the crowd of spectators behind me and remembered how my former commander, Captain Rock Bookman, had stood before our sixty-man unit at bunco-forgery and stated he wouldn't consider me or any female officer for promotion simply because we were women. He had said, "No woman on this department could possibly compete against men for promotion or field assignments." His words had stung, cutting deep into my pride. At least now, I was making the case for the women on the force who couldn't afford to make it for themselves.

"Your decision must be to resolve and provide an honorable career for the one hundred and eighty policewomen who have patiently awaited this fulfillment. This great city, the city council, the board of police commissioners, and the manager of the police department are not above the law of the land. The issue is mandated by Title VII of the Equal Opportunity Employment Act to provide opportunity for promotion and assignment without consideration of sex.

"Will this be a courageous turning point in the history of law enforcement in this city? Will you right a wrong of long-standing in your police department and let a veteran policewoman who has devoted twenty-five years to the protection of you and your loved ones, and who many times reiterated her willingness to lay down her life in the line of duty, continue to go unrewarded for faithful, loyal, loving service to her city, merely on the flimsy excuse that she is a woman?"

What a relief! I had finally aired not only my grievances but my female fellow officers'. At long last, we had officially made some noise.

The room erupted with applause from the women and loud commentary from the men. Kohn hammered the gavel. "Please, Sergeant. One minute." He waited for quiet as I tried my best to control any show of emotion.

"Chief, do you desire to question the sergeant?" Kohn asked.

Davis whispered to Deputy Chief Collins. "Tell me, Sergeant," Collins said. "What do you think about 5'0" policemen?" He stifled a grin and whispered something back to Davis.

I couldn't believe these two would ask such a stupid question. "I've given that question a lot of thought. What is germane is whether a 5-foot-tall person can perform as a qualified police officer. Is it mandatory for only giants to be police officers? Military records reflect millions of 5-foot men throughout history who have fought gallantly in bloody wars. Many have come home heroes."

In response to questions from the commissioners, I said that I saw no reason why trained 5'4" women should not be given "combat" experience walking beats and riding in radio cars. "I'm not saying every woman born is capable of this. I know it's kind of a mind-blower when you think about a woman being shot at. But despite statements to the contrary, in 1948, '49, '50 and '51, LAPD policewomen did walk beats. We did ride in radio cars both in uniform and in civilian clothes. And we did make arrests off the street in combat situations."

No other woman stood to speak, and my words made no difference. I would find out almost as soon as I had finished my plea for equity that in private session earlier that day, the commission had voted to send Chief Davis' Unisex Plan to the city council. That would assure its passage. The commission wasn't even going to consider what I had said. I might as well not have gone.

I had done what I could to convince the department to treat its female officers equally. Over the years, my ambitions had been thwarted. Although I had made the grade of detective sergeant, I had been denied the chance to take a written examination for promotion to lieutenant. Now things were about to get much worse. I wouldn't let the chief continue to imperiously ignore the law and set himself above what he had sworn to uphold. After unsuccessful appearances before the city council and the police commission and years of opposing the system from within, a single recourse remained.

The only way to interrupt this intolerable set of circumstances was to exercise my freedom and fight through the courts. The thought of suing the LAPD sent chills down my spine. On the other hand, if it got too hot, I could retire immediately since my pension was now secure. There had to be a sacrificial lamb right now, and it might as well be me.

"Why don't you broads stay home?" a policeman yelled as I prepared to leave the hearing room. "Most of you don't even need to work, and you don't belong behind the badge."

I exited with wet eyes and intensifying anger as the sound of the men slapping each other on the back boomeranged in my ears. For twenty-five years, I had been held back in my career just because I was a woman. I was so frustrated, I was ready to burst. "I'll be damned if I'll accept this stupidity," I said out loud. Chief Davis had underestimated me, just as he underestimated the women under his command. He had made a significant mistake on both counts.

I sped down the hall to the lobby, then around the corner to the press room. Hansen was napping on the newsroom's lumpy couch. I grabbed his sweater and shook his shoulder. "Wake up, Hansen. Come with me. It's my turn to pay back the coverage you gave me. I've got an exclusive, just for you."

He yawned, cleaned his glasses, picked up a pad and pencil, and followed me outside. "What's up?" He stretched. "Can't we stay inside where we can be comfortable?"

"I don't want any leaks until I can set up what I must do. I don't trust the telephones in our building. They can all be bugged upstairs in scientific investigation's electronics center. And I don't trust ears that might hear what I have to say to you."

He looked at his wristwatch. "If you can talk fast, I have time to make the afternoon deadline on the paper."

"That won't be necessary, Ken. This story can't break yet. I need your solemn promise you won't tell another soul."

"For the love of God, woman. What's this all about?"

"Promise?"

"I can't keep anything from my editor and he'll undoubtedly assign a writer to this. But I can promise this. He'll honor your request. Now, what's cooking?"

"I'm angry. Really angry. The police commission just finished backing Davis's Unisex Plan."

"What are you going to do?"

"I'm filing a formal complaint against the LAPD for discrimination." Just uttering those words made me straighten up and smile.

He wrote fast, not looking up as we talked. It took a split second for the impact of what I had said to register. "What a sweet story! I'll love ya forever. But Jesus, do you know what you're doing?"

"No. But it must be done, assuming I don't lose my nerve."

"All hell is going to break loose," he said. "You're going to be in deep trouble. I'll hightail it the two blocks to the *Times* building. Don't go home tonight until you hear from us. Don't worry—we'll be there to back your action. You're going to need all the help you can get. But for God's sake, be careful, will ya?"

"Sure. They're already upset with me today, but just wait."

My phone was ringing when I stepped into the empty squad room after calling the Equal Employment Opportunity Commission from a corner payphone. I quickly picked up the receiver.

"This is Dorothy Townsend, feature writer for the *Times*. I'm assigned to your story. Hansen has filled me in on what you're doing. Have you made contact with the EEOC?"

"I don't like talking on these phones, Miss Townsend, but I'll take a chance. Yes, they've given me an appointment for Friday, March 16th at ten o'clock."

"Sergeant, I'd like to meet you there with our photographer. Will that be alright with you?"

"I'd be grateful."

"Let me assure you, nobody will know until this hits the paper."

I hung up. I had decided to kick the fear of retaliation out of my life and move forward. For years, I had done all I could to change things to no avail. Now all I had to do was keep my mouth shut. I would be a nervous wreck from now until that Friday morning. I couldn't even tell Shannon or my son Kelly. It wasn't fair to them, but I couldn't risk a leak. It was hard enough to make the decision; I couldn't stand any additional pressure at home, which would inevitably result from my sharing this.

On the morning of March 16, 1973, I pulled out of bed after not sleeping all night and showered. I needed a trip to the beauty parlor, but there would be no time for that. I would just have to brush my hair and go with it. No policewoman dared appear on duty in pantsuits, so I picked the loudest one I owned, a pink and white striped knit. After all those years of being told how to dress on duty, I decided I wouldn't wear a girdle. I knew my choices would drive the department image-makers crazy, but that would be nothing compared to what I was about to do. Since the battle for equal pay decades ago, no female officer had dared to confront the LAPD or seek redress for grievances. That was about to change.

The ache in my chest returned as I parked in the lot behind the Federal Commission building, so I popped a nitroglycerin tablet. I knew that going up against the chief would take guts, but I hadn't realized it would hurt this much. I sat in my car until the pain subsided and then made my way to the building.

A woman and a man waited for me in the foyer.

"Sergeant Blake?" the woman asked. "I'm Dorothy Townsend and this is my photographer, James Caccavo." We shook hands. "Best we go on up," she said. Then she turned to the photographer. "Have your camera ready. We may not be able to get more than one good shot."

We all stepped off the elevator onto the third floor. A receptionist escorted us into a partitioned cubicle and went to summon my interviewer. The instant she left the room, Townsend said, "James. Quick. Get behind the table. As soon as we're seated, snap a picture. We're not supposed to be here."

A young Black woman soon approached from an office and sat down across from me. "Sergeant Blake?" she asked. "I'm your interviewer." She noticed Townsend and frowned. In that moment of hesitation, Caccavo snapped several pictures. The young woman stood. "I'm sorry, but the press isn't allowed," she said in clipped tones, her smile gone. "You'll have to leave."

"Even if I want them here?" I asked.

"I'll have to talk to my supervisor."

She returned with a senior gentleman who escorted Townsend and Caccavo out.

"This is for your legal protection," he said. "They'll wait for you downstairs. Now you can complete your interview." He left and the interviewer sat down and handed me a form.

"All you have to do, Sergeant Blake, is write a statement of your complaint," she said. "Call me when you've completed what you want to say in your own words."

I froze. Once I signed this document, there would be no turning back. It was like getting married. Did I really want to go through with this?

Yes, I did. Most people don't realize just how awesome police power is. If the police don't stay true to the law, we can lose our democracy. In this case, someone had to step forward and invoke the law to bring to Chief Davis' attention that he couldn't overstep his bounds and treat us as second-class citizens. I had to fill out the paper, my last recourse to claiming first-class citizenship.

Feeling very alone, I pulled a statement I had already prepared out of my jacket pocket and picked up the pen. Carefully, I copied the words before me:

> *I allege that myself and others similarly situated are being discriminated against because of our sex (female), in violation of Title VII of the Civil Rights Act and the Equal Employment Opportunity Act.*

I leaned back in my chair and drew in a deep breath. It no longer mattered what happened; I felt exhilarated. The deed was done. Whatever I had to face would be worth it. They could not undo what I had initiated this day.

A pregnant woman approached from an office near the reception desk. Although she looked ready to deliver at any moment, she moved with ease and seemed unconcerned. I would learn many years later that her husband, the late Norbert A. Schlei, had been the principal draftsman of the Civil Rights Act of 1964, upon which my case would hinge. "I'm Barbara Schlei, attorney for the Commission," she said. "We have work to do, Sergeant." When I stood to shake her hand, she said, "Sit down, Sergeant. I need to discuss your understanding of your status now that you've filed the complaint."

"My status?"

"Do you realize the position you put yourself in today?"

"To be honest with you, Mrs. Schlei, I've been so upset that I haven't considered anything. I'm just trying to save my job."

15

TARGETED

I sure didn't know what I was getting into.

"Do you have a lawyer?" asked the EEOC attorney.

The pain in my chest quickened. "A lawyer? That's why I came here. Why do I need a lawyer?"

"You not only need a lawyer, Sergeant, but you also need money."

Barbara Schlei leaned on the table to hold eye contact with me, her delicate features not betraying her thoughts or feelings. Her pregnancy made her seem huge.

"I came here believing the EEOC handled everything. Money and a lawyer are needs I cannot meet." My stiff upper lip trembled as I fought back the tears. "I have only myself."

She moved next to me and rested her hand on my shoulder. "Listen very carefully. You must clearly understand that your status since signing the complaint has changed. Do you comprehend what I'm saying?"

"I feel like the biggest ass on earth." I looked up into her face. "Sometimes, Counselor, I'm also a slow learner. Yes, I comprehend. What do I do now?"

When I had left home that morning, I was only afraid of filing the complaint. Now, I felt terrorized. I understood all too clearly that by challenging the LAPD and taking on the City establishment, I had put myself and my job in jeopardy.

"Do you want me to represent you until you can find adequate help?"

"Without question, Mrs. Schlei. I'd be grateful for your assistance."

"For the record, Sergeant, I accept your request. As your counsel, I now advise you not to make any commitments until you clear them with me. Understand?"

"Yes, ma'am." A throbbing headache beat at the back of my skull, and my neck muscles felt tight.

"Before you and I can proceed, you must go downstairs and meet the media. Pull yourself together. They're clamoring for an interview with you. As soon as that's completed, come back to my office. We have work to do before you leave today."

In the elevator, I tried to tuck, push, and pull my clinging knit pantsuit into a respectable appearance. Without my girdle, I felt almost nude. I dabbed on fresh lipstick, blotted my mouth on a tissue from my pocket, and prayed my complexion wouldn't look too washed out. I stepped out into bright sunshine, and two dozen microphones bristled into my face. Pinned against the building, I felt like the knife thrower's lady on stage. I answered questions hurled at me from every well-known television commentator, radio announcer, and news reporter in the city.

Why did you file a complaint against the police department?

"They won't promote women past sergeant."

How do you feel about the proposed new height and weight standards?

"They're a discriminatory solution to discrimination."

The chief, Sergeant. What about the chief?

"He won't listen to our grievances."
Do you think women should be shot at?
"My life is no more valuable than a man's."
Do you want to be chief?
"I'd like the opportunity."
What's going to happen when you go back to work?
"I have no idea."
Are you scared, Sergeant?
"I'm petrified."

The members of the press disappeared as quickly as they had materialized. I would eventually become quite adept at this media business, sharing stories about how less qualified men had been promoted past other women and me, and how women's lives were ruined by the City's discriminatory practices. But this barrage had been an unexpected first. In the hot, bright sunshine, I took a moment to pull away from the support of the building and regain my composure. Soaked with perspiration, I thought about Shannon and Kelly, and hoped they would understand. I hadn't warned them about today. I had no idea every reporter in town would be here.

Schlei sent me to the California State Fair Employment Practices Commission at First and Broadway to inform them that I had filed with the Federal Commission. The state agency waived jurisdiction in the case because it was a complaint on behalf of all Los Angeles policewomen and returned it to the federal commission for action, giving me a release of jurisdiction. As I drove back to Schlei's office, I turned on the news, heard my voice, and almost hit a parked car. It was on the air already! If Shift thought I was a celebrity in February, wait till he caught this.

I went directly to Schlei's office. All the telephones in the reception area rang at once. "You're famous, Sergeant," Schlei said. "You're making history. Sit down. I need to know how you arrived here at the Equal Employment Opportunity Commission. Have you been through department channels?"

"Yes, ma'am. How I got here is a long story. Months ago, I asked Judge Joan Dempsey Klein for advice. She told me to sue. I tried going through channels, but that didn't work. So now I'm doing just that."

"Sergeant, all you've done today is file a complaint with the EEOC. You'll need a lawyer to pursue your redress. This must proceed through federal court. We'll protect you through every step of the process."

"Barbara. May I call you Barbara? I asked the Police Protective League to help me. It was a shock when they turned me down. I've been a dues-paying member all my police career."

"How do you feel about this morning?"

"The power of the police department is awesome. I've seen it misused. I worry that a hothead on the force might physically hurt me. Last night, I dreamed the chief put a hit on me." Saying it out loud made it sound melodramatic, although years later, in 1990, Officer Shilah Johnson would tell reporters, "We panicked. I was afraid for her and us. It was like going up against God, only God doesn't wear a gun, so it was worse."

"You don't have to be afraid now, Fanchon," Schlei said. She put her arm around my shoulders. "I'm your friend. Here's my card. Keep it in your wallet. If there's any trouble, call, no matter what time of day."

"This will give me strength to return to work on Monday."

"You've done a very brave act." She walked me to the door and handed me a paper. "Here are your referrals to find a lawyer. It isn't ethical for me to recommend, but I can give you a list to pick from. And remember that the United States government is now backing you 100 percent. Even the LAPD understands that!"

On the drive home, I wondered about being called brave. I didn't feel brave. My family's reception didn't help. After drinking a glass of wine and falling asleep on the couch, I roused myself enough to fix dinner. We ate in silence. Shannon wouldn't speak to me, having caught the blast of my publicity while still at work. Kelly turned stoic—a frozen young man, totally incapable of understanding his mother—and retreated to his room. Neither one showed any indication of support.

That Monday morning, after a decidedly uncomfortable weekend at home, which I survived by cleaning house, I parked on the upper deck of the LAPD building. By now, most of the men would have heard the broadcasts. I forced myself to return to work, even though I was scared to walk into that police building because of what the men would say or do. I would rather have been beaten at the public pillory than go to my office, but I had to.

The best defense was a good offense. Determined to be positive instead of cowardly, I took the stairs, two at a time to the third floor, instead of the elevator. As I rounded the corner from the stairwell, the detective headquarters desk sergeant yelled, "You sure got a line of bullshit! Saw ya on TV." He stood up, came around the corner and stood spread-legged in front of me.

"Good for you, Smithy. After all these years, you finally heard the message. We are all tired of bullshit! Now, be a good lad and step aside. I need to go to work."

It had begun. I brushed by him and made my way to the bunco-forgery squad room, where I paused and breathed deeply. I wanted to turn tail and retire. Instead, I grabbed the knob, pulled the door open, stepped in, and stopped. Fifty-nine pairs of eyes, none friendly, focused on me. A young white male officer I did not know sat in my chair. The buggers! They couldn't wait.

While not happy at being displaced, I wasn't surprised. I had anticipated some kind of reaction. Besides, this new guy had my total sympathies. He had no idea how hard he would have to work on misdemeanor checks. I wondered where I had been banished to.

Lieutenant Shift, all six feet plus of him, popped out of his chair and addressed me with a sneer. "No more investigations for you. You are now assigned to the desk." In a sarcastic tone, he added, "We all know how much you love working the desk."

The men tittered as they elbowed each other and whispered. I didn't know what I had expected, but it was more than a change of assignment. I could handle that. Quietly, I turned.

"Hold up a minute, Blake." Shift was every inch the 'boss' as he boomed, "You are not to leave this room without my permission, and that includes latrine relief!"

"I don't like being harassed just because I've filed a complaint against this department," I countered. "You've made your point. I'm no longer working investigations. But don't you think it's a bit much to make me ask permission to make a pit stop?"

In a pig's eye, I'd ask permission to visit the ladies' restroom. I'd go when I damn well had to! This was elementary-grade-level harassment meant to cut me down to size. They wanted me under their thumb, but I wasn't going to play along.

The squad room broke into laughter and talk. Of course, they had to do something to show their disapproval. I had fallen from grace for daring to challenge the LAPD, and they would make me pay. It could have been worse. I hated working that stinking desk, but I would work it better than it had ever been worked before.

The phones, which had been almost conspiratorially silent, started ringing at 8 a.m. Calls were flooding in from around the world with journalists asking to interview me. I was having the time of my life talking to England, Japan, and South America before Shift stopped me.

He stood by my side, glowering. "You get any more calls about your activities, refer them to the public information division for handling. Do I make myself clear?"

I grinned. "I hear you loud and clear. Is there anything else, Lieutenant?"

He turned and stomped back to his desk.

This was no time for me to be sarcastic, I realized. I needed to bite my tongue, hold my temper. I felt sorry for Lieutenant Ryan Shift. His stress would come from the top down as well as from the bottom up every time he had to deal with me. Management was stuck with my sudden celebrity status—heady stuff that I had never experienced to that degree.

It only took a couple of days before the LAPD time-honored use of the silent treatment was applied to me by everyone on the force. I didn't even hear from my police friends or the policewomen I was trying to protect as they capitulated to the fear of administrative reprisal. It was like the earth had opened up and swallowed me. I felt betrayed—not an award-winning emotion. Still, if the department expected me to become a sniveling wimp, they were due for disappointment. Driven by the belief that everybody should be guaranteed a fair opportunity to realize their dreams and visions, I wasn't about to back down. Besides, the department had already taught me how to withstand this kind of pressure.

On the following Wednesday after filing the complaint, a commander eased into the reception area. He paused in front of me on his way to the captain's cubical to wave a finger in my face. "Bad girl! You should be ashamed of what you've done to the department." He walked into the captain's office before I could reply. That bastard had called me a girl!

When one of the men came through the door, I grabbed his arm. "Hey, fella. Cover the phones. I need a latrine run." I glanced over my shoulder at Shift as I bolted into the hall. He started to rise, but I left before he could object.

Upon my return, I found him waiting at my desk. "I'll have to write an incident report on you," he growled. "You disobeyed orders; you didn't get permission to leave."

"Who am I to tell you what to do, Lieutenant? But you would do well to check with the chief's office before you write that incident report or take any action against me. I don't think the chief is interested in antagonizing the EEOC. I suggest you call his office and find out what the ground rules are about me."

"What are you trying to say?"

"I was informed by the EEOC lawyer that once I filed my complaint, my whole legal life changed."

He snapped to a standing position, his smug attitude replaced with a clenched jaw, strode back to his desk, grabbed the phone and dialed. I watched him deflate and sink into his chair.

Not caving into Shift's abuse did not spare me from other kinds of harassment. After work, late one afternoon, as I headed to the law offices of a couple of attorneys I hoped would represent me, I spotted two officers in my rearview mirror. I had seen the same pair a couple of days earlier and thought it was just a coincidence, even though I knew they worked internal affairs. The fact that they were once again behind me in an undercover police vehicle had to mean they were tailing me.

Despite feelings of trepidation, I decided to find out for sure. I hung a right off the freeway, and they stuck right with me. I whipped onto a surface street west of downtown L.A. and headed down an alley in a residential area. I gunned the motor and sped through to a side street, skidded around the corner, went through another narrow alley and changed direction onto a cross street. Spotting an open and empty residential home garage, I shot in, shut off the engine, and slammed the door.

Inside a stranger's garage and worried about getting caught by the occupants even though the house seemed empty, I watched through a crack at the side of the door. The internal affairs officers rolled past, slowed to a crawl and stopped. After talking to each other, they threw up their arms and drove on. I waited to see if they would circle back. They slowly cruised by one more time. When they didn't return after that, I backed out of the garage and parked on the street.

Why would internal affairs waste their time tailing me? Just then, I caught a reflection in my rearview mirror. A senior lady had pulled her Chevy sedan in the garage I had just vacated. I quietly started my engine and left the neighborhood. That had been a close call. I didn't want to think what would have happened to me had the homeowner come home and found me, without her permission, parked in her garage. But I had bigger things to worry about. For years, the LAPD had equated dissent or criticism of the LAPD with disloyalty. By filing with the EEOC, I had indulged in both. Clearly, the department had decided to make me pay. Thankfully, I had escaped that day's intended reprimand.

I headed for my attorneys' office for a short meeting. Although I had signed with a prominent law firm, I had quickly realized they couldn't handle my case. They needed funds and had suggested I raise money through benefits. That thought sent me into a depression. I couldn't devote the time and energy, nor seek the expertise my case demanded, and still work full time. I decided to stick with them only until I could find another source of help.

On my way home, the pain in my chest made me turn around and drive to Receiving Hospital. After an EKG, the doctor decided that stress had caused my illness. He gave me Valium and took me off duty for ten days, telling me to go home and go to bed, and to call if the pain persisted.

A week later, feeling more relaxed and rested, I talked to a friend on the telephone. In the background of the conversation, I heard tell-tale clicks that sounded like a wiretap. I asked my friend to hang up and call back. I still heard the clicking. I wouldn't have paid any attention if internal affairs hadn't tailed me, but I was now on high alert.

When I completed the call, I went outside and circled my house to check for anything that might confirm my suspicions. I didn't see any telephone linemen hanging from any poles close by and didn't find any evidence of line tampering. The phone company denied any complicity and advised me to file a police report. That would have been funny had I not felt so frightened. If the department wanted to know about me, they were quite capable of bugging my telephone, car, or house without even the phone company knowing.

Lawful or unlawful, true or false, I concluded the clicking was real. From then on, I didn't want to pick up the phone. Not being able to call people like my sister added to the emotional strain. I was at a total loss about what actions to take to make things better for myself. I seemed to be out of options.

No matter how tough I thought I was, harassment is like drops of water on a forehead; eventually, it takes a toll. When I returned to duty on April 12th, the silent treatment at work, the increase of vicious barbs and profanities from the men as they passed by me, and imprisonment at the reception desk wore down my nerves even further.

Despite their clear bias against policewomen, I had never dreamed that so many of the men on the job would turn surly toward me. The silent treatment at work was a bitch to endure, but the cruelty of their angry remarks scared me. The subtle undercurrent of hatred frightened me even more. There would be no protection from any policeman who might take out his anger about women's liberation on me. How far would someone go to retaliate? Surely the men wouldn't dare harm me. Or would they?

Trying not to succumb to paranoia, I couldn't stop wondering whether the department I revered was capable of placing me in danger. Had a contract been put out on my life for real? That seemed crazy, but I had to wonder what the two guys from internal affairs would have done had they caught up with me.

Although their numbers were small, I knew male officers who enjoyed brutality. I remembered a time when I walked a beat at Sixth and Hill Streets and was interrogating a male teenager about curfew violation. Two policemen I knew came up, grabbed the boy, dragged him into the dark alley, and beat him with their gloved fists. I could hear the teenager cry. When the white-faced boy came out of the alley, followed by the police officers, he apologized to my partner and me for lipping off. "That'll teach you to respect cops," one of my colleagues said.

Now I had become a target for their abuse, the person who needed to be taught a lesson.

16

GETTING HELP

I needed to think out my options and explore what actions I could take to protect myself and stop the harassment. Thumbing through the paperwork on my case, I looked again at Schlei's referral list of lawyers. So far, the calls I had made hadn't been encouraging. Most were eager, but a lack of money prevented me from committing.

In sheer desperation, I wrote a letter to the American Civil Liberties Union (ACLU). If the LAPD found out, I would be branded a communist. However, the women's lot at the LAPD wasn't going to get better until I found help.

Within a week, the ACLU answered. "Your request for help will be presented to the board of directors for consideration. You will be contacted." Now what had I done?

Ramona Ripston, the fiery spokeswoman for the ACLU, called me at home, assured me of their backing, and put me in contact with Southern California ACLU's Women's Rights Project director Jill Jakes, who made an appointment with me. I parked in downtown L.A. as directed and waited for her station wagon to pull up behind me. She slid out of her car.

Her dog, a huge Great Dane, sat up front and growled when I approached her.

"Sergeant Blake?" she asked.

I nodded.

"Don't mind my dog. Let's walk." She moved with the ease of a dancer, her long brown hair flying in the breeze. "Sergeant, I've been assigned by Ramona Ripston to your case. I'll be here to help you all I can. I want you to know that I am a lawyer, but I will not be representing you through the litigation."

"I need help," I said. "I need it now."

"The ACLU knows that." She stopped to face me. "You're invited to appear before their executive committee in Century City on April 22nd at noon. Can you keep that appointment?"

"Yes, yes, yes," I sputtered. "But what's this meeting about?"

"There'll be a vote to decide whether they should become a friend of the court on your behalf when appropriate." She proceeded to explain that a friend of the court, while not being a party to a case, assists with relevant information, expertise, or insight.

"I have to say, Ms. Jakes, this is the first good news I've heard since I filed my complaint. I'm worried about money. I can't cover any costs at this point."

"The ACLU doesn't fund the procedure of pursuing justice through the courts. But be assured, Sergeant, we'll find the right help. There are people who are following your case. They'll not let you fall through the cracks."

Just hearing her speak those words made me feel better. The upcoming meeting with the ACLU's executive committee buoyed my spirits even further.

On April 22nd, I drove to Century City and met Jill in the foyer of one of the high-rise buildings fronting Olympic Boulevard. "I'm nervous," I said as we shook hands. "I have mixed feelings about the ACLU. Ever since I was a rookie, I've been told by the LAPD that the ACLU is full of card-carrying commies bent on overthrowing the government."

Jill explained that the ACLU defended anyone's rights as defined by the Bill of Rights, regardless of political persuasion. "Overthrow the government? No," she said. "Overthrow the government's violation of our civil liberties? Yes. Do you understand?"

"It's hard for me to admit to myself that I have blindly followed the LAPD's castigation of the ACLU without question. You're the first person who's ever said to me, 'It's a free country. People have a right to carry any card they please.' I'm in shock at my ignorance."

"Come on, Sergeant," she said with a grin. "You have more mind-openers awaiting you. When we enter the conference room, you'll be amazed at who you see sitting there."

We stepped into the room, and she pointed to a vacant spot at the conference table. "That's your seat," she said. "I'll sit behind you." The other chairs were filled with the top lawyers of our time. I couldn't put names to faces, but most of them were highly visible professionals whom I had seen frequently on television and in the news.

Jill wasn't wrong. The setting and those present awed me. I noticed the legal-sized agenda given to each person at the meeting. Item 2: *Sergeant Blake versus Chief Davis—Title VII. Sex Discrimination in the Los Angeles Police Department.* I also noted that although eighteen items covered many rights, I was the only litigant present.

Betty Gallo, a tall woman whom I had met the previous week for less than fifteen minutes, rose from her seat and rapped her gavel to get the attendees' attention. "It's your turn, Sergeant," she said with a smile. "Tell the panel why you're here."

Schlei hadn't mentioned that Gallo held a prestigious position with the ACLU. Had I known that, I wouldn't have called her. But there she stood, conducting that meeting.

I cleared my throat. "I'm here to ask for your help." Oh God, this was hard. "First, I have a confession. I've been told by the LAPD that you're communistic. That makes my being here difficult."

They laughed!

"You're not the first person to come before us with that misconception," Gallo said. "It's expected, Sergeant. There's only one reason for the American Civil Liberties Union to invite you here today. Are your rights as a woman sergeant on the Los Angeles Police Department being violated?"

"Without question. Chief Davis not only wants to continue the discrimination against promotions for women, but he's also informed us that he wants to terminate women as police officers. There hasn't been a female hired since he became chief, and he's openly announced that by the time he's through, only twelve of the one hundred and eighty current female officers will be left on the force. Because of these abuses, I filed a complaint with the EEOC. When I did that, I didn't understand how the process works. I was shocked to learn that I need to fund this case and hire my own attorneys. So I need legal and monetary help. I can't fight the Los Angeles Police Department without both."

"I ask for a show of hands," Gallo said. "How many support the sergeant in her quest for help?"

The vote was unanimous.

"You must know, Sergeant, we do not furnish either a lawyer or fund litigation. We'll assist you in locating appropriate legal representation and the funds will follow. You have more interested, concerned friends than you can comprehend. Don't be afraid. As you know, Jill Jakes will guide you through the process.

"Now, before you go, let me address your fear about the communists. Some of our members may be communists, or democrats, or republicans, or whatever. As an American, under our Constitution, it's guaranteed that they can belong to any organization they choose. Defending all civil rights, no matter how unpopular, is at the heart of the American Civil Liberties Union."

Where had I been all my adult life that I had allowed the police, politicians, religious leaders, or others to control my thinking? I had to become more knowledgeable and not allow myself to be manipulated.

"I want to thank each of you," I said. "I feel honored that you invited me today. In my legal and financial pursuit to help the careers of women on the LAPD, your participation gives me the first solid hope of success."

Jill and I made our way to the door. One of the male lawyers stopped me and shook my hand. "What took you so long, Sergeant?"

Startled at his question, I wondered why it *had* taken me so long. "Fear," I sputtered. "I've been afraid of the Los Angeles Police Department. And I loved my job."

Jill and I exited onto the Avenue of the Stars in Century City and headed to our vehicles parked in the adjoining lot. "What now?" Jill asked. "What's your next move?"

"I need an appointment with Barbara Schlei at the commission to talk about decisions I must make."

"Stay in touch, Sergeant." She smiled. "We're on a great adventure."

In the weeks preceding my appearance before the ACLU and my meeting with Schlei, council member Billy Mills had voiced his opinion that all policewomen should be given the opportunity for advancement. He had also suggested that if the present class of policewomen was being held down, their salaries would reflect that. After Mills' comments, the city council ordered the chief to prepare a ninety-day pilot program for the women. On May 9th, Chief Davis submitted his recommendations through the police commission to the Los Angeles City Council. His plan included only two new assignments to patrol and traffic functions for active-duty policewomen volunteers who met the minimum male requirements of 5'8". (His Unisex plan would subsequently drop that requirement to 5'7" and later to 5'6".) The women would have to wear the male uniform. They would have to volunteer to retrain with male recruits and perform all functions required by male officers.

When I heard that the chief's Unisex Plan had moved forward to the L.A. City Council, I believed it would be approved without further debate. I called the city council clerk and asked to be put on the agenda to rebut the plan.

My request to appear before the city council was approved for the June 12th agenda.

In the first part of that month, I met with Schlei in her office. By then, I was so frustrated with my inability to find legal representation and so scared about what I had done that I was about ready for a nervous breakdown. "I'm frightened," I said. "I'm not making up the harassment that's been taking place at work. They deny it, but I know better."

"I'll contact the EEOC." She made notes as she talked. "They'll send a letter to the city council and the chief, and they'll copy you. It will remind them of your right to sue without harassment. If that doesn't calm down your life, call me. Now, what else is troubling you?"

"I'm at my wit's end looking for adequate legal help. The lawyers I've hired can't handle my case. Didn't you mention something about some center?"

"It's on the list I gave you. Let me call for you right now. If Tom Hunt is there, I'll set up an appointment."

"Before you do, can you tell me something about him? I wish I could have a woman lawyer, but that doesn't seem to be working out."

"There isn't another lawyer in the United States better qualified to handle your case than Tom. He's the most compassionate man I know when it comes to equal opportunities for minorities and women. He recently left the Justice Department's Civil Rights Division to join the Center for Law in the Public Interest. He believes in what he does, and he's brilliant."

She immediately sent me to Tom's office in Century City, across Olympic Boulevard from the high-rise building where I had met with the ACLU. I parked on a side street and rode the outside, glass-enclosed elevator to the third floor. A receptionist gave me directions to Tom's office, which looked west toward the Mormon Temple.

He sat in a swivel chair, its back turned toward me, talking on a telephone. A table stretched before him covered with stacks of files and cluttered documents. More files and books lay piled in front of a couple of six-drawer file cabinets and along the walls. He bounced up from his chair. "Sergeant Blake, let me clear this so you can sit down."

With perpetual deep-blue circles under my eyes, I must have looked to him like I had crawled out of a storm. To say I was tired was an understatement.

He quickly put the chair's foot-high contents on the floor. "We're running out of space in this building," he said. I was surprised at his youthfulness. His boyish face radiated a smile and his eyes flashed beneath rimless glasses, which offset a thatch of curly dark hair with just a hint of a receding hairline.

As we shook hands, I could see I stood a bit taller than he. I looked directly at him.

"Did you talk to Barbara Schlei about my case?"

"That was her on the phone when you came in. Yes, she filled me in on your complaint. Let's get acquainted. Your case is very interesting; we need to talk."

"Do you think you can accept my case?"

"Do you have other questions before I answer that?"

"I'd like to know more about you. It's hard for me to believe that a man will honestly pursue equal rights for women."

"Let me show you something," he said, grabbing a picture of three boys. "These, I'm proud to say, are my sons. Pidge—that's my wife—and I feel deeply about injustice. The white boy is ours by natural birth. We adopted our other two sons early in their lives. One is Black and one Brown. All three are within a year of each other in age." He put the picture back on his desk.

I would later learn that Tom Hunt had more experience with Title VII employment discrimination cases—and had done more to bring racial parity into the workplace—than any other lawyer in Southern California. I also learned that Tom was nationally recognized as a leading attorney in the employment discrimination field. At the time, however, that photo was enough for me. This was a man who clearly cared about all kinds of people.

"I just changed my mind about needing a woman to represent me," I said. "You're it."

"Sergeant, think before you answer. What do you want from this case?" Hunt asked, barely acknowledging my pronouncement.

"I don't have to think about that. I know what I hope to accomplish. I want a federal judgment that will ensure a law enforcement career, without harassment, for women on the Los Angeles Police Department."

"What's in it for you?" he shot back.

"Nothing. I'm finished on the LAPD."

"What about money?"

"I haven't any."

"Come now, Sergeant. What monetary gain do you think you'll realize if you win?"

"Mr. Hunt, perhaps you don't understand me." I started to get up. "I'm not here to fleece the taxpayers of Los Angeles."

"Sit down, Sergeant. This isn't the time for you to leave. I had to know if you were for real. The center has funding, but we select clients motivated by principle, not monetary gain. You pass. We'll handle the expenses during litigation."

"But, Mr. Hunt, I don't understand. You mean I don't have to come up with money?"

Hunt confirmed that the Center would fund my case.

"Barbara Schlei must have told you that I was with the Justice Department," he said. "While I was in the Washington, D.C., offices, I tried only Title VII cases, mostly for minorities facing discrimination in the South. I have as much experience with the 1964 Equal Employment Opportunity Act as any other lawyer in the United States. That's my specialty. If you're willing, Sergeant, I'll accept your case."

I reached across his desk and grabbed his hand. "You need to know I signed with another firm, but nothing has happened. What do I do about that?"

"Not to worry. I'll have you sign the necessary papers before you leave. I will need more information from you. Tell me what you've already done on the department and elsewhere."

He pulled out a yellow legal pad to take notes.

"This is a good case," he said when I finished briefing him. He sat back and smiled. "It's a great challenge."

"I can't tell you, Mr. Hunt, how grateful I am that I've found you. Do you have more questions?"

"Questions? We haven't even started to ask the questions. But I need to have a clear understanding with you." He wheeled around to face me. "I must have your complete trust. This lawsuit will be for the class of women as a whole, rather than for you individually. I will need your total support for any decision I make throughout the entire litigation. And because the case will be a class action, I must have the final authority to make all decisions as to how to litigate the case. Understood?"

"It's clear to me." I sat still. "I wouldn't want it any other way, but I must know what's happening."

"I'll keep you informed of every legal move. We'll have many bull sessions to explore all options. I'll rely on you to help me."

"One more item, Mr. Hunt. I am to appear before the city council on June 12th to refute parts of Unisex. Is that okay?"

"Sure."

"You must also know that I've appeared on several talk shows."

"The more publicity, Sergeant, the more education there is on correcting blatant discrimination. The old dinosaurs like Chief Davis will go to their graves believing they're right. They will not change voluntarily. Title VII is a remover of resistance to equal rights. And remember this, we have nothing to hide. Our job is to expose and find the truth. I have a lot to do before filing your class action complaint against the LAPD in federal court."

The day I appeared before the city council, the councilors unanimously voted to consolidate classes of *policeman* and *policewoman* into *police officer*. The city council then asked the civil service commission to establish new height and weight requirements. They further instructed the police department to provide retraining for current policewomen volunteering for patrol duty. However, they ignored the mandate of the 1964 Equal Employment Opportunity Act and all that I had to say about it. In addition, they brushed aside the continued discriminatory practices against the women, paying no attention to the wise recommendations of either Muriel Morse, general manager of city personnel, or Councilwoman Pat Russell.

Nevertheless, I left the L.A. City Council chambers feeling smug because I knew something they didn't. Tom Hunt would soon be filing papers that would legally start my case and challenge the LAPD's entrenched discrimination against women. I had no idea at the time that the lawsuit against the LAPD and the City of Los Angeles would be the first of its kind in the nation, nor that it would turn out to be a major case in the advancement of women in law enforcement.

When I returned from City Hall, Lieutenant Shift met me at the door. "Before you get busy and before the men return for the day, let's step into the captain's office," he said. He carefully picked up a paper from the desk. "This is the month for efficiency ratings. Here's your copy so we can go over it together."

I knew immediately that this would constitute further punishment for filing the complaint against the LAPD. But this time, a biased rating without foundation would highlight the administrative abuse and add to my case.

I quickly scanned the boxes with check marks. "Lieutenant, how can you believe that this report is true?" I demanded.

I wouldn't have traded places with him. He knew this report was a lie and kept his eyes focused on the papers in his hand. "That's the way I see it," he said, biting his lower lip. "And the captain agrees with me."

"Please tell me how you arrived at your conclusions. You've said absolutely nothing about my job performance since the last rating. I'd like to know how I could possibly go from an upper 10 percent down to 50 percent."

"The captain . . ." His voice faded.

"Speak up, Lieutenant. I can't hear you."

"You've been disloyal. You can't deny that!"

"I have never been disloyal to you, the captain, or the chief."

"You've been disloyal to the department." His cheeks puffed. "You know what you did."

"If you're referring to my suit against the LAPD and the City and you're using that as a basis for this rating, you've reached a new low." I sat forward. "If anyone is to be accused of disloyalty, it's the department's practice of discrimination against me. Pursuing my grievances through the federal court has absolutely nothing to do with my loyalty."

He shot out of his chair, bent over, shoved the paper across the desk, and pointed to a line. "All you have to do is sign here."

"Not now, not tomorrow, not ever." I stood, my back held straight and tall. "You can't make me sign anything that's not true." I could hear my voice rise and swallowed to bring it back under control.

"You have to sign. It's departmental orders," he snarled.

"Not in a million years," I said. "I'll never allow another rating to be used against me when I know I've done my job." I folded my rating copy and tucked it into a pocket of my blouse.

"If you refuse to obey a lawful order, I'll have to bring you before a trial board." He turned to look out the window.

"I feel that you're threatening me."

"No. Damn it, all your signature means is that you acknowledge I've talked to you, and you've seen your report."

"I know, and you know, that five ratings at 50 percent is your way of telling me I'm not wanted in this division. I also know I couldn't get a decent transfer out of here with that hanging over my head. And one more thing. If I'm transferred out of this division, I'll raise so much hell you'll wish you'd thought out just what you were doing."

"What am I supposed to tell my captain if you don't sign?" He stood, towering over me.

"He's my captain, too. Just offhand, I think you have a problem. There's only one entry on your report at 50 percent that I'd never challenge, and that's my health. Every sick day I've taken is for real illness, and not something I've lied about to avoid coming to work. But the rest of this evaluation is blatantly unfair."

"It's only an administrative tool. It happens every six months."

"You're using it this time to humiliate me," I said. "I'm supposed to swallow my integrity and sign. I'm supposed to ignore the favoritism I see you give the chosen few in this division, those gentlemen who regularly receive a solid upper 10 percent rating. That guy's hands shake so badly he can't hit the target and qualify by himself," I said, pointing to one of the older sergeants. "I've heard you tell Sergeant Willie Gough to go with him to the firing range, to stand next to him and shoot his target for him to qualify for the monthly requirement. I'm sure no one would dare report any of the gross personnel violations in this division. Do I need to say more?"

"I'll have to talk to the captain." He dropped into his chair. "You're putting him in a terrible position with the chief."

"Look at that report and the position it's putting me in," I said. "Can you honestly tell me it's the truth?"

"I'll give it to the captain." He rose to leave. "Don't say I didn't warn you."

"Am I supposed to tremble?"

Captain Jackson was not pleased with me, but he had the good sense to hold the report pending his observation of my work and conduct. He indicated that he would re-evaluate it after a six- or eight-week wait.

Before June ended, I received a copy of a letter from the EEOC, just as Schlei had promised, requiring that no harm come to me during the process of litigation. The LAPD had to make sure I wasn't harassed or hurt in any manner. I copied the letter and drove into work on Sunday. Using the master key I still possessed from when my job had been to take people on tours of the building, I entered the chief's office and placed a copy of the letter on his desk. I wanted to be sure he saw it with his own eyes.

Chief Davis's office was strange territory to me. I had never been there before and couldn't resist looking at the autographed pictures on the mahogany lined walls. A two-foot-square, five-foot-tall podium with a glass-enclosed top caught my eye. It contained the Fickle Finger of Fate award from the Smother's Brother's television show *Laugh-In*—a hand cast with the third finger extended in the universal salute. My chief's pride and glory was to have been singled out by an award designed to poke fun at outrageous behavior by well-known national figures. No wonder the press had dubbed him Crazy Ed.

Of course, he had very consciously and willfully fueled that moniker with his incendiary sound bites. When asked about how to deal with hijackers at LAX, for example, he replied, "I recommend we have a portable gallows, and after we have the death penalty back in, we conduct a rapid trial for a hijacker out there and hang him with due process out there at the airport."

The next morning at work, I was still reliving my delivery of the EEOC's letter to the chief's office and wondering how long it would take before the silent treatment would end when Sergeant Betty Finch, who worked across the hall, breezed into our office. She stopped to talk to my partner, her back to me. "Can you imagine that old blister going to the ACLU," she said as her thumb flew to her shoulder and pointed at me. "Everybody knows they're a pack of reds."

I'd had it. I would not sit there and accept that kind of abuse. It was time to take action. I bolted up three flights of stairs and burst into the reception room of the chief's office. Deputy Chief Dale Speck rose from a chair. "Slow down, Fanchon. What's the problem?"

"It's been bad enough living through the silent treatment," I said. "But I won't tolerate anybody calling me a commie."

"We haven't any control over how the troops treat you."

"Come on, Dale. I've been discussed at roll calls."

"What do you want me to do?"

"I want you to call Betty Finch. She's the one inferring I'm a commie."

"Well, I don't think—"

"I'm angry. I've taken all the harassment and barbs I'm going to take. I'm about to sue the LAPD for character assassination in addition to discrimination. This office has the power to take action. I know you can do something."

"I'll take care of it, Fanchon." He walked with me to the door. "Try to calm down. It's not as bad as it seems."

"And the peer pressure? Are you going to take the heat off?"

"I said I'd handle it." He scowled.

"Just want you to know, I have a copy of the EEOC's letter that states the LAPD has to protect me. And I have a lawyer. I'm not walking away from the complaint I filed with the EEOC, even though I've been pulled off investigations because of that filing. I can live with that for right now, but I don't have to tolerate abuse, and I won't."

I had no idea what action Speck took, but after that, I could come to work and do my job with some degree of peace. The officers still avoided me, but at least the overt harassment, along with some of my fear, diminished.

On July 1st, Tom Bradley, a former LAPD cop and the first Black man ever elected mayor, was sworn into office. Most of the men on the LAPD were not happy with his election, and their outrageous verbal comments about him made me wince. I took the time to call and wish him great success.

Five weeks later, Captain Jackson summoned me into his office. Two hot cups of coffee steamed on his desk, and he indicated that one was for me. "Sergeant, we've some unfinished business to complete. I've monitored your work since your chat with Shift. Here is your new rating. It's upgraded in three categories to the upper 25 percent. That should make you feel better." He smiled as he pushed the report over for me to sign. "We can clear this matter up right now."

"What about my loyalty, Captain?"

"That one has been corrected."

I read the report. It didn't matter now whether it was accurate. A single change would enable me to prove their persecution through the rating system. "May I keep a copy, sir?"

"Take the last one and sign the rest. As you can see, I've already signed the report." He seemed pleased with my signature.

My hand shook as I removed the last signed copy. I folded the paper and held it in my hand. "Thanks. Now, this one goes to my lawyers along with the copy Shift went over with me." I stood up. "It establishes harassment after I filed with the EEOC."

"You mean," he stammered as his eyes widened, "you mean, you have a copy of Shift's report?" He sank back into his chair. I barely heard, "Oh shit!"

I smiled, tipped my fingers to my forehead in salute, and sailed back to my desk.

17

GAME ON!

On August 20, 1973, Tom Hunt filed a complaint in the federal district court against the LAPD and the City of Los Angeles. The complaint alleged that the segregation of women into the inferior "policewoman" category and the related virtual total exclusion of women from the uniformed LAPD jobs violated Title VII of the Civil Rights Act of 1964 as well as the United States Constitution. It also alleged that the City's hiring practices—notably the height requirement—violated federal law because those job-related mandates were statistically discriminatory and not justified by scientifically valid evidence. Finally, it alleged that denying women the ability to promote above sergeant violated both the Constitution and the 1964 Civil Rights Act. By lottery, the case was assigned to Judge William Matthew Byrne, Jr.

Simultaneously, Tom filed a motion for preliminary injunction with the Los Angeles Federal Court to require that women be hired in ratios that were legitimate. Although the LAPD had hired more than two thousand new police officers over the prior three years, not a single new woman had been appointed to sworn positions. Tom asked that this de facto hiring freeze against women be rescinded and that women be hired at a 25 percent ratio.

A big break occurred when Sergeant Leola Vess contacted me. She had been promoted to sergeant in 1945, the first woman to reach that rank, and had since acquired a master's degree in psychology. She was an outstanding police professional from a two-police-officer family without blemish against her character or police performance, and eighteen years of experience. Even though she was one of the most highly regarded women in the department, she, like the rest of us, couldn't be promoted because she was a woman. She entered the case as a co-plaintiff with me.

That fall, I was duly subpoenaed, and Shift had to let me attend federal court to hear a motion related to my case that Tom Hunt would be making. I walked the half-block north from the police building to the cavernous, marble, Spring Street courtroom—a slow, dull headache marring the excitement. I met Jill Jakes, and we seated ourselves directly behind Tom at the plaintiff's table. I leaned over the railing, tapped my attorney on the shoulder, and wished him the very best. Across the aisle of spectator seats, several members from the police department sat together. They scowled when they saw me. I smiled.

My headache intensified. I found two aspirin in my purse and swallowed them without water. Judge Byrne entered. "Are the lawyers for the plaintiff prepared to commence?" he asked.

"Yes, Your Honor." Tom stood, waiting for the judge.

"You may proceed, Counselor."

"Thank you, Your Honor." Tom stood before the court, his dark blue suit jacket buttoned, his eyes intent as he spoke.

As the pain in my head forced me to shut my eyes, I heard Tom's quiet voice intone, "The complaint calls for an injunction in connection with hiring and work practices that discriminate against women by the Los Angeles Police Department."

I opened my eyes and found myself unable to focus the right one. I didn't say anything to Jill. I couldn't have even if I had wanted to since we couldn't talk while court was in session. I sat in misery, not daring to move, and tried to pay attention to what Tom was saying. He asked that the next class of male recruits be held up until the women could compete. The pain at the back of my head felt like hot needles. I heard Tom ask that the suit be deemed a class action, to include all the women on the department as well as all past, present, and future female applicants for police officer positions. If class certification were granted, the potential liability against the City would balloon, thereby turbocharging the case. "And, Your Honor," Tom concluded, "we shall prove the illegal practices that the defendants have pursued for many years."

I closed my eyes and hoped the pain would abate. I heard Judge Byrne order the case continued. That would happen again and again during those early days until the case was finally transferred to another judge the following year.

It was just as well that I had no idea of the delays in store because I felt ill enough as it was. When I stood, a wave of nausea hit. Dizziness made me shaky. As we exited the court building, we were met by a battery of TV cameras. "Sergeant, why do you think women make good officers?"

"Women neutralize violence," I said, as I fought fainting. "We're not interested in proving anything to the old boys club. We don't have to be gladiators."

"You mean you don't need brawn to subdue suspects?"

"I'm saying that women don't provoke situations. Men do. But I'm just as lethal with a weapon as any man if I have to be. I've arrested men and women as well as children."

The interview was over, and I made my way back to the office. By then, a numbing sensation shot down my right arm, and I could no longer see out of my right eye. I thought the back of my head would burst open.

As it turned out, I'd had a mild stroke. Elaborate tests by a neurosurgeon followed. After three weeks, the numbness on my right side abated, and my right foot didn't drag. My eyesight returned, and I could talk since my tongue was finally back to normal. Although the tests conducted did not show any deterioration, I became aware that my ability to recall names and telephone numbers had diminished. The stroke wiped out all my sick days, and I had to drop to 75 percent of my pay until I could qualify again for a full paycheck. But I had survived, and that was all that mattered.

During my three weeks on sick leave, nobody called from the department, sent flowers, cards, or visited. After two-and-a-half decades, I felt as if I had never been a member of the LAPD. It left me with a sad feeling. It also made me realize that the action I had taken to sue had become far more critical than I could have imagined. I remained baffled by the resistance from the men and their inability to change. How could they deny equal opportunity for both men and women? Maybe I would never see the healing process in my lifetime, but no matter the outcome, my fight against discrimination was worth it.

In late October 1973, Tom Hunt called and asked that I meet him at the police academy on Friday after work. There wasn't much activity when I arrived. In the fading late afternoon light, I could see a Black man in a complete professional umpire's uniform talking to a white woman in shorts.

The high hills of Elysian Park had already cast their shadows on the academy's athletic field. "We'll have to hurry before we lose daylight," Tom announced by way of greeting. "I brought a registered National Baseball League Umpire to officially time Michael Wendler, one of the failed female academy applicants, through the academy agility test. Come on. I'll introduce you."

Tom walked toward the six-foot wall. "Over here, Fanchon," he said with a wave. "I didn't have time to explain when I called. The department gave me permission to use this facility to retest Wendler. I've got a sneaking hunch that the results are going to be very interesting."

"Your message to meet you here made Shift terribly curious."

Tom grinned. "The PD must have been concerned when they set up this test. I'm surprised they don't have somebody here to monitor us."

I didn't know it then, but during this period, the physical agility test was failed by 50 percent of the women and only 3 percent of the men who took it. Still, I figured that Tom was on to something. In the meantime, I had to be patient and watch the test play out. "Do you have the official timing requirements?" I asked.

"Yes, but I don't know which comes first."

"Do you have the hand gripper for testing strength?"

"Wendler scored a passing grade on that one. It's the six-foot wall, dragging the dummy, and running the track that are in question. I need to know how well she can perform. She swears she passed. I've got to know if she can. When I checked the records for the day she took the examination, the documents had been altered. Her scores were scratched out and failing scores written in their places."

"I don't want to say out loud what I'm thinking!"

"I know," he said. "That's why we're here."

I marked off the run before the wall. The umpire fired a gun with blanks and started his official stop-watch. Wendler, a tall, 35-year-old woman, took off, her legs stretching as her toes bit into the dirt. She hit the wall with her feet, grabbed the top, flipped her lean body over the top and kept going. Her legs pumped through the flat tire maze. Next, she grabbed the 150-pound dummy and dragged it the required distance before taking off on the oval track. Her legs drove at a fast pace as she pushed her speed to the max around the dirt lane. After the finish, she coasted to a slow trot, stopped in front of us, and bent over. Bracing her arms on her knees, she gasped for breath.

"She's scored high," the umpire said. "Not one failure." He stared at the timer in his hand, jotting the results in a small notebook.

"Give me your written results," Tom said. "Please sign, time, and date them. Blake and I will sign as witnesses." He shook his head. "I knew they messed with her and marked her as failed. They didn't even bother to worry about blotting out her passing scores."

"Tom, this places the police academy instructors in suspicion of tampering with official city documents," I exclaimed. "Right?"

"Exactly."

"That's outrageous! I wonder how many other women didn't make it because of fraudulent testing."

"That's why Wendler is now a plaintiff in your case," Tom said. "Since Judge Byrne first ordered the processing of the women's applications, all testing results of females are suspected of having been tampered with by the police academy."

I couldn't imagine they had been so stupid as to alter scores. But look at what Wendler had done just now. She was way over their failing scores.

My stomach churned. How could any officer on the LAPD take part in anything as despicable as falsifying official city testing?

"Wendler," I said. "I want to thank you for cooperating with Mr. Hunt. I can't tell you how bad I feel that you were washed out. I understand you've passed your 35th birthday. That makes you ineligible to be retested."

"That's right, Officer Blake. But I'm grateful I can be of help."

"When police officers violate their integrity to this degree because they can't accept women as police officers, they need to be prosecuted."

"Hold your anger, Fanchon," Tom said. "Your case will right a lot of wrongs. It's not worth our energy to blow the whistle on bad conduct by individual officers. That's up to the department to clean up. We want to keep our sights on the big target. This kind of discrimination is one reason why the LAPD cannot defend against your case. Right now, I'm feeling pretty good about what we're uncovering."

I felt awful about the potential tampering. As we walked toward our parked vehicles, I looked more closely at Wendler and wondered if the men had decided she was a lesbian and washed her out for that reason. True or false, the slightest inkling that an applicant might be a homosexual still stirred hatred among most LAPD males. Never mind that homosexuality is not a choice. Never mind that they often jumped to assumptions without any foundations. Wendler, because of her build and her physical ability, could easily have been just such a target. Either way, her deposition on November 5, 1973, would only help our case.

The following week, Tom invited me to attend a lunch with him to get me better acquainted with the personnel at the Center for Law in the Public Interest. When I arrived, he escorted me into another office. "My God, Tom," I said when I saw the woman sitting behind the desk. "You didn't tell me I'd be working with an actress!"

"This is Linda Douglass," he said, laughing. "Wife of the center's managing attorney, John Phillips."

Linda, one of the center's paralegals who would become a

top network television commentator and, in 2009, President Obama's chief healthcare spokesperson, stood and held out her hand. "Finally. I'm privileged to meet you, Fanchon. I've pestered Tom for days since I first learned about your case." She smiled and squeezed my fingers. "You've become a role model for me." Her modulated voice flowed without hesitation.

"After what I've endured, it feels strange to hear a compliment."

"Let me share with you how much your case means to me. I've named my cat *Fanchon Blake*."

"My whole name?"

"Your whole name."

"You mean, every time you call or talk to your cat, you say my whole name?"

"She won't respond if we don't. She's a holy terror. That's why I named her after you."

"Good grief, Linda. You're going to get sick of hearing *Fanchon Blake*."

"As soon as we can, I'll take you home and introduce you to your namesake. She's a very independent calico who mouses once in a while and loves to climb trees and chase birds."

Imagine having a cat carry your name, I thought to myself.

"Have a seat," Tom said. He grabbed a chair for me and continued. "Both of you. We might just as well have our conference right now."

Linda handed me a pad and pencil from her desk. "You'll want to make notes."

"I need help with the legwork," Tom said. "We have a tremendous task to accomplish. We must gather everything that can be used when we go to trial. I'm counting on you two to contact as many retired policewomen as possible and interview them in person. I want their individual stories of what happened to them on the LAPD."

"I've got an up-to-date address file on most LAPD women, both active and retired," I said. "I can bring that in for starters."

"Linda will have to coordinate your activity. It will be tough for you, Fanchon, while you're still on active duty."

"We can handle it, Tom," Linda said. "We'll start by making appointments with those willing to be interviewed. I'll try to set up the interviews on Fanchon's off-duty hours."

"I'm afraid we'll have trouble," I said. "Even those on retirement don't want to be connected with me under any circumstances. I don't mean to be negative, but you need to know it will be challenging."

"Bring me your list, Fanchon," Linda said. "I'll start right away."

Linda was a no-nonsense graduate from the University of Southern California, and I liked her determination. "I may be able to spend more time on it than you think," I said. "Since I got sick, I've been wondering if I should retire."

Tom nodded his head. "I know it's been tough on you, Fanchon. There's no reason for you to stay because of the case. Go ahead."

That was a great relief. "When I go to work this afternoon, I'll find out when I can leave," I said without the slightest hesitation. "I'd like to stay until January, but I'll have to see what they say. I'll be available to help seven days a week once I've completed my last day at work."

I went back to my office, knowing that no matter how painful it would be to put my police career behind me, staying under adverse conditions had to end. In the squad room, each person I saw ignited a flood of memories. Slowly, I picked up my purse and made my way to police personnel on the fifth floor.

Once at the counter, I whispered, "I'd like to file for a service pension."

The woman handed me a form. "Fill out the essentials. It will take a minute to figure your total time."

This was it. I felt oddly detached from what was happening. No feelings. I just stood there and waited as the desk clerk searched the files for my records and calculated when I could retire. "Sergeant Blake," she said when she returned to the counter, "taking into account your vacation time, your last paid day will be the 4th of January, 1974. You'll need to return your badge, key, hat piece, and police buttons before that date."

"Will that give me over twenty-five years of service?"

"With extra days to spare."

And just like that, my career on the LAPD was essentially over. It was unreal. I went back to my office and straight to Shift.

"My Christmas gift to you, Lieutenant. I've filed for retirement."

"Isn't this rather sudden?" He stood. "When do you leave?"

"You'll have to check with personnel. The last paid day will be January 4th."

Shift didn't say another word.

I ended my career with the LAPD in December 1973. Now officially retired from the police career that I loved, I had to come to terms with the inability to fulfill my dreams as a felony investigator. For me, the struggle to rise in rank in accordance with my capabilities was over.

The next day, Pat Russell summoned me to the city council to receive the resolution traditionally presented to retiring officers. Before a resolution can be presented to a recipient, the council must vote approval for the award, concentrating on the potential recipient along with the citation it contains. The vote is usually routine and without challenge, but I was an active plaintiff in an ongoing, unresolved federal lawsuit against the LAPD and the City.

I watched the fifteen council members vote electronically from their seats in the semi-circled structure, inside the beautiful colonnaded chambers. Then Pat called me to the public microphone. When I turned to face the audience, I saw that although the chief was notably absent, Shift had come in by himself to pay his respects to me. Russell pulled a large folder from her desk and stood beside me.

"It's my honor, Fanchon, to present you with this City of Los Angeles Resolution." She read:

"NOW, THEREFORE LET IT BE RESOLVED that the City Council of Los Angeles commends and thanks SERGEANT FANCHON BLAKE for her outstanding service to the Los Angeles Police Department and to the citizens of this city, and wishes her continuing happiness and service in retirement that should be complete with the knowledge that HER CONTRIBUTIONS TO HER FELLOW MAN ARE DEEPLY APPRECIATED AND WILL BE LONG REMEMBERED."

She handed me the colorful resolution with the large gold city seal affixed at the bottom. The council members stood, and one by one came to shake my hand. Shift stayed right behind me the whole time, even though he didn't have to be there. Tears dripped unabashedly down my face.

Although this resolution is given to all retiring LAPD officers, this one signaled the city council's tacit acceptance of my legal battle against discrimination on the Los Angeles Police Department. Who else in Los Angeles's history had ever received such a resolution while suing the City?

18

THE TOLL

For the legal system to work, the lawyers have to initially ferret out and then meticulously develop the facts, so that when the judge applies the law, irrefutable logic leads to victory. But so many human factors enter into the process, it's inevitable that legal filings, continuances, and re-assignments of judges, to say nothing of issues involving the judges themselves, prolong the movement toward justice.

I just never realized how long my case would last or the toll it would exact on my health. The pressures I had confronted at work and continued to face at home, along with my new retirement and the slowness of the court, all combined to keep me popping nitroglycerin pills. Added to that, the heart doctor had unwittingly mentioned that drinking a glass of wine before bedtime would help me relax. Little did he know that I had always felt if one glass of wine was good for me, then two or three would be even better.

When Judge Byrne transferred my case to newly appointed Judge Robert Firth in 1974, the case was set in limbo until Firth got accustomed to his judicial robes. At the time, it was impossible to estimate how long that might take. In the meantime, Linda Douglass and I interviewed retired women officers. I developed tremendous respect for her ability as an investigative interviewer. We never failed to bring back excellent material for Tom to use in court.

By then, Tom had captured my total attention. I would come to know that he possessed a heart that beat for humanity. I stood in awe as he began slogging through the muck of discrimination. He pursued the case with pure passion and analytical brilliance, following a methodical pattern of thinking out every possible option regarding each decision, sometimes out loud, punctuated by bombastic *ah-ha*s as he walked around the office. He found many discriminatory, illegal practices in the Los Angeles Police Department, but wisely opted to narrow his focus to the most egregious discriminatory practices against women. He chose to make the LAPD prove by scientific evidence that the height, physical strength, and agility hiring requirements (which statistically had an adverse impact on women) were job-related and, therefore, legal under standards set by the United States Supreme Court.

On March 8, 1971, the United States Supreme Court had decided *Griggs v Duke Power Company*, a landmark case in the employment discrimination legal field, which Congress had extended to state and local governments the following year. The essential holding in *Griggs* is that any hiring or promotional requirement that operates detrimentally against women, minorities, or any other protected group, violates the Civil Rights Act of 1964. The employer is liable unless it can show by scientifically-valid, empirical (i.e., not anecdotal) evidence that the requirement is genuinely job-related and that people who do better on those hiring or promotional requirements make better employees. So the LAPD had to prove that their hiring requirements were valid indicators of who would be an effective police officer.

Just two years after that U.S. Supreme Court decision and the same month I met Tom for the first time, Tom had won a class-action suit on behalf of minorities against the Los Angeles County Fire Department using that very principle. I was confident that we would have the same success in my case, not only because the height, strength, and agility requirements were so clearly not indicative of job performance, but because Tom Hunt was spearheading the battle.

The case had been going just shy of a year and a half when Tom summoned me to his office for a conference. Failing to realize the many hours of overtime he worked, weekends included, to prepare this case, I had been bugging him with telephone calls because it seemed as though nothing was happening. Delighted that Tom had information to share, I waltzed into his office that morning and caught him standing in front of his window with his hands in his back pockets. He had stripped off his tie and opened the top buttons of his shirt. Tom flashed a smile upon seeing me. "I've got a surprise for you," he said. "He'll be here any minute."

When Tim Flynn (he would later change his name to McFlynn when he and his bride Donna McGuirk merged their names) arrived at the center, I was instantly entranced. He wore his shoulder-length reddish hair parted in the middle and sported an outrageously huge handlebar mustache. I judged him to be in his 30s, which made him a contemporary of Tom's. Despite a muscular and robust physique, Tim exuded a sense of tenderness.

"Tim's been hired by the center," Tom said. "He's a former special prosecutor. We stole him from the L.A. County District Attorney's Office."

Tim may have been gentle with me, but he was fierce when it came to the case. As a special prosecutor, Tim had focused on police misconduct. That misconduct would be sanitized regularly, as the cops closed ranks to protect their own. So while essentially policing the police, he handled a lot of excessive police force cases where he saw up close police officers committing perjury and falsifying evidence. Unlike Tom, who focused on Title VII cases like mine as a means of redistributing job opportunities and economic parity for classes of people who had been left behind, Tim's interest in my case revolved around making the LAPD a better department. He figured that bringing in women—who excelled in conflict resolution, tension de-escalation, and cooperation—would civilize the police. Years later, when talking about the case, he would sum it up with the words: "Okay, LAPD, we're coming after you, and we're going to kick your ass."

I had no idea at the time how perfectly Tim, who had started volunteering with the center the year before, and Tom would work together. Not only had Tim specialized in police cases, but he also had tons of trial and media experience. I simply noted how refreshing it was to see a professional man defy convention with his physical appearance. I bet his abundant red hair raised eyebrows when he appeared in court.

"Welcome to Blake versus Los Angeles and the LAPD," I said upon meeting him.

"From what Tom has shared," Tim said. "I feel lucky to join him."

"Let's get down to business," Tom said. "We've lots of fertile areas to attack the LAPD. Tim, I want you to file this motion today. We're requesting to maintain certification of the Blake case as a class action." He handed the papers to Tim, who would wind up making a lot of the statements and arguments in court while Tom worked on the briefing and technical legal arguments.

"When does this have to be filed?" Tim glanced at the documents.

"You have time to make it down to the federal district court this afternoon. Firth isn't too swift. He was appointed in May of last year and hasn't ruled on four other pending motions hanging up the case. Today's filing will get the attention of Cecil Marr in the city attorney's office. Maybe this motion will prompt the judge to take action."

I left the center quite happy. Tom hadn't gone to sleep as I had feared. Instead, he was doing all he could to broaden the lawsuit. Class action certification would throw open the floodgates if we won. For now, however, there wasn't anything more I could do to help him. He needed Tim and his legal experience.

Things weren't going quite as well for me on the personal front. Bewildered by depressed feelings I didn't understand, I couldn't see the real danger signs that engulfed me. On April 1, 1976, I sat at my rolltop desk and wrote in my journal:

> *April Fool's day. I'm wondering who's the fool. I'm stuck in a marriage that's dying. Stuck in a lawsuit that has no end. Stuck with a body that wants to fall apart. Stuck at home with nothing left to do but clean house, wash clothes, cook dinner, and save my sanity with a glass of wine.*

Turning to alcohol was nothing new, but it now became a real problem. Finally, after much encouragement, I checked myself into a facility called Raleigh Hills. The aversion treatment and my subsequent daily intake of Antabuse reduced my consumption of alcohol to nothing. But, neither the treatment nor the pill stopped the horrible craving to drink. Nobody had told me that after a month of not drinking, I would be alcohol-free, but not sober. Nobody had told me about being a dry drunk.

In the meantime, the case was dead and destined to remain so until Judge Firth ruled on the motions Tom had filed eighteen months prior. At the three-year mark from the date of the case's filing, the two cops working with the deputy city attorneys brought in a birthday cake to celebrate the fact that after all this time, the case remained stalled. For them, that lengthy delay was almost as good as winning. If this kept going, our funds would likely run out, and we—along with the case—would just go away.

Back home again and frustrated as all get-out, I dove into the breakers and surfed onto Manhattan Beach. Unbeknownst to me, I was following the same path that most public interest plaintiffs travel: fear, frustration, anger, questioning the process, and wondering if they can cope with all that's transpiring.

Once ashore, I walked back to my towel and flopped down. How different my life was—lazing on the sand, watching white gulls circling above. But that wasn't what I wanted. I hated being beached like some old seafarer. My potbelly that mounded under my black bathing suit and my inner thigh skin that hung like so much bread dough didn't help my morale. I couldn't even enjoy the beauty of the ocean as it ebbed and flowed, or its misty salty air. I ached to go back to the excitement of the police department.

Unable to doze, I set up my beach chair, put on my straw hat, and reached for a copy of the inner-city *Los Angeles Daily Journal*. An article about the police department's affirmative action plan surprised me since I hadn't heard about that before I had retired. I read that Assistant Chief Daryl Gates had apologized to the City for a recent delay, explaining that

Davis's request for a thirty-day continuance for further study was required "because of the Blake case." I couldn't help but let out a chuckle. Davis had been so confident that day in the police auditorium that nobody would oppose his plan to eliminate most of the policewomen from the department.

I continued to read. "Two city council committee members expressed grave doubts over goals in the LAPD plan for hiring women and minorities, fearing they were in fact quotas. Quotas, they said, would eventually result in reverse discrimination."

Forced quotas made me feel uncomfortable, but nobody had come up with a better way of making up for sixty-six years of onerous police employment practices. Did quotas mean that women would be hired in disproportionate numbers for a few years? Sure. But you can't get to where you're supposed to be if you don't accelerate. As my attorneys explained to me, if you leave a stop sign at the same speed as the car that's a block ahead of you, you'll never catch it.

This talk of reverse discrimination seemed like just another ploy by the City and the department to try to keep women out. If the city council was beginning to swing in his direction, no wonder Davis wanted a delay.

I put the *Journal* down. Had anything changed for policewomen since I had hired on in 1948? Nothing, really. A few more sergeants and token assignments. I watched the ocean, its fluctuation constant. Nothing stayed the same, I reassured myself.

I returned to my towel, picked up my belongings, and strolled past the seawall and up the short block of low squatty cottages to my house. Inside, I showered, dressed, and began to fix dinner, unable to get Davis out of my head. Why did men like him keep refusing policewomen their careers? Davis could have led the way when it came to dealing with discrimination against women. Instead, he had doggedly held onto his old-fashioned ideas about females.

I knew it would take a mighty blast from the federal courts to pry open opportunities for women on the LAPD. If I won my case, the federal process would mandate quotas through affirmative action. By the time Davis and his staff understood the legal thrust, their policy of police management by discrimination would be changed forever.

The telephone rang, breaking my thoughts. I dried my hands and answered. Tom sent my spirits soaring. "Good news is pouring in, Fanchon. I waited to bring you up to date. Judge Firth came back to work last month."

"You mean the case is moving again?"

Yes, the case was moving, but only because Tom and Tim had effectively placed a firecracker under the judge's rear by filing papers outlining how, after eighteen months, he still hadn't ruled on five pending matters. They had even analyzed the number of backlogged cases for all L.A. federal judges and discovered that while the average judge had eighty cases pending, Firth had five hundred. The papers delineated Tom and Tim's plan to go to the Court of Appeals to compel Firth to rule on the five matters pending in our case, implied that they might ask that he be removed from the bench, and asked that he remove himself from the case.

Eight days before the public hearing on the motion, the judge's clerk called Tom and Tim and asked them to see the judge for an off-the-record meeting. They joined Firth and two city attorneys in the judge's chambers, where Firth apologized to Tom and Tim for the delay and promised that if they took the matter off calendar, he would rule on the five issues within six days, i.e., two days before the scheduled hearing he was asking us to take off calendar.

Delays always favor one party. To this point, that certainly hadn't been us. So when Tom started to agree, Tim, never fearful, said he would withdraw the motion, but only after the judge had ruled on the pending matters. A pink hue washed over the judge and Tom's faces. As promised, six days later, Firth ruled on the five points. And despite the pressure that Tom and Tim had exerted, he ruled in our favor on all five.

"Firth barred the Police Protective League from joining the case," Tom told me jubilantly when he called. After their initial refusal to help me, the league had filed a motion to become a friend of the court. The Police Protective League fell under the political dominance of the chief's office, and Tom suspected that the legal maneuver had been initiated by the chief to help fight me.

"We don't need any more soldiers in the war against us," Tom said.

"That's what I call justice."

Tom laughed. "There's more. Firth certified the case as an across-the-board class action on behalf of past, present, and future women applicants, employees, and retirees."

The court had placed the City on notice that all police employment practices that discriminate against women would be scrutinized under the stringent standards of the Civil Rights Act.

"That's comprehensive," I said, barely managing to suppress a hoot of joy. "What happens now?"

"We move forward without further delay! But that's not all the good news. Do you understand that there are federal agencies—namely the employment section of the Justice Department's Civil Rights Division and the Law Enforcement Assistance Administration, better known as the LEAA—that are vitally interested in your case?"

"I knew that the EEOC had protected me when I filed with the Commission, but I've never heard about the LEAA. What does it mean, Tom?"

"It means that the LAPD is gonna hurt. The LEAA is threatening to withhold $10 million of federal grants from the City because of the LAPD's hiring irregularities and promotional system regarding women and minorities."

I had to let that comment sink in. Finally, I said, "Really? Maybe that's why Davis asked for a thirty-day delay of all City affirmative action plans. Can the LEAA really hold back those funds?"

"Yes," he said. "They know how to get results. The City is now trying to rectify police hiring rules."

Again I was silent. What was Tom telling me? Was my case over? "Tom, will their action stop our lawsuit? I didn't go through all this to end up without a federal court decision."

He laughed. "No. If we go to trial, we'll subpoena the LEAA to testify on your behalf."

"That's a relief. For a moment, my heart stopped. I thought the case had died."

"We're in this until we win. There's a tremendous amount of work ahead. Tim is heading out to interview police departments in six of the country's largest cities. He'll be gone at least four months. It's too soon for us to get excited, but I do feel good about the LEAA shaking up the City and the PD."

I hung up the receiver wanting to celebrate the first good news in two years. I hadn't taken Antabuse in a long time or touched a drop of alcohol for over a year. One happy little snort couldn't hurt. After all, the tide had turned. No reason in the world why I couldn't celebrate with a drink.

I reached up over the refrigerator for an open bottle of Jack Daniels whiskey. "I'll be damned!" I said out loud. "Shannon doesn't trust me. He's left a mark where he last topped off." I set the bottle on the counter, found my old double jigger shot glass tucked behind the china, and poured it full. If I pinched my nose, I wouldn't smell the alcohol and get nauseated. I closed my eyes and downed the amber fluid. The old familiar fire traveled to my stomach, and I waited for a happy feeling. Nothing. No upset stomach. Not even a buzz. Maybe I needed one more. Before I had quit, it had usually taken a couple of belts to feel high. I poured another double jigger, gulped it, and waited. Nothing. I held the bottle under the cold water tap until it filled to Shannon's mark, carefully dried it, and put it back exactly where I had found it. He would never know the difference. Then I closed the cupboard door, washed the jigger glass, and put it away.

Back in the kitchen, I peeled potatoes at the sink. As the skins dropped into the garbage disposal, I wondered how my case would end. If I won, I would be lucky to see the LAPD change in my lifetime.

Maybe Judge Firth would speed up the process. I would just have to wait to see how my case played out.

After brushing my teeth and rinsing my mouth to cover my intake, I finished making dinner, prepared the table with a white tablecloth, candles, and flowers, and turned on the stereo with pianist Marion McPartland, a favorite of Shannon's. Then I lowered the lights and placed empty wine glasses by our plates.

When Shannon came home, I was all smiles as I convinced him that I wasn't an alcoholic and could handle wine when I ate. Kelly didn't say a word. We enjoyed our old happy selves, and dinner was a huge success. But thereafter, I struggled to keep from drinking during the day. I went through hell waiting for my highball while Shannon showered and changed after work. The times he didn't want to drink meant I didn't dare, which triggered a burning ache in my nerves. When we did drink, one was never enough. I found I could eat a candy bar before I went to bed to help quiet my craving. When the candy didn't work, I kept a pint hidden in a shoebox in my closet.

Shannon and I continued to go through the motions of getting along, never acknowledging the deep chasm in our marriage. The subject was never broached in part because there wasn't much to talk about. Quietly, I went to counseling. The first book I read, *When I Say No, I Feel Guilty*, planted the seed of self-growth. Fortunately, I had no comprehension that such a tiny seed would take painful years to sprout or that the journey would be bewildering, confusing, and lonely. Eventually, Shannon simply packed his things and left me.

I turned my attention back to work and decided to apply for a private investigator's license as a backup. It would take a couple of months to pass the examination, and I wouldn't receive the credentials until after the first of the year. Of course, I still hadn't quit drinking because I had concluded that I didn't have a problem.

One morning, I arrived early for my morning Women's League Bowlers. I walked past the dark alleys to the bar and grill, sat in a booth, and ordered a highball. After two drinks, feeling easy-going, I noticed that my bowling ball hadn't been washed and decided I had time to give it a bath.

I went into the restroom. There was no vanity, so I piled my purse on top of the bowling bag on the floor. Gently, I lifted the twelve-pound blue ball into a small, gleaming sink. I lathered my hands with the liquid soap, rotating the ball until the surface shone. Then I turned on the faucet to rinse. Just as I lifted the ball six inches out of the basin, my soapy hands lost a firm hold. The ball zipped down with the speed of a comet, taking the bottom of the sink with it. The ball hit the floor between my feet, zoomed under the latrine stalls, and bounced against the commodes until it finally stopped.

I stood there, hands still frozen where the ball was supposed to be, looking down through the hole at the vacant space between my feet. Great balls of hell, what had I done! I dropped to my knees to look under the stalls and was relieved to find that I was the only one in the restroom.

Shaking, I bagged the soapy ball, picked up my purse, mustered what courage I could find, and casually sauntered out to the man at the main desk. The lights were on, and women had begun to arrive.

I waited for my turn. "Sir," I said when he was free. "Excuse me, but I have a confession."

The rosy-faced gent shut the till and faced me. I took a deep breath and set my jaw. "I just dropped my ball through your sink in the ladies' room. I was trying to wash it, but it went straight to the floor. How much do I owe you?"

He stared at me and burst out laughing. "Busted the sink?"

"Yes, sir. It's got a hole as big as my ball."

"As big as your ball?" He laughed harder. By now, the incoming women had stopped to listen, and I could feel my face reddening. He finally dried his eyes with a white handkerchief. "Tell ya what, your honesty won't cost you a penny. My insurance will take care of it. For a quarter, you can wash your ball in that machine right over there. It's pretty safe."

My team applauded even though I couldn't look a single member in the eye. We settled down to bowling and cinched first place. But all through the competition that day, I thought about having ordered those two drinks. I vowed to find a job after the first of the year. That would help.

My health improved. Armed with a revised resume, I contacted a retired LAPD police lieutenant who owned a security company. I wanted a job while I waited for the case to settle, and I needed to know that I could take care of myself now that Shannon and I had separated.

Toward the middle of October, Tom called. "Judge Firth's health has taken a serious turn," he said. "Our case is off calendar until further notice. It means another delay until he can come back to work, or they decide to assign another judge."

Another delay. I settled the receiver in its cradle, headed for the liquor shelf, and poured a drink. I sat on the couch. Would we ever get my case resolved? Firth had been nothing but a pain. Since the case had been filed in August 1973, more than three long years had elapsed, two of them on his watch. How many more years would pass before this ended? Would the chief wind up winning by default?

At the end of October 1976, Tim got married. When a wind suddenly came up at the outdoor wedding reception, it ripped off an enormous palm tree husk that landed pretty darn close to me.

"Ed Davis is out to get you, Fanchon!" Tim announced with a grin.

I was almost ready to believe him.

19

SOMETIMES IT TAKES A WOMAN

"Don't panic, but our new Judge Curtis just threw a ringer into the case," Tom said over the phone when he called on Friday the 13th of May, 1977.

Judge Jesse William Curtis, Jr., an elderly federal judge who had grown up in an era before women had joined the legal profession, was as pleasant and respectful as Chief Ed Davis was bombastic. But when it came to females doing police work, I would quickly find out that the two men had everything in common and were in complete agreement. During a press interview that Sergeant Jackie Howell, then president of the Policewomen's Association, had participated in, Davis had said he would put women on patrol only when football coach Tommy Prothro put women on the Rams' front line. Curtis would try to use the law to support that discriminatory position.

"Now what?" I asked. "What else can happen?"

"Plenty," Tom said. "Curtis didn't wait for the pre-conference hearing coming up on May 16th. Today, he granted the City's motion to dismiss your case in all aspects on the ground that the City's employment practices are legally valid as a matter of law."

Curtis had ruled that "The City of Los Angeles has decided to establish a police force with certain characteristics that are related to the proper exercise of its police powers. The fact that proportionately more men than women possess the desired characteristics does not invalidate the City's decision ... [Although] women can perform all the ... [job-related] tasks to some degree, the fact remains that many men, because of their physical characteristics, can perform certain important functions better than a large majority of women . . . Certainly, a sane chief of police would not dispatch a group of women of average female height, weight, and strength to contain a public uprising such as the Watts riots when the same number of men possessing the height, weight, and strength of average males is available."

Tom and Tim had told me there was no way the City would win its motion for summary judgment (a verdict without a trial), which stipulated that since there were no legal facts in dispute, no trial of the case was necessary. In actuality, there were plenty of factual issues in contention, even though the evidence that the LAPD had recently put together was so weak it was laughable. But sometimes opinion and bias trump facts, even on the bench.

"The bastard!" I exclaimed, my heart sinking into my ankles. "You mean we've lost?"

Devastated doesn't even begin to describe how I felt.

"I told you not to panic," he said. "We filed an emergency appeal with the Ninth Circuit Court of Appeals this afternoon. We haven't lost, but we have a fight on our hands. It will tie us up for another long delay while the appeals court makes its ruling."

"I'm not a happy plaintiff," I said. "To put it bluntly, I'm disgusted. Do you have any idea how long it will take the appeals court?"

"Who knows? But I have it on good authority that the Justice

Department will file a companion suit in U.S. District Court by June 2nd against the LAPD for employment discrimination."

He was right, but, of course, I didn't know that then.

"Judge Curtis is turning out to be worse than Firth, and I didn't think that was possible."

"Remember, I told you about judges. They're unpredictable. We lost this ruling, but we haven't lost the case. As long as the LAPD refuses to end their grossly discriminatory practices, the appeal process would have had to happen sooner or later."

"True," I said. "We wouldn't be in this mess if they'd been reasonable."

Curtis's Friday the 13th ruling wasn't the last of him. I went shopping for my 56th birthday and stopped short when I caught a *Herald-Examiner* headline: "POLICE UNISEX UPHELD." The subsection read, "Fitness Tests Held Unbiased." I paid for the paper and snatched it from the stand. Shaking, I read:

> Los Angeles Police Department physical fitness standards do not have to be lowered simply to allow more women to qualify as officers, a federal judge has ruled here in a precedent-setting sex discrimination decision.

The judge, of course, was Curtis, who, several weeks later, would reveal just how biased he was when he told the papers, "It does not appear to this court that the plaintiffs' ultimate success, in this case, is probable."

The evening sun disappeared on the horizon and silhouetted the Manhattan Beach pier against a darkened sky. I shivered on my way home as the damp evening air made overhead electrical wires crackle. Slumped at my desk, I called Tom. "Can you imagine the nerve of Curtis declaring that current fitness rules do not violate anyone's rights?"

"We've only been fighting skirmishes. That's why we had to appeal," Tom said. "The heart of your case is that we can't let the LAPD place restrictions against women. Don't fret over Curtis. That's what you've got me for."

I poured a drink. I knew there was terrible pressure both for and against equal rights. One could never know how much the belief systems of each lawyer, judge, plaintiff, or defendant would influence the outcome. Meanwhile, I, the instigator of this vital process and a player in this drama, had become a shadow alluded to as the Blake Case.

Following Tom and Tim's appeal of Judge Curtis' dismissal, Walter Cochran-Bond, an attorney with extensive experience in workplace investigations, joined the fray. Over the many months that followed, he handled a good share of the highly technical appellate briefing regarding the requirements for showing job-relatedness. Assuming fairness from the three judges who would make up the Ninth Circuit appellate panel, we had a sure winner.

One week before the oral argument, as per standard procedure, we were informed of the identity of our three-judge panel. A grand slam home run! First, Shirley Hufstedler, a brilliant, highly respected judge, whose prior opinions showed clear feminist leanings. Second, Thomas Tang, himself a minority and a victim of racial discrimination, whose previous decisions demonstrated a strong sympathy for civil rights claims. Third, Gus Solomon, a Jewish district judge from Seattle, with a reputation as an "old-line liberal."

Tom and Tim had just thirty minutes to make our case orally. Tim presented the technical merits of the case. Those clearly showed that the City had not met its burden of proving by valid empirical evidence that the LAPD's height, weight, and physical agility test hiring requirements were predictive of performance in police work. Tim also argued the crucial rhetorical part of the presentation, which Tom kiddingly called the Irish Blarney part of the case.

Starting in 1975, Tim had networked to find those large, urban police departments that in recent years had collectively put thousands of female police officers on uniform street patrol, as well as in plainclothes, detective, and undercover assignments. These departments hadn't required a pre-employment height or strength test and had allowed them to promote.

The on-the-ground research had been his idea. "I didn't even know that Title VII used a Roman numeral," he had told Tom when he first started working on the case. "Let's use my strengths. While the LAPD tries to prove that women can't do the job, I'm going to prove that they're doing an exemplary job across the nation."

So he crisscrossed the country, interviewing scores of such women, along with their male partners, trainers, supervisors, and chiefs. He returned with sworn depositions from police departments in six cities, including Boston, New York, Washington, D.C., and Dallas, which undercut any possible claim by the LAPD that the exclusionary height, strength, and agility standards were job-related or in any way predictive of job performance. "I found woman after woman who, on a scale of one to ten for what you need to be a good police officer, were tens in terms of performance," he would later say.

From the top people to the bottom, the depositions all showed that a woman's height or whether she could climb a wall or do chin-ups couldn't possibly predict job performance. In the opinions of their superiors, the women in these urban areas were doing the job just as well as men, receiving commendations of valor and the support of their fellow officers.

Besides, these women on patrol brought different skill sets to complex police work. "Mark my words," the highest-ranking female officer in the New York Police Department, who served as a commander in the Bronx, told Tim before being deposed. "Women are the most revolutionary new resource to policing since the motorcar."

The fact that a woman was 5'2" or 5'1" or 5'3" made no difference even when arresting violent suspects. Indeed, the women's inability to just wrestle a suspect to the ground had compelled them to find alternate ways to handle the situation. Perhaps that explained why they were more skilled than men at conflict resolution. The women police officers didn't get hurt more than their male counterparts. They didn't file more workers' comp claims or take more time off than the men. And they won just as many distinguished service awards.

The evidence Tim had gathered was convincing, and the LAPD's so-called evidence did nothing to disprove it. When the other side began to make its case before the Court of Appeals' three-judge panel, Judge Solomon interrupted the city attorney's argument. "Do you know the joke about the parade going by?" he asked. "The lady is watching her son, who's in the parade but is out of step with everyone. 'Look,' she says. 'Everyone is out of step but Johnny.'" He was referring to Tim's evidence and letting our opposition know very clearly that the LAPD's attitude about women was out of step with city police forces across the country.

Federal law stipulated that anything adversely impacting women had to be shown by empirical evidence to be job-related. If the City of Los Angeles and the LAPD had had proof that the wall climb and the height requirements were predictive of job performance, none of this would have mattered. But they didn't. Their evidence was a joke. They submitted results from a practice session, for example, during which officers were judged while carrying out arrests with a resisting suspect. The only problem was that people doing the judging and those acting out the part all knew that the exercise was intended to judge the height requirement as job-related. "If I could set up that kind of a test, I could prove that only short people can be good basketball players," Solomon said critically, taking the LAPD's position to its absurd conclusion.

Hearing Solomon's comments, clearly in our favor, and realizing that all three judges had suffered discrimination made Tom and Tim want to pinch themselves. They were pretty sure that we had won this round, but just to be safe, they didn't say a word to me.

As we waited for the outcome of our appeal, Chief Edward M. Davis announced that he would retire and run for governor. "If ever I should decide to run for public office, I should have my head examined by a proctologist," he had once said. The memory made me chuckle. As an individual, I liked Chief Davis. I just couldn't swallow his archaic attitudes about women or his inability to obey Title VII of the Civil Rights Act of 1964. And it irked me to no end that he would escape being held accountable for his policy about women officers.

On the second of May, 1979, Tom, Tim, and I waited in Tom's office for word on the ruling from the Ninth Circuit Court of Appeals. None of us could talk, all too aware of the tremendous importance of the appeals court finding. I closed my eyes to stop all the worry. Instead, I thought about Tom. Just remembering that he had accepted my case put a catch in my throat. No lawyers could have worked harder or better than Tom and Tim.

Tom's phone rang.

"Here it comes," he said. He listened intently, writing information, his face withholding any clues from Tim and me. Finally, he turned to us. "The Ninth Circuit Appeals has ruled in our favor."

Vindication at last!

I yelled, raced around Tom's desk and hugged him. "Bless you, guys," I said, backing away. "What's next?"

"Right now," Tom said, "the city attorney is filing a writ of certiorari petitioning the Supreme Court of the United States to review the decision. So we wait. We should be okay because Shirley Hufstedler, who wrote the opinion on behalf of the court, is sharp and known for her ability to expose the heart of a case. She's written that the LAPD's evidence fails to prove that height and agility requirements do not discriminate against women. If the Supreme Court agrees to hear this case, we'll have to prepare to make our arguments before them."

More waiting. On the other hand, this case was important enough for the City to appeal to the Supreme Court. My case would set precedent throughout the United States if we won.

"Can you guess how long it will be before the Supreme Court will act?" I asked, my morale high despite the prospect of yet another holdup.

"They could hear it as early as this fall's calendar or next spring. But once they make a decision, the long delays should come to an end. It costs the City a bundle of money every time something like this pops up."

I had to live with that pronouncement and go back to my personal life. That day, no matter what the results of my case, Judge Shirley Hufstedler had won my total admiration and gratitude. In time, I learned that she had written a gem of a ruling. Judge Curtis had said that the evidence presented by the LAPD, now led by Chief Daryl F. Gates, was sufficient for them to win. Judge Hufstedler's thirty-five-page opinion, which follows as an Appendix to this book, established that it wasn't. In the first part of her opinion, which reversed Curtis' summary judgment, she wrote:

> We conclude that the LAPD's use of sex-segregated job classifications prior to July 1, 1973, violated Title VII. Appellees completely failed to carry their burden of proving a business necessity to justify the Department's discriminatory system maintained in violation of Title VII.

Her words were just as definitive when she addressed the physical abilities test:

> We cannot conclude that appellees [the LAPD and the City of Los Angeles] met their burden of justifying use of the physical abilities test as a business necessity. The fact that the LAPD hired thousands of male police officers between 1968 and 1973 without using any pre-employment physical test suggests that the practice is not essential to safe and efficient job performance. Moreover, the modest correlations between scores of successful candidates on the physical test and scores during academy training on peer evaluations, tests of physical ability, and shooting skills, hardly establish that the physical test is so intimately related to job performance as to be a business necessity. Appellees had to demonstrate that their measures of training success are themselves significantly related to important aspects of job performance and they utterly failed to do so.

The Ninth Circuit sent the case back to the district court for trial. Since the trial judge would have to follow the law of the case—i.e., the ruling from the Court of Appeals—when it conducted the trial, there was no way the City could now win in the district court. Assuming that the U.S. Supreme Court saw it our way, they would have nowhere else to turn. The case would once again be returned to district court, with the Ninth Circuit's ruling establishing the law the trial judge would have to adhere to. Even though I had taken on the LAPD as a lone wolf with scant support apart from my attorneys, the department and the City had essentially been checkmated and would be forced to settle with us.

I was overwhelmed. After six years, this sex discrimination challenge, which I knew had also severely impacted the women still at the LAPD, might actually get resolved. Maybe one of them would even rise to chief of police before I died.

20

SO CLOSE

Even though things seemed to be going our way, the case would lag for close to a year while we waited for the U.S. Supreme Court to accept or deny review of the Court of Appeals' decision. During this time, the U.S. Department of Justice joined the fray, filing an employment discrimination lawsuit that added claims for minorities and then consolidating its case with ours. Having the United States Government on our side substantially strengthened our case.

Tom and Tim made offers to the City to settle, waiving back-pay claims in exchange for a court-ordered affirmative action numerical goals-and-timetables program for women and minorities. But they also said that once the Supreme Court denied review, we would not settle for only goals and timetables, but would also be demanding $2 million (about $7 million in current dollars) in back pay.

"The price is too high," replied one of the mayor's chief deputies—a guy by the wonderful name of Easy Burts—in a meeting with Tom and Tim.

"No, the price will go up by $2 million unless the mayor acts now," Tom said somewhat naively.

"I'm not talking about *that* price," Easy countered. He was talking about *political* price.

Shortly thereafter, Tom and Tim went to a Dodgers game, and on the ballfield's giant, illuminated announcement board, a large message blared that the LAPD was going to hire hundreds of new officers within a month and that applications were welcome. Tom almost stood up from his seat to return to work right then and there to stop this last-gasp hiring of an all-white male group before we got the LAPD under a court order.

Although he and Tim did stay for the rest of the game, within days, they filed a motion for injunctive relief. Given the rulings in the Court of Appeals and the City's patently clear inability to succeed at trial, they stipulated, if the City needed to hire hundreds of new officers, 25 percent should be women. The Justice Department lawyers actively joined the effort to seek this temporary goals-and-timetables court order.

Jesse Curtis was *still* the judge on the case. Since Tom and Tim knew he would rule against us on our motion for a preliminary injunction, they served the other side. They also sent Judge Tang (one of the three appellate judges who had just ruled in our favor) the papers in support of a request for a temporary injunction from the Court of Appeals, to be formally filed just as soon as we had lost the next round with Judge Curtis.

As expected, Judge Curtis denied our motion, deeming it "unreasonable and unnecessary." It would be inappropriate for him to interfere with standard police hiring practices, he concluded.

That was at about 11 a.m. on Tuesday, December 18, 1979. At 3 p.m. that same Tuesday afternoon, Tom and Tim argued the matter on the phone to Judge Tang, who had read the papers even before they had been officially filed. This kind of timing happens once in a hundred thousand cases. At the end of the argument, Judge Tang ruled, orally, in our favor, ordering that the goals and timetables be in force until the matter could be heard and decided by a regular three-judge appellate panel in three weeks.

The next morning, Wednesday, December 19, 1979, the big story in the *Los Angeles Times* was that Judge Curtis had ruled against us the day before. Nothing was said in the newspaper about Judge Tang's subsequent oral order in our favor.

That afternoon, Tom and Tim got a call from Judge Tang's clerk, instructing them to go to the federal district courthouse in downtown L.A. to get a fax of Judge Tang's written order, which they were to then serve on the City. They did so gladly. As they walked down the courthouse steps with the order in hand, two attorney friends passed them on the way up.

"We see Curtis screwed you guys again," one said, referring to that morning's news story.

"Not to worry," Tom responded gleefully, holding up Tang's order.

"How did you get that?" his friend responded with astonishment.

To this day, this accomplishment remains one of the great moments of both my lawyers' lives.

When Daryl Gates complained that the preliminary injunction was interfering with the police department's ability to hire the hundreds of new officers he needed, Tom and Tim took to the media. They pointed out that this in no way curtailed the department's ability to hire, just their ability to hire only white men. "This should lead to a settling of the case," they concluded, planting a seed that reporters picked up on.

Three weeks later, Tom and Tim argued to the court that the goals and timetables governing hiring at the LAPD be imposed on any hiring done before trial. A special panel chaired by the chief judge of the Court of Appeals for the Ninth Circuit had been constituted to hear the motion. One of the other justices, Joseph Jerome Farris, was a Black, former civil rights lawyer.

We had gotten lucky again. The U.S. Court of Appeals for the Ninth Circuit covers eight states (including Alaska) and includes forty-seven judges, several of whom had served for many years. At one hearing, one of the justices had hit his head on the bench with an audible thump after dropping it to shield his eyes from the sun that was streaming in through the court's back windows. He was so old that when he didn't move, the other two justices bent over to make sure he hadn't taken ill or died.

We could have easily drawn a panel with a judge like that, especially since most of the judges on the court at that time had grown up before the women's movement. There were many more Jesse Curtises than Shirley Hufstedlers, and an overwhelming majority of white males. And yet, by some miracle, we had drawn not only a woman and two minorities the first time around but a seemingly receptive panel this time as well, which was headed up by Chief Judge James R. Browning.

Tim argued persuasively for our side. Again, the judges seemed most impressed by Tim's evidence about the success of policewomen in other major cities despite lacking the LAPD's pre-employment prerequisites. The evidence wasn't truly relevant, because if L.A.'s practices could be shown to be job-related, they would be legal regardless of what was going on elsewhere. Even so, Tim's Irish Blarney worked its common-sense magic again.

The court indicated that it agreed with Tom's theory that a goals-and-timetables hiring order would not lower the quality of the people hired. Evidence revealed that the people at the middle and bottom of the City's civil service hiring list were just as qualified as those at the top. It also showed that there were sufficient numbers of women and minorities on the City's civil service list of qualified applicants to meet the goals and timetables we requested. All that needed to be done was to order that the City "dip down," i.e., go out of order on its civil service list to get whatever number of women were needed to meet the 25 percent hiring order.

After Tim finished, Deputy City Attorney Cecil Marr got up to argue. "May it please the court," he said. "After hearing the appellants' argument and the court's questions, I feel a little bit like the coyote howling at the moon," he told the panel, which had indicated that it agreed with Tom's theory and was ready to rule in our favor.

"Just like the coyote can see the position of the moon, you can see this court's position. So howl away, Counsel," Judge Farris said.

The court's formal order, issued a few days later, overturned Curtis's weak, prejudiced ruling, and constituted a preliminary injunction with the goals and timetables we had asked for. The Chief of Police, Daryl Gates, was on the TV news that evening, mad as hell, which made Tom, Tim, and me feel just great.

On April 29, 1980, Tom called from Los Angeles. "Great news," he said. "The Supreme Court denied the City's petition for certiorari and has returned your case to our district court for resolution."

We had prevailed. As I would find out, however, we still had a ways to go.

"Do I fly down now?" I asked, barely able to contain my excitement. Even though I had relocated to the state of Washington, twelve hundred miles away from the action, I had impatiently anticipated the results of this legal case and couldn't wait to celebrate its conclusion.

"No," he said with a laugh. "That's a bit premature, but I'll let you know. The case isn't over. We could still go to trial. Or we could save time and dollars and negotiate with the city attorney through a consent decree that has the power of a court order. By the way, this makes the Hufstedler opinion the law that governs this case."

We had changed the law of the land in fifty states!

Even though there was a chance we could still go to trial if the other side wouldn't work with us on quota-hiring terms as well as back pay claims, I remained optimistic.

"I'll keep a suitcase packed and set aside money for an airplane ticket."

"Don't expect this to close that fast, Fanchon. But with any luck, we could come to a conclusion before the end of another year."

"And what about the LAPD? Do you think Chief Gates will cooperate and settle?"

"My guess is that in your case, the Supreme Court has started the dominoes falling. It's a matter of time, planning, and patience. I'll call when anything develops."

Almost without exception, the fundamental goal in any employment-discrimination class action case is to integrate the defendant's workforce. So, although we held some powerful cards, Tom and Tim offered to settle for a solid court-ordered affirmative action plan, plus $2 million. In short, we wanted a 25 percent hiring order for women to be in effect until 20 percent of the police force was female. The goal was only about half of the 50 percent female general population because legitimate studies showed that, at that time, only half as many women as men, proportionately, wanted to be cops.

With the Court of Appeals' preliminary injunction still in

effect, there was no pressure to negotiate in a crisis mode, so it took months to hammer out the language and get everyone to sign off. At one point, the Los Angeles Police Commission's chair Stephen Reinhardt, a good friend of Tom's who became a United States Circuit Judge of the United States Court of Appeals for the Ninth Circuit, came to Tom's office and begged him, "like a good fella," to drop the $2 million demand. The City needed the money, he argued, and the people who would be getting the $2 million didn't necessarily deserve it. Tom refused, saying that employer defendants like the City, who are guilty of wrongs and litigate for years, have to pay for their refusal to settle quickly.

"Will it help if I get down on my knees?" Reinhardt asked.

"Nope," Tom replied.

21

DONE DEAL

Tom and Tim saw a lot of action during the more than six months it took to carve out a settlement, which ultimately would be expanded to include Blacks and Latinos.

Conversely, I was like a kid waiting for Christmas. Each day dragged, and I couldn't concentrate. My craving for alcohol worsened. I started to eat pie and drink malts, both loaded with sugar, to stay in control. That didn't last long.

"This is your lawyer," Tom said when he called after my latest recovery. "How are you feeling?"

I brought Tom, who would wind up successfully fighting his own alcohol-related demons some years later, up to date on what had happened since my relapse. Recovering from drinking posed a problem for me every day. Recurring nightmares, sweats, and uncontrollable tears plagued my life. I wondered if I would ever feel normal again. Daily attendance at AA meetings helped me through the trying moments of rehabilitation, but I resented my physical condition. At least I finally recognized that I was an alcoholic.

"We need you here on Thursday, November 20th, at 10 a.m. sharp," he said. "Think you can make it?"

Was he kidding? Aside from my drinking and recovery, I had thought of little else for months.

"I can fly down tomorrow. What's so important?"

"We need you here for the wrap-up," he said. "We have a court date with Judge Curtis and the City Attorney at the U.S. District Court."

"What are you telling me?"

"We have a fantastic binding agreement with the City of Los Angeles," he said. "It's to be signed Thursday morning. This is the big one we've worked hard to obtain. We've won, Fanchon."

I couldn't say a word. My tongue refused to move, and I couldn't make my vocal cords respond. My eyes filled with tears.

"Are you still there?" he asked. "Speak to me, say something."

"I'm so emotional right now; it's hard to talk. It's been such a long, long time. It's hard to understand that it's over. Nothing will stop me from coming down. Of course, I'll be there."

I had no idea even then that this class action lawsuit would be hailed as a landmark case, which would prompt hundreds, if not thousands, of law enforcement agencies across the country to drop their exclusionary policies, or that it would impact recruitment, training, and appointment standards at all levels. I just knew that at long last, this fight was over. We had wanted a federal ruling, and we had gotten it. The result affirmed my belief in the American system of justice.

"I don't know how to thank you and Tim, but I'll see you in court. This is one date I won't miss."

After our goodbye, I stood still by my window. A bald eagle rose from a high, twisted, dead limb of old-growth fir and lifted itself on mighty, white-tipped wings. As I watched that magnificent bird soar, my spirits rose, and I felt the weight of seven years slipping away. My case and sobriety dove-tailed at that moment into a double miracle. The day got quiet. Not a leaf rustled, nor did I hear the chirp of birds. There was no drone of high-flying planes or traffic driving by. No human voice filled the air. I sank to my knees, held my hands together on the sill, bowed my head, and through tears I could not stop, I gave thanks for my life. A surge of elation washed me clean inside. At that point, I didn't know the ramifications of the win or its potential to effect change. I could only hope.

Thursday morning, I stood in the sunshine on the steps of the U.S. Courthouse in Los Angeles waiting for Tom. My jacketed, dark blue pantsuit felt good as the November breeze cooled the temperatures to a livable seventy degrees. I watched him emerge from the public parking lot across the street, looking dapper in a blazer, accompanied by Tim, and Jill Jakes, who had become a state court judge. We hugged each other like little kids, and Jill looped her arm through mine. "Come on, Fanchon. We'll sit together this time and enjoy it. It's a bit different from that first day your case was filed in this very court. What a great moment."

"I've a lot to be grateful about," I said. "I won't forget how you helped. If it weren't for Ramona Ripston and the ACLU, I never would have known you."

We all walked together into the courtroom, shortly after the city council had approved the decree in executive session. Tom and Tim headed for the lawyer's table on the left. Jill and I sat in the row directly behind them. Somber members from the police department sat behind their current city attorney, one of several we had dealt with during the seven years it had taken the case to resolve. The quiet courtroom made me feel like we were sitting in a cathedral. My heartbeat sounded in my ears. I didn't want to talk.

The LAPD had been the only major U.S. police department not covered by a federal court order to hire women and minorities. My launching this suit had finally changed that. "This settlement is one of the biggest in Justice Department and federal law history," Tim had told the press. After seven years and more than five hundred separate documents filed by my attorneys, it was hard to take in.

Judge Jesse William Curtis, Jr. stepped up to the bench, adjusted his black robe, and slid into place. I watched his ruddy face for any signs of acknowledgment. If the opportunity presented itself, I would never let him forget his newspaper pronouncement that the Blake case had no chance for success. I hoped his injudicious opinion would make him feel uneasy.

I wondered whether it had bothered him to have been chastised by Judge Shirley Hufstedler's ruling. Did it bother him that the Supreme Court had supported her findings by returning the case to his court for disposition? Were I to sit there in his place under the same circumstances, I would find presiding over the agreed-upon consent decree a most challenging task and probably be just as meek as he was now. On the other hand, what poetic justice that the very judge who had ruled against us four years prior, now had to approve a settlement that would set up a permanent program for women and minorities.

The sweeping court order:

- Banned discrimination in the hiring, promotion, training, discipline, discharge, compensation, employment terms, or conditions of any employee or job applicant
- Ordered a 20 percent annual appointment goal for women for the first year, a 22.5 percent annual appointment goal for the second year, and thereafter a 25 percent annual appointment goals for women, to be in effect until 20 percent of the police force was female

- Ordered an annual hiring goal for minorities of at least 45 percent (approximately 22.5 percent Blacks and 22.5 percent Latinos), to be in effect until population parity
- Stipulated increased quotas to be put into place to compensate for the failure to meet the above hiring goals
- Set the height requirement at 5'0"
- Ordered that at least six eligible women who could pass the examination be promoted to lieutenant
- Granted women and minorities monetary relief in the amount of $2 million and a back pay fund of $1.5 million to be split evenly between current or retired officers deemed eligible, and women and minorities who had applied to become police officers on or after August 20, 1970
- Set aside $500,000 for recruitment
- Awarded me $50,000 for being denied permission to take the examination for lieutenant, Leola Vess $25,000, and the other plaintiffs $1,000 each. Leola and I would not receive any other monies, but the other three plaintiffs would.

I strained to control a demonstration of joy. I didn't care a hoot about the monetary part of the settlement; this case had set a precedent for civil rights case law. It impacted not only the Los Angeles policewomen but all working women nationwide, especially women seeking to be police officers. Chief of Police Daryl Gates may not have been thrilled with the order, but to his credit, he would not only comply with the quotas specified by the order, but he would exceed them.

"We have a terrific chief of police who has implemented the decree with great enthusiasm and really supported the women," Officer Shilah Johnson, former president of the Policewomen's Association, would say ten years later. "Without Fanchon and Chief Gates, we wouldn't be where we are today."

As I watched Tom, Tim, the city attorney, and the judge complete the signing, I heaved a sigh of relief. The last big domino had fallen, and the Los Angeles Police Department was now required to change. When the court adjourned, I jumped to my feet and shook Tom's and Tim's hands. I needed to get outside. Tom, Tim, and Jill followed me. My attorneys were so giddy they could hardly walk. They had put in such long hours, giving up sleep, holidays, and time with their families. Now, all that sacrifice had paid off.

When I hit the steps, I leaped up and out into the air, letting go of a victory yell that could be heard in the police building a short block away.

"How do you feel, Sergeant?" a reporter from the *Los Angeles Herald Examiner* asked.

How do I feel? What a question! My feet were still treading air.

"I stand today, recognized as a first-class citizen," I exclaimed. "The women on the Los Angeles Police Department have a federal order that prohibits the police department from ever again shutting them out. They can compete for promotions and assignments. How do I feel? I'm bursting with pride; that's how I feel."

I couldn't resist shoving my fists straight up. This case had affirmed a powerful message that was bound to resonate among police departments throughout the country. It was mind-blowing.

After the interview, I drove back to Tom and Tim's office. As I walked in, Pat Russell called me. "Congratulations," she said. "We're all so excited and happy for you."

"It's hard to understand that it's finally over and I've won," I said.

"My office is sponsoring a celebration in your honor—5 p.m. Monday night in City Hall's Tower Room. Please tell Hunt, Flynn, and their office that they're invited."

"I don't know if I can stand that kind of attention, Pat. Seven years is a long time to be an outcast."

"We haven't received a *no* from anyone we've contacted," she said. "That must tell you something."

"I'm only three months away from the treatment center. I'm not sure I can handle the serving of alcoholic beverages."

"No problem," she said. "We're not going to this gathering because of cocktails. It will be a new experience to host an event without alcohol. It's an idea that could set a new trend."

That startled me. "But, Pat, you mustn't deny them just because I can't drink."

"Relax," she said. "It will be fun to watch their faces when they take that first pure swallow. See you there, my friend; 5 p.m."

Tom said he wouldn't miss it, especially after what we had been through. "It's been my experience that the lawyers are forgotten after the thump of the final gavel," he said.

"I won't let anybody forget," I said. "I don't want to accept any credits without you. There wouldn't be anything to celebrate if I hadn't filed the EEOC complaint, and you hadn't accepted my case."

He walked me to the elevator. "Of course, it isn't over for Tim and me. We still have to monitor what the consent decree orders. We'll be surveying the LAPD's compliance each year to make sure they follow through on what the court has directed."

Monday morning's *Los Angeles Times* dedicated its lead editorial to the case. Titled, "The Open Door," the commentary read:

> *The rules are clear now. The Los Angeles Police Department can get about the business of filling 500 vacancies, mindful of the requirement that more of those jobs than ever before must be filled by women, African-Americans, and Latinos.*
>
> *The consent decree frees the City from the possibility of a long trial and would only have further undermined the police department's*

reputation and its recruiting ability. The decrees do come much too late to be of help to Fanchon Blake, who brought the suit in 1973 and who now lives in retirement in Washington State. She helped open the door of opportunity for others.

I put the newspaper down and yelled to my sister, with whom I was staying while in Los Angeles. "Jeannie, wait till you see today's paper!"

She poked her head around the corner from her kitchen, "What are you prattling about?"

"I never thought I'd see the day when I'd end up in an editorial," I said, delighted to be top banana for a brief moment.

"Impressive," she said as she set out breakfast. "Come on, luminary. Come down to earth, or you'll never make Russell's gathering tonight."

At 5 p.m., I rode the small elevator at City Hall with my sister and retired policewoman Marilyn Owens. I had been disappointed not to hear from more of my colleagues that day, but I knew that for the LAPD, the enforced change was like swallowing a broomstick sideways. Now I was going to face the very people my case would so radically impact.

"Jeannie, I'm scared to death. I don't think I can step off this elevator into that crowd."

The door opened. "Go on," Jeannie said. "They're waiting for you. I'll see you when it's all over." She gave me a gentle nudge, and I stepped into the room. My former partner and friend, Sergeant Dorothy Pathe, greeted me first. She hugged me and whispered, "Remember when I said the devil made you do it?"

I stepped back, laughing. "Of course. That's what helped me survive. Thanks for coming tonight."

"Wouldn't have missed it. Congratulations from all of us."

Even by this point, nobody I spoke with could believe the lawsuit's outcome. Pat Russell steered me to the podium across the room. I stood next to Mayor Bradley, and we waited for quiet. Some sixty to seventy people, including a less-than-elated Chief Daryl Gates, city council members, Commissioner Ula Pendleton among other commissioners, and many police officers had managed to attend despite the short notice from Pat Russell's office. Twenty to twenty-five active and retired policewomen bunched together near the elevator, there, despite a climate that even in the face of my win had remained hostile to those who supported me.

"Thank you for your attention," Pat Russell said. "You all know why we're here. Last Thursday closed a seven-year litigation between Fanchon and the Los Angeles Police Department. There are some among us tonight who have asked to express their remarks. Mayor Tom Bradley, would you so honor us?"

Tom Bradley didn't try to hide his smile. His tall, muscular physique dwarfed the podium as he stepped up to speak. He had risen from retired LAPD lieutenant to city council member to mayor and would be elected an unheard-of five consecutive times. He spoke quietly in a measured delivery. "This is a great moment that I shall always remember. This victory tonight is for all employees who work for this city. I want to acknowledge the courage it took for Fanchon to come forward and file a complaint against discrimination. The consent decree filed a few days ago will establish new changes in hiring, assignments, and promotions for the policewomen on the LAPD. It also recognizes the overlooked, qualified minorities who can now become police officers." He turned toward me. "It is my pleasure to thank you." He took my hand, squeezing gently, then hugged me before stepping aside.

It required every ounce of control to keep from crying as the compliments continued. I blushed so many times that I wanted to bolt and run. Praise was foreign to my ears.

"And, now ladies and gentlemen, the main plaintiff, Fanchon Blake."

I stood in front of the group and without thinking, blurted, "My name is Fanchon, and I'm a recovering alcoholic."

Nobody moved. I watched their faces. Eyes widened and jaws dropped. Had a mouse run across the spacious floor, it would have been heard, but probably not seen since they were all staring at me. It took a moment before I could find my voice. I continued. "It's true. I've just blown my anonymity. No big deal." I watched the faces relax and smile as they turned to each other to make quiet comments. For the first time since my recovery, the internal shakes subsided.

I stood before them with my old self-assurance and felt my voice grow strong as I continued. "The fact that this long ordeal is over, the fact that we now have guidelines for both men and women, the fact that changes to unfairness must be made—all of this has been addressed. I want to thank all of you for appearing here with me and to thank Pat Russell for honoring my sobriety by not serving alcohol tonight.

"Before I stop talking, I want to introduce my lawyer, Tom Hunt. He's accomplished a miracle for the women on the LAPD."

As people clapped, I reached for Tom's hand and raised it with mine. He held back and whispered that he didn't want to speak.

"Also, I want to introduce retired Sergeant Leola Vess, who holds the distinction of, in 1945, being the first woman on the Los Angeles Police Department appointed sergeant. She waited in vain to compete for further promotion. She came forward, fighting guilt about her loyalties to the department. Under great personal stress, she applied for retirement earlier than planned to become a plaintiff in this case. Thank you, Lee." She came forward, and I raised her hand in acknowledgment of the applause.

I continued. "You must know that I did not file my complaint against the LAPD for monetary reward. What I wanted was granted last Thursday: a federal order to correct inequities. Seventy years is an incredible length of time for male management to ignore the tremendous human talent of our policewomen. I want to thank those of you who are active-duty women officers on the police department for your support this evening. Over the past seven years, you have endured some of the most unbelievable treatment because of my case. You have endured intense brutality against women recruits at the police academy. You've suffered physical abuse, with one woman's leg being broken by a man during one-on-one combat training. You've suffered emotional abuse. During physical agility testing, male training officers at the academy altered the passing scores of women applicants, so they failed. This blatant display of control and power made your silent support for me heroic. And we haven't even mentioned the daily verbal abuse you were forced to ignore."

My remarks surprised some of those in attendance, but I kept going. "I do believe it's unheard of for a successful plaintiff suing the City to be greeted with thanks from some of the City's elected officials. This act of acknowledgment tonight penetrates far deeper than an accolade for me. Mayor Bradley's appearance this evening is a refreshing signal from the top that many among us rejoice in the change ordered through the federal court. This historic decree guarantees that women officers cannot be shunted into the shadow of the badge. For the first time in the history of Los Angeles, we've come together to celebrate the liberation of women officers from the silent force."

* * *

You don't change your stripes overnight, but over the next few years, despite ongoing de facto segregation and racial tension in the department according to a *Los Angeles Times* study, more and more women were hired and promoted on the LAPD, which also improved on the diversity front. Every time I heard about somebody getting promoted on the department, I would call them up and say, "Congratulations. *You* did your part."

By 1986, half of the academy's fifty-three recruits were women. Recognizing that the increasing numbers of female officers needed facilities in which to train, a two-story women's locker room and weight-training facility was erected at the Los Angeles Police Academy. It seemed fitting that it had been constructed with recruitment funds initially budgeted by the City to meet the consent decree hiring goals, which had proved unnecessary.

At the dedication ceremony on January 6, 1986, I discovered that the building had been named after the late Sergeant Jeannie Eisentraut, who was killed in a 1981 traffic accident, and me. That wasn't all. The plaque by the front door reads: "This building was made possible through the efforts of Sergeant Fanchon Blake."

Wow! I had sure come a long way since those days of feeling like the earth had opened up and swallowed me when no one at work would talk to me. This new acceptance was like an impossible dream come true.

In 1990, on the tenth anniversary of the settlement, the City had a big ceremony at the police academy to honor the women who had been hired under the decree. Among the female police officers present were sergeants, captains, and lieutenants, along with women who now worked as bomb technicians, motorcycle officers, helicopter pilots, and patrol officers—all positions that had once been exclusively male. The department would still need to work on the retention of female recruits and officers, but the doors were now unlocked.

The officer in charge of the ceremony had told me that I wouldn't be able to address that audience. "We don't think it's appropriate," he said. But, thanks to the Los Angeles City Council president, I got my chance. I was heralded with a standing ovation. That was quite something after all those years of going it alone, at least on the LAPD front.

"You have my commitment: I shall never sue the police department again," I promised the crowd.

I added a few words about the fact that even at this point, women officers faced challenges. Nothing was going to be given to them, I knew. "Don't give up your dreams," I urged.

In a surprise tribute, Chief Gates said a few words as well, noting that the number of women on the LAPD at that point had topped one thousand. "I was wrong," he said about his prior objection to women being on the force. He didn't just acknowledge that once. He admitted it five times in that speech. His conclusion: "The LAPD is a better department now because of the women on the force."

Within six years of that gathering, the number of women officers would swell to almost 1,600, coming within three percentage points of meeting the mandated 20 percent marker. In the meantime, several thousand Blacks and Latinos would also be hired, helping to make the LAPD a more civilized and effective department.

After the ceremony, I went over to take a last look at the plaque.

"You realize that will be up there 100 years from now?" my good friend Hy Kravitz, a retired sergeant, said after hugging me. "People will say, 'Who the hell was Fanchon Blake?'"

I laughed. "And I'll pop right up and say, 'Here I am.'"

EPILOGUE

When I wrote this in 2010, thirty years had passed since my lawsuit against the LAPD was settled. At that point, 1,884 female officers, including seventy-four who rank above sergeant—the ceiling when I served—were on the department. One in five officers was female, with half of those working street patrol. So when I received an invitation to participate in a luncheon honoring 100 years of policewomen on the LAPD, I accepted gladly. The fact that women in the LAPD could rise or fall according to their ability rather than their sex didn't wash away the years of discrimination or any lingering issues. With hardened attitudes, any switch of this magnitude requires years to achieve. But the LAPD, in the face of many other police problems, is a tremendous success in reversing discrimination practices that denied women, Blacks, and other minorities their right to equal opportunity. The victories on that front, along with the struggles and the achievements of so many women along the way, are worthy of celebration.

The car that took me to the Los Angeles Police Academy, where the luncheon was to be held, drove through the red brick gates and then past the building that bore my name. At the September 13, 2010 event, I was seated right by the chief's table at the front of the room. Immediately, women of all colors, in and out of uniform, came up and gave me hugs. Black, Latino, and Asian men lined up as well. "Thank you," they all said one after the other. I suddenly realized that without the lawsuit, none of them would hold the jobs they do.

Some of the old-timers, women as well as men, told me, "Oh yes, I was told to keep my mouth shut and not make waves." But if you don't talk about a problem, no matter how much trouble you might be courting, how can you correct it?

The positive energy in the room revealed that the LAPD was a different place to work than it used to be. Male attitudes had clearly changed. Midway through the luncheon, my former antagonist William Wagner put his arms around me. "I'm sorry," he whispered in my ear. That three of his female family members had wound up serving on the LAPD told me he truly understood that we cannot condone prejudice that denies individuals the right to compete for employment, assignment, and promotion, no matter what their occupation. That applies to policing for a number of reasons.

Research at several major universities has proven that increasing the number of qualified women in law enforcement is an effective strategy for reducing police use of excessive force, improving police response to family violence, and improving community and police relations. The only conclusion any sensible person can come to is that increasing the number of qualified women in law enforcement is an effective strategy for changing police culture.

Charlie Beck, then the chief of police, sought me out soon after his arrival at the luncheon and hugged me. "I'm very happy to meet you and to thank you for what you did," he said. I knew that along with having his head on right, Charlie Beck had a good heart, so I was thrilled when he became chief and loved

Epilogue

how he led the department. His words touched me and helped to further heal the part of me that still felt fractured.

A couple of days later, I attended the annual LAPD Legendary Ladies' Luncheon where the LAPD's top-ranking woman at the time—whom I had never met—Deputy Chief Sandy Jo MacArthur, came up to me. As we reviewed the past, I mentioned that early on, before I became aware of the limitations imposed on women at the LAPD, I'd had ambitions. "I would have loved to have been the chief of police," I said.

Without saying a word, she reached up and removed her chief's stars from her left lapel. "I want you to have these, Fanchon," she said as she pinned them on me. "If it hadn't been for you, I wouldn't be here."

She gave me a big hug, and I started to cry.

After all the bitter tears over the years, these tears were welcome. So many women had been able to compete for promotion, for assignments worthy of them. As a result, so many had risen through the ranks. As I looked around at the new face of the LAPD, I knew that, if I had to, I'd do it all over again.

AFTERWORD

by Congresswoman Pat Schroeder

Recent law enforcement controversies raise compelling questions about police culture and the infamous code of silence that many observers have advanced as a key component of police culture. This book serves as a fascinating window into that police culture, written from the perspective of someone who was simultaneously a Los Angeles Police Department insider and, because of her gender, forever an outsider.

A newspaper might report Fanchon Blake's story in a single article headlined, "Court Orders End to LAPD Discrimination Against Policewomen." The newspaper reader might say, "I thought that stuff ended years ago," and turn the page. The story, however, is much richer than such an article could convey, and it is that rich story that this book sets out so compellingly.

History teaches us that many principles of justice and fairness that seem self-evident have, in fact, been stubbornly difficult to establish in practice, and at great personal cost to the people who worked to establish them. I think often of Susan B. Anthony, who worked her whole life—was even convicted in a criminal trial—to establish the right of women to vote. She devoted decades of her life to this goal and died more than a decade short of seeing women's suffrage become a reality. I think of Harriet Tubman and the underground railroad. I think of Margaret Sanger in earlier times, and Sarah Weddington in our time, working to make reproductive rights a reality for women.

These great struggles involved countless women and men of courage, many of whose identities have been lost to us; but each of these struggles also involved people whose individual names and stories are treasures that inspire us.

Fanchon Blake, fortified by her military experience and training, devoted much of her life to establishing the principle that the Los Angeles Police Department, and by extension, all law enforcement agencies—traditional bastions of male power—are obliged to afford equal opportunity and treatment to women. Congress enunciated this principle in the groundbreaking Civil Rights Act of 1964 (an act, by the way, which was amended to include sex discrimination in an effort to defeat the entire measure). But laws are not self-executing, and many people have worked hard, both before and since 1964, to bring about equal opportunity and treatment for women in the workplace.

Fanchon Blake invested seven years of her life in the court case against the LAPD—and those seven years represent just the last part of her twenty-seven year struggle.

Time, however, is only one way to count the price Fanchon Blake paid to establish this principle. To read Fanchon Blake's story is to understand that the courage required to seek justice is not usually the kind that can be demonstrated in one fine, blazing moment of truth; rather, it must be summoned day by day, year after year, in the thousands of painful and humiliating incidents, both petty and large, that comprise prejudice in action. It is to understand that if a woman today finds her workplace free of discrimination or harassment, a host of other women have paid a heavy price to achieve that.

This isn't to say that Fanchon Blake's story is a litany of wrongs. The march of characters through her life—ranging from a few truly odious people to a fair number of people who are likeable but do not, for a variety of reasons, rise to the occasion, to a handful of courageous souls—is a fascinating parade indeed; but never in this parade is there a character more fascinating than Fanchon Blake. There are times when you want to grab her by the shoulders and shout, "No, Fanchon, don't do that!" There are times when she acts courageously in full knowledge of the enormous risk she is taking, and there are times when she responds to an injustice with the kind of brilliant clarity that can only issue from naïveté. In common with every human being, she makes her share of mistakes. But her courage flows through it all, like the river that carves, over time, a magnificent canyon.

It is fashionable today to use terms like affirmative action to whip up division and anger. This book reminds those of us old enough to remember, and teaches those who are too young to have lived through them, how bad the "good old days" could be. I know, from what I hear every day from women around the country, that sex discrimination is not entirely a matter of the past. Fanchon Blake's story illuminates how ugly and wrong, how corrosive and destructive, is discrimination. She shows us how difficult discrimination is to dislodge, yet she inspires us to work diligently to end it.

We have been fortunate, in our times, to have witnessed courageous people who, though having suffered tremendously at the hands of powerful forces, have emerged free of bitterness, committed to justice and reconciliation. Nelson Mandela and Daw Aung San Suu Kyi have exemplified this extraordinary quality on the world stage. Fanchon Blake's ordeal at the hands

Afterword

of the LAPD consumed decades of her life. Her case took so long that she never benefited from it in her own career. Even so, of the many notable images in this book, the one that will touch your soul most deeply is the image of Fanchon Blake emerging at the end without bitterness, her hands clasping the prize of justice, her heart open to reconciliation.

APPENDIX

Shirley Hufstedler's opinion became the law of the land because Fanchon Blake—the woman whose story you just read—was not willing to accept the discrimination to which she and those around her were subjected. She stood up and said no. Here is Judge Hufstedler's opinion in its entirety.

FANCHON BLAKE, et al., Plaintiffs-Appellants,
v. CITY OF LOS ANGELES, et al., Defendants-Appellees.
Nos. 77-3595, 77-3601
UNITED STATES COURT OF APPEALS,
NINTH CIRCUIT
595 F.2d 1367; 1979 U.S. App. LEXIS 15011; 19 Fair Empl. Prac. Cas. (BNA) 1441; 19 Empl. Prac. Dec. (CCH) P9251; 27 Fed. R. Serv. 2d (Callaghan) 567; 53 A.L.R. Fed. 1
May 2, 1979

COUNSEL: Cecil W. Marr, Deputy City Atty. (argued), Los Angeles, Cal., for plaintiffs-appellants.

A. Thomas Hunt, Jr. and Timothy B. Flynn (argued), Los Angeles, Cal., for defendants-appellees.

Appendix

JUDGES: Before HUFSTEDLER and TANG, Circuit Judges, and SOLOMON,[1] District Judge.

OPINION BY: HUFSTEDLER

Appellants brought this class action charging the City of Los Angeles, the Los Angeles Board of Civil Service Commissioners, and Edward M. Davis, then chief of police of the Los Angeles Police Department, with sex discrimination in employment in the Los Angeles Police Department ("LAPD"). The appellants represent a class of women who are past, present, and future applicants for, employees in, and retirees from sworn positions in the LAPD. Appellants claimed violations of Title VII of the Civil Rights Act of 1964, as amended (42 U.S.C. §§2000e Et seq.), the Fourteenth Amendment of the United States Constitution, and the Civil Rights Act of 1871 (42 U.S.C. §1983). [**2] After certifying the class, the district court granted summary judgment to the appellees. Appellants appeal from the summary judgment, and the City cross-appeals from the class certification order.

We reverse the summary judgment and hold that (1) appellants met their burden of proving a prima facie case that the appellees violated Title VII before July 1, 1973, by maintaining sex-segregated job classifications, and after July 1, 1973, by using selection devices, including a height requirement and a physical abilities test that disproportionately [*1371] excluded women from employment, (2) appellees' use of sex-segregated job classifications between March 24, 1972, and July 1, 1973, violated Title VII because it was not mandated by business necessity, (3) appellees were not entitled to summary judgment with respect

---

1 Honorable Gus J. Solomon, Senior United States District Judge, District of Oregon, sitting by designation.

Appendix

to employment practices used after July 1, 1973, because they failed to show that the questioned employment practices were justified as a matter of law under the required standards for business necessity, (4) the gender-based classification system used by appellees before Title VII became applicable to governmental agencies violated the [**3] equal protection clause of the Fourteenth Amendment. Because we reverse and remand the case to the district court for trial, we decline to reach the merits of the class certification order.

FACTUAL BACKGROUND

Prior to July 1, 1973, the LAPD maintained separate, gender-based job classifications in entry-level police positions. Men in the "policeman" classification performed general police patrol assignments and could be promoted through all ranks of the department. Women in the "policewoman" classification generally performed "tasks relating to women and children, desk duty, and administration." Policewomen were barred from regular police patrol assignments and were ineligible for promotion above the level of sergeant. Between 1970 and 1973 no women were appointed to sworn positions in the LAPD, although the department hired more than 2,000 men. The percentage of women in sworn positions in the LAPD declined from 2.62 percent in 1970 to 2.15 percent in 1973.

Beginning on July 1, 1973, the LAPD abandoned the sex-segregated job classifications and established a single entry-level position of "police officer" for both men and women. The department unified its lines of promotion and imposed identical entry [**4] requirements on both male and female applicants for "police officer" positions. "Police officers" initially were required to be at least 5'7 in height; this requirement subsequently was lowered to 5'6 where it remains today. The department also instituted a physical abilities test, which all applicants for "police officer" positions were required to pass. In 1976, three years after the "unisex" job classification program had been established, women occupied only 2.08 percent of all sworn positions in the LAPD and only 0.48 percent of all positions in the ranks of sergeant and above.

The district court found that appellants' sex discrimination claims spanned three time periods of distinct legal significance. The first period antedated March 24, 1972, when Title VII became applicable to governmental agencies. The district court held that the dual classification system in effect during this period did not violate the equal protection clause of the Fourteenth Amendment because it was "substantially related to and serve(d) . . . the important governmental objective of providing an effective police force." (Blake v. City of Los Angeles (C.D. Cal. 1977) 435 F. Supp. 55, 61.) [**5]

The second period was between March 24, 1972, and July 1, 1973, the date when the LAPD abolished the sex-segregated job classification system. The district court held that the dual classification system did not violate Title VII during this period because its continuation was justified by "business necessity." The dual classification system was found not to be a violation of the Fourteenth Amendment for reasons mentioned above.

The final period was the time after July 1, 1973, the date when the unisex "police officer" classification was instituted. The district court held that "undisputed facts" established that the entry requirements for police positions, including the height requirement and the physical abilities test, violated neither the Fourteenth Amendment nor Title VII. Appellants' Fourteenth Amendment claim was rejected because the district court found no evidence of discriminatory intent. The district court held that discriminatory intent also must be proved to establish a Title VII violation by an agency of local government. Thus appellants' [*1372] Title VII claim was rejected, although the district court concluded that the LAPD's height requirement and physical [**6] abilities test "imposed a severe adverse impact upon women." (Blake v. City of Los Angeles, supra, 435 F. Supp. 55, 62.) The district court held, alternatively, that no Title VII violation could be shown even under the impact standard of Griggs v. Duke Power Co. (1971) 401 U.S. 424, 91 S. Ct. 849, 28 L. Ed. 2d 158, because the height requirement and physical abilities test "are appropriate for the selection of qualified applicants" as a matter of law. (Blake v. City of Los Angeles, supra, 435 F. Supp. at 66.)

I
TITLE VII CLAIMS

Appellants contended that the LAPD violated Title VII before July 1, 1973, by maintaining sex-segregated job classifications, and after July 1, 1973, by using selection devices, including a height requirement and physical abilities test, that disproportionately exclude women from employment.[2] A three-part inquiry is required to decide whether Title VII has been violated. (Dothard v. Rawlinson (1977) 433 U.S. 321, 329, 97 S. Ct. 2720, 53 L. Ed. 2d 786; Albemarle Paper Co. v. Moody (1975) 422 U.S. 405, 425, 95 S. Ct. 2362, 45 L. Ed. 2d 280; DeLaurier v. San Diego Unified School District (9th Cir. 1978) 588 F.2d 674, 676.) [**7] The first question is whether plaintiffs have

---

2 Title VII provides in pertinent part: "(a) It shall be an unlawful employment practice for an employer (1) to fail to refuse to hire or to discharge any individual, or otherwise to discriminate against any individual with respect to his compensation, terms, conditions, or privileges of employment, because of such individual's race, color, religion, sex, or national origin; or (2) to limit, segregate, or classify his employees or applicants for employment in any way which would deprive or tend to deprive any individual of employment opportunities or otherwise adversely affect his status as an employee, because of such individual's race, color, religion, sex, or national origin." (42 U.S.C. §2000e-2(a).)

established a prima facie case of employment discrimination. (Dothard v. Rawlinson, supra, 433 U.S. at 329, 97 S. Ct. 2720.) If a prima facie case has been shown, the burden then shifts to the employer to justify the employment practice in question. (Griggs v. Duke Power Co., supra, 401 U.S. at 432, 91 S. Ct. 849.) If the employer meets his burden of justification, plaintiffs may then show that alternative selection devices exist that would serve the employer's legitimate interests without discriminatory effects. (Albemarle Paper Co. v. Moody, supra, 422 U.S. at 425, 95 S. Ct. 2362.)

[**8] Prima Facie Case of Discrimination

Although the district court recognized that, under Griggs v. Duke Power Co., supra, a prima facie Title VII violation can be established by "the mere showing of a disproportionate impact" of an employment practice on a group protected by Title VII (Blake v. City of Los Angeles, supra, 435 F. Supp. at 63), the court held that the Griggs impact standard could not constitutionally be applied to agencies of state and local government. Relying on Scott v. City of Anniston (N.D .Ala. 1977) 430 F. Supp. 508, the district court reasoned that Congress had no constitutional power to impose on state and local governments antidiscrimination standards greater than those compelled by the equal protection clause of the Fourteenth Amendment. Because the Supreme Court in Washington v. Davis (1976) 426 U.S. 229, 96 S. Ct. 2040, 48 L. Ed. 2d 597, held that proof of discriminatory purpose was needed to establish a violation of the equal protection clause, the same standard must be engrafted on Title VII in actions against state and local governments. The premise of the argument is that "it is simple logic that [**9] a statute can be no broader than its Constitutional base." (430 F. Supp. at 515.) The premise is wrong because it misconceives controlling authority interpreting both the Fourteenth Amendment and Title VII.

Appendix

In Katzenbach v. Morgan (1966) 384 U.S. 641, 86 S. Ct. 1717, 16 L. Ed. 2d 828, the Supreme Court held that [HN1] Congress' power under Section 5 of the Fourteenth Amendment to enforce that amendment by "appropriate [*1373] legislation" is not limited to prohibiting state action that itself violates the Constitution. Katzenbach upheld the constitutionality of Section 4(e) of the Voting Rights Act of 1965, prohibiting certain uses of a literacy test to determine voter qualifications. Although the Supreme Court previously held that use of literacy tests to determine voter qualification did not violate the Fourteenth Amendment (Lassiter v. Northampton County Board of Elections (1959) 360 U.S. 45, 79 S. Ct. 985, 3 L. Ed. 2d 1072), Katzenbach held that Congress could determine that legislation banning use of literacy tests was "appropriate" to enforce the Fourteenth Amendment. In upholding congressional determinations of the efficacy of imposing [**10] bans on the use of such tests to implement the Fourteenth Amendment, the Supreme Court observed that "(i)t is enough that we may be able to perceive a basis" for the legislation. (384 U.S. at 653, 86 S. Ct. at 1725.)

The 1972 amendments extending the coverage of Title VII to state and local governments were enacted by Congress pursuant to Section 5 of the Fourteenth Amendment.[3] (Fitzpatrick v. Bitzer (1976) 427 U.S. 445, 453 & n.9, 96 S. Ct. 2666, 49 L. Ed. 2d 614.) In enacting this legislation, Congress clearly intended to apply the Griggs "impact" standard to state and local governments. As the Supreme Court said in Dothard v. Rawlinson (1977) 433 U.S. 321, 332 n.14, 97 S. Ct. 2720, 2728, 53 L. Ed. 2d 786: "Congress expressly indicated the intent that [HN2] the same Title VII principles be applied to governmental and private

---

3 Section 5 of the Fourteenth Amendment provides: "The Congress shall have power to enforce, by appropriate legislation, the provisions of this article."

Appendix

employers alike. See H.R. Rep. No. 92-238, 92d Cong., 1st Sess., p. 17 (1971); S. Rep. No. 92-415, 92d Cong., 1st Sess., p. 10 (1971)." In reviewing the constitutionality of Congress' extension of the Griggs impact standard to state and local governments, we need only consider whether the 1972 amendments to Title VII were "appropriate [**11] legislation" to enforce the equal protection clause of the Fourteenth Amendment. (Katzenbach v. Morgan, supra, 384 U.S. at 651, 86 S. Ct. 1717.) The 1972 [HN3] amendments are appropriate legislation to enforce the equal protection clause if they are "plainly adapted to that end" and . . . not prohibited by but . . . consistent with "the letter and spirit of the constitution." (Katzenbach v. Morgan, supra, 384 U.S. at 651, 86 S. Ct. at 1724 (Quoting McCulloch v. Maryland (1819) 17 U.S. 316, 4 Wheat. 316, 421, 4 L. Ed. 579).)

Congress enacted the 1972 amendments to Title VII after taking notice of findings "that widespread discrimination against minorities exists in State and local government employment." (H.R. Rep. 92-238, 1972 U.S. Code Cong. & Admin. News, pp. 2137, 2152.) It was plainly within Congress' authority to [**12] determine that implementation of the equal protection clause required extension of the Griggs impact standard to state and local governments. (See Katzenbach v. Morgan, supra, 384 U.S. at 653, 86 S. Ct. 1717.) The means chosen by Congress are rationally related to the goal of enforcing the equal protection clause's prohibition of discrimination. The 1972 amendments are consistent with the letter and spirit of the Constitution. Because Congress acted pursuant to Section 5 of the Fourteenth Amendment, the Tenth Amendment does not foreclose application of the Griggs impact standard to state and local governments (Cf. Fitzpatrick v. Bitzer, supra (Eleventh Amendment does not bar congressional provision for awards of backpay and attorneys' fees in Title VII actions against state)), regardless of

Appendix

any limitations it may impose on Congress' Commerce Clause powers (See National League of Cities v. Usery (1976) 426 U.S. 833, 96 S. Ct. 2465, 49 L. Ed. 2d 245).

We agree with the Seventh Circuit that "since the 1972 Amendments are clearly rationally related to and consistent with 'the letter and spirit' of the Fourteenth Amendment, and the means chosen [**13] were not in themselves unconstitutional, . . . Congress could constitutionally incorporate the Griggs test into the 1972 Amendments." (United States v. City of Chicago (7th Cir. [*1374] 1978) 573 F.2d 416, 423-24.) We therefore hold that Title VII applies the Griggs impact standard to both public and private employers alike, as numerous courts have recognized. (United States v. City of Chicago, supra ; United States v. Virginia (E.D. Va. 1978) 454 F. Supp. 1077, 1084, Overruling Friend v. Leidinger (E.D. Va. 1977) 446 F. Supp. 361, 384-87; Harrington v. Vandalia-Butler Board of Education (S.D. Ohio 1976) 418 F. Supp. 603, 607; See also United States v. City of Buffalo (W.D.N.Y. 1978) 457 F. Supp. 612; League of United Latin American Citizens v. City of Santa Ana (C.D. Cal. 1976) 410 F. Supp. 873; Officers for Justice v. Civil Service Commission of San Francisco (N.D .Cal. 1975) 395 F. Supp. 378.) The district court erred in holding that appellants were required to present evidence of discriminatory intent to defeat the City's motion for summary judgment.

The district court [**14] concluded that even if the Griggs impact standard was applied, appellees would still be entitled to summary judgment. This conclusion was based in part on the district court's holdings that continuation of gender-based job classifications and use of the physical abilities test and height requirement was justified by "business necessity" (issues we discuss Infra). But the district court also concluded that appellants' evidence about the impact of the post-1973 selection

Appendix

standards would be insufficient to establish a prima facie case of sex discrimination even under the Griggs standard.

The City does not claim that appellants failed to show a prima facie case of discrimination under the Griggs standard for the gender-based job classifications in effect before July 1, 1973. The district court recognized that appellees "do not claim that the dual classification system for Policemen and Policewomen in effect during this period would comply with the requirements of Title VII." (Blake v. City of Los Angeles, supra, 435 F. Supp. at 61.) The undisputed total exclusion of women from regular police patrol work and positions above the level of sergeant unmistakably established [**15] a prima facie case of sex discrimination. Thus, the burden shifted to appellees to justify use of these practices after March 24, 1972.[4]

The undisputed evidence revealed that the 5'6 height requirement excluded 87 percent of all women, but only 20 percent of all men between the ages of 18 and 79. The 5'7 requirement excluded 95 percent of all women, but only 32 percent of all men. (See also Note, "Height Standards in Police Employment and the Question of Sex Discrimination," 47 S. Cal. L. Rev. 585, 588 n.13.) The physical abilities test excluded half of all women who took it, but only 2.6 percent of all men who took the test. Although the district court recognized that the height requirement and the physical test had a severe adverse impact on women (435 F. Supp. at 62), it nevertheless concluded that appellants had failed [**16] to show a prima facie case of discrimination arising from the use of either or both of these qualifications.

Despite the court's recognition that most disparities of this

---

4 The question whether defendants met their burden of justification with respect to the gender-based job classification is discussed at pp. 1375–1376, Infra.

Appendix

kind based upon statistical comparisons "often give rise to an inference of racial discrimination," the court concluded that "the same inference does not necessarily follow when a claim of sexual discrimination is asserted." The district court did not explain why gross disparities established through statistical comparisons are probative of racial discrimination, but not similarly probative of sexual discrimination. However, the district court did not have the benefit of Dothard v. Rawlinson (1977) 433 U.S. 321, 97 S. Ct. 2720, 53 L. Ed. 2d 786, which reached the opposite conclusion. Dothard, decided six weeks after Blake, held that a prima facie case of sex discrimination was established from national census statistics showing that a 5'2 height requirement disproportionately excluded women from positions as Alabama Correctional Counselors. Dothard leaves no doubt that [HN4] a showing of disproportionate impact is all that is required to establish a [*1375] prima facie case of discrimination, whether [**17] it be racial or sexual discrimination. "(T)o establish a prima facie case of discrimination, a plaintiff need only show that the facially neutral standards in question select applicants for hire in a significantly discriminatory pattern." (433 U.S. at 329, 97 S. Ct. at 2726.) No inference of discriminatory purpose need be drawn for the statistics to establish prima facie discrimination, because discriminatory intent need not be shown in Title VII actions. (United States v. City of Chicago, supra, 573 F.2d 416.)

The conclusion follows that appellants established a prima facie case of sex discrimination by establishing a disproportionate impact by statistical methods indistinguishable from those in Dothard. Thus, the burden shifted to appellees to justify use of the challenged selection devices. (See, e.g., United States v. City of Buffalo (W.D.N.Y. 1978) 457 F. Supp. 612, 622, 625 (disproportionate impact of written test and height requirements establishes prima facie case of discrimination); Officers for Justice, supra, 395 F. Supp. 378, 380, 382 (disproportionate impact of height requirement and physical test established [**18] prima facie case of discrimination).)

Appellees argued that the disproportionate exclusion of women was not as bad as it looked from the statistics because fewer women than men were interested in police work. The contention is not relevant. The challenged qualifications disproportionately excluded women who were interested enough to apply. Moreover, even if appellees had proved that women were less interested than men in police work, which they did not, the disinterest itself may be traceable to the Police Department's use of selection devices that would disproportionately exclude women. As the Supreme Court observed in Dothard: "The application process might itself not adequately reflect the actual potential applicant pool, since otherwise qualified people might be discouraged from applying because of a self-recognized inability to meet the very standards challenged as being discriminatory." (433 U.S. at 330, 97 S. Ct. at 2727.)[5]

[**19] The fact that there are physical differences between males and females, including the fact that men, as a group, tend to be taller and physically stronger than women as a group, does not erode the prima facie inference of discrimination that flows from a showing of statistically disproportionate

---

5 See Note, "Height Standards in Police Employment and the Question of Sex Discrimination," 47 S. Cal. L. Rev. 585, 598–99 (1974). Nothing this court said in United States v. Ironworkers Local 86 (9th Cir. 1971) 443 F.2d 544, supports appellees' notion that plaintiffs are required to go beyond a showing of disproportionate impact to establish a prima facie violation of Title VII. Our statement that the use of statistics "is conditioned by the existence of proper supportive facts" meant only that statistics should be used properly and should not be used to make inferences they do not support. Appellants here properly used statistics to establish the disproportionate impact of appellees' selection devices. They did not need to make any greater showing to establish a prima facie case of sex discrimination. As we stated in Ironworkers: "It is our belief that the often-cited aphorism, 'statistics often tell much and Courts listen,' has particular application in Title VII cases." (443 F.2d at 551 (footnote omitted).)

impact. "Similarly, the statistical disparity here between male and female performance on the physical agility test establishes the Prima facie case of sex discrimination, with the burden shifting to the defendants to show that the selection device is job-related. If defendants establish to the court's satisfaction that the upper body strength which the test primarily measures is necessary to patrol work, they will prevail, not because the plaintiffs have not established the Prima facie case, but because the necessity for proper job performance of the skills measured by the selection device permits use of the device despite its adverse impact. Defendants' argument errs in that it takes as given the precise fact that the law requires defendants to prove." (Officers for Justice, supra, 395 F. Supp. at 382 n.1.)

"Business Necessity" Defense

Because undisputed evidence before [**20] the district court established a prima [*1376] facie case of sex discrimination, the burden shifted to defendants to show that "business necessity" justified their employment practices. (Griggs, supra, 401 U.S. at 431, 91 S. Ct. 849.) As the Dothard Court explained: [HN5] "once it is thus shown that the employment standards are discriminatory in effect, the employer must meet 'the burden of showing that any given requirement (has) . . . a manifest relationship to the employment in question.' Griggs v. Duke Power Co., (supra,) 401 U.S. at 424, 91 S. Ct. 849, 28 L. Ed. 2d 158." (Dothard, supra, 433 U.S. at 329, 97 S. Ct. at 2726.) Administrative convenience is not a sufficient justification for the employer's practices. Rather, "a discriminatory employment practice must be shown to be necessary to safe and efficient job performance to survive a Title VII challenge." (Dothard, supra, 433 U.S. at 332 n.14, 97 S. Ct. at 2728; DeLaurier v. San Diego Unified School Dist. (9th Cir. 1978) 588 F. 2d 674, 678.)

Appendix

Until July 1, 1973, the LAPD maintained sex-segregated job classifications that barred all women from police patrol [**21] work and prohibited women from being promoted above the level of sergeant. The district court recognized, and appellees conceded, that the dual classifications system did not comply with the requirements of Title VII. Yet the district court, citing Robinson v. Lorillard Corp. (4th Cir. 1971) 444 F.2d 791, held that continuation of the practice was justified by "business necessity." The district court reasoned that "the City made a good faith effort to comply with the Act, and that the time required to put the revised hiring practices into effect was not unreasonable under the circumstances." (Blake, supra, 435 F. Supp. at 61–62.)

The district court misapprehended the impact of Robinson v. Lorillard Corp., supra, 444 F.2d 798. The Robinson court had held that [HN6] "(t)he test is whether there exists an overriding legitimate business purpose such that the practice is necessary to the safe and efficient operation of the business. Thus, the business purpose must be sufficiently compelling to override any racial impact; the challenged practice must effectively carry out the business purpose it is alleged to serve; and there must be available no acceptable [**22] alternative policies or practices which would better accomplish the business purpose advanced, or accomplish it equally well with a lesser differential racial impact." (444 F.2d 791, 798 (footnotes omitted).) There was no evidence before the district court that the use of sex-segregated job classifications was necessary to the safe and efficient operation of the Los Angeles Police Department; moreover, there was abundant evidence that less discriminatory alternatives were available. Indeed, the very fact that the Department has successfully functioned since the dual classification system was abolished suggests that the old system was not required by compelling business purposes. (Cf. Schick v. Bronstein (S.D.N.Y.

Appendix

1978) 447 F. Supp. 333 (height requirement does not serve an important governmental objective as department acknowledged by abolishing it); Schaefer v. Tannian (E.D. Mich. 1974) 394 F. Supp. 1128, Remanded on other grounds (6th Cir. 1976) 538 F. 2d 1234 (former practice restricting women to positions in Women's Division does not meet "business necessity" test).) No changed circumstances have been suggested that would justify [**23] the former prohibition of police patrol assignments for women in light of their subsequent successful performance on patrol. Thus, the LAPD's use of the dual classification system cannot be justified on the grounds of business necessity.

The district court attempted to justify a continuation of the dual classification system after March 24, 1972, on the ground that continuation of the discriminatory system was necessary to maintain a functioning police department during the transition period. The district court's conclusion was based upon its prior erroneous conclusion that the earlier segregative system was justified on business necessity grounds and on the further assumption that a grace period should be implied similar to that accorded private employers when Title VII was first enacted in 1964. The inference properly to [*1377] be drawn by Congress' express grant of a one-year grace period to private employers in 1964, and an omission to grant a similar grace period when public employers were added to Title VII in 1972, is that Congress deliberately withheld any grace period. The legislative history of the 1972 amendments to Title VII enforces our conclusion. "Legislation [**24] to implement this aspect of the Fourteenth Amendment is long overdue." (H. Rep. 92–238, 1972 U.S. Code Cong. & Admin. News, pp. 2137, 2154.) Nothing in the history suggests that Congress intended to permit public employers to delay compliance because immediate compliance with the law would be administratively inconvenient.

Appendix

We conclude that the LAPD's use of sex-segregated job classifications prior to July 1, 1973, violated Title VII. Appellees completely failed to carry their burden of proving a business necessity to justify the Department's discriminatory system maintained in violation of Title VII.

We turn to the selection devices used by LAPD after July 1, 1973. Despite their exclusionary impact on women, the appellees sought to justify the Department's height requirement and physical abilities test as "job-related" measures of qualities important to successful performance of police tasks. The district court accepted the appellees' contentions and held that "(t)he undisputed facts before this court are such that the court must conclude as a matter of law that the qualifying tests are appropriate for the selection of qualified applicants for the job in question." (435 F. Supp. at 66.) [**25] Accordingly, the district court granted summary judgment to the appellees despite the proved exclusionary impact on women of these qualifications in the period after July 1, 1973.

The district court's conclusions appear to be, once again, based upon a misunderstanding of the "business necessity" defense and of the relation of the concept of "job relatedness" to the business necessity defense. *HN7* "Job relatedness" is relevant only for the purpose of trying to prove that the characteristics which the various tests select are directly related to the business necessity. The term "job related" generally is used to refer to the capacity of selection devices to measure traits that are important to successful job performance. The process of determining whether a selection device is sufficiently job related to comply with the requirements of Title VII has been referred to as "validation." It is not enough that the device selects characteristics that may have some rational relationship to job performance; "a discriminatory employment practice must be shown to be necessary to safe and efficient job performance to survive a Title VII challenge." (Dothard, supra, 433 U.S. at 332, n.14, 97 S. Ct. at 2728.) [**26]

Because the "business necessity" defense is very narrow, it is not easy for employers to demonstrate the job relatedness of selection devices shown to be prima facie violations of Title VII. (See Albemarle, supra, 422 U.S. at 425–36, 95 S. Ct. 2362.) An employer who tries to show job relatedness as a matter of law on a motion for summary judgment faces an even greater challenge. [HN8] Summary judgment, of course, is appropriate only if the evidence before the district court shows "that there is no genuine issue as to any material fact and that the moving party is entitled to a judgment as a matter of law." (Fed. R. Civ. P., Rule 56(c).) All of the intendments are against the party who is moving for summary judgment. (Adickes v. Kress & Co. (1970) 398 U.S. 144, 158-61, 90 S. Ct. 1598, 26 L. Ed. 2d 142; United States v. Diebold, Inc. (1962) 369 U.S. 654, 655, 82 S. Ct. 993, 8 L. Ed. 2d 176; Stansifer v. Chrysler Motors Corp. (9th Cir. 1973) 487 F.2d 59, 63.) Meticulous review of the record convinces us that the appellees were not entitled to summary judgment because appellees failed to show that their selection devices were so job related [**27] as to be justified by business necessity.

The district court did not specify the legal standard it applied to determine that the LAPD's selection devices were "appropriate" as a matter of law. Yet it is apparent from the district court's opinion and the evidence in the record that proper [*1378] Title VII standards were not applied. For example, the district court concluded that "(t)he situation here is similar to that in Washington v. Davis, supra, 426 U.S. at 245–46, 96 S. Ct. 2040, where the Supreme Court stated that it was 'untenable' that a verbal abilities test for a police officer position was improper, even if it excluded a large number of Negroes." (435 F. Supp. at

Appendix

66.) However, when the Supreme Court reached this conclusion in Washington v. Davis, it was applying the Constitution and Not Title VII. (Washington v. Davis, supra, 426 U.S. at 245-46, 96 S. Ct. at 2050 ("it is untenable that the Constitution prevents the Government" from using a verbal abilities test).) The Supreme Court recognized that Title VII imposed a more stringent standard. [HN9] "Under Title VII . . . it is an insufficient response to demonstrate some rational [**28] basis for the challenged practices. It is necessary in addition, that they be 'validated' in terms of job performance. . . . However this process proceeds, it involves a more probing judicial review of, and less deference to, the seemingly reasonable acts of administrators and executives than is appropriate under the Constitution. . . ." (Washington v. Davis, supra, 426 U.S. at 246-47, 96 S. Ct. at 2051.[6])

The degree of justification [**29] the district court required for the LAPD's selection devices fell far short of the "business necessity" required by Title VII. The district court stated that because the asserted relationship between the LAPD's selection devices and police duties was "obvious," a less-searching inquiry into their job relatedness was necessary. Noting that there is no single, appropriate method for validating employment test, the district court held that "defendants need only supply competent and relevant evidence on this issue." The district court based its award of summary judgment on defense affidavits, which "for the most part, merely point out what is obvious and needs little proof." (435 F. Supp. at 65.) We disagree with the district court

---

6 The district court's erroneous application of the constitutional standard of Washington v. Davis apparently was the source of its conclusion that the LAPD's selection devices were "appropriate" as a matter of law. Selection devices that are insufficiently job related to comply with Title VII may be able to pass muster when the less stringent constitutional standard is applied. See Smith v. City of East Cleveland (N.D. Ohio 1973) 363 F. Supp. 1131, Rev would in part, aff'd in part sub nom. Smith v. Troyan (6th Cir. 1975) 520 F.2d 492.

that, under Title VII, use of the selection devices could be justified in this manner.

HN10 To justify the use of pre-employment selection devices as a business necessity, an employer must show that the tests or requirements are so closely job related that their use is "necessary to safe and efficient job performance." (Dothard, supra, 433 U.S. at 332 n.14, 97 S. Ct. at 2728.) Thus, the burden of demonstrating the job relatedness of [**30] selection devices cannot be easily satisfied. (See Officers for Justice, supra, 395 F. Supp. at 384 (the large exclusionary impact of certain selection devices requires "a very high degree of persuasion" for defendants to justify their use).) It is not a burden that can be carried by the assertion of an "obvious," but unmeasured, relationship between selection standards and qualities thought necessary for job performance. (Dothard, supra, 433 U.S. at 331, 97 S. Ct. 2720.) Rather, it is essential that selection devices be "validated" by professionally-acceptable methods. (Albemarle, supra, 422 U.S. at 431, 95 S. Ct. 2362; See Washington v. Davis, supra, 426 U.S. at 247 & n.13, 96 S. Ct. 2040.)

In Albemarle, the Supreme Court explained the legal standard for determining the job relatedness of selection devices: *HN11* "discriminatory tests are impermissible unless shown, by professionally acceptable methods, to be 'predictive of or significantly [*1379] correlated with important elements of work behavior which comprise or are relevant to the job or jobs for which candidates are being evaluated.'" (422 U.S. at 431, 95 S. Ct. at 2378.) [**31] The validation process thus involves at least two distinct aspects. The employer first must determine what "important elements of work behavior" are. Then he must demonstrate that his selection devices are "predictive of or significantly correlated" with the elements of work behavior that have been identified as important.

Appendix

^HN12^Validation studies must employ professionally-acceptable methods to increase the likelihood of obtaining trustworthy results. Courts have recognized that a number of validation techniques are professionally acceptable. (See Washington v. Davis, supra, 426 U.S. at 247 n.13, 96 S. Ct. 2040 (describing three professional methods of validation).) The Equal Employment Opportunity Commission ("EEOC") has incorporated these techniques into guidelines that outline minimum standards for professional validation studies. (29 C.F.R. $1607.) The Supreme Court has held that the EEOC guidelines are "entitled to great deference" from courts determining whether employment selection devices comply with Title VII. (Griggs, supra, 401 U.S. at 434, 91 S. Ct. 849. See Washington v. Davis, supra, 426 U.S. at 247 n.13, 96 S. Ct. 2040; [**32] Albemarle, supra, 422 U.S. at 430–35, 95 S. Ct. 2362.) Although compliance with the EEOC guidelines is not mandatory, an employer's burden of justification is much heavier if the guidelines have not been followed. (United States v. City of Chicago, supra, 573 F.2d at 427.)[7]

When the proper legal standard for determining business necessity under Title VII is applied to the evidence in the record, it is apparent that appellees [**33] were not entitled to summary judgment. Appellees failed to establish that the LAPD's selection devices were so closely job related that their use was justified by business necessity. At most, they showed that there was

---

7 The EEOC guidelines are designed to help employers determine whether their selection devices comply with Title VII: The reason that it is important to follow the EEOC guidelines is because they incorporate professional procedures for test validation that are thought to insure more reliable results. The fact that it may be difficult to professionally validate selection devices does not excuse non-compliance with professional procedures; rather, it suggest that employers should be more cautious in employing selection devices that have discriminatory impacts. Shorter officers may have certain advantages in observing field situations (E. g., the ability to look under objects, the ability to squeeze through narrow passageways) that taller officers lack. The City failed to demonstrate that the net advantages of height in observing field situations were sufficiently great to make the 5'6 height requirement a business necessity. [**35]

Appendix

some rational relationship between their selection devices and certain elements of job performance by police. While this may have been sufficient to satisfy the district court's relaxed standard of review, it fell far short of demonstrating business necessity for the selection devices.

Appellees offered two general justifications for use of the height requirement. They argued that taller officers could more easily control resisting suspects with a minimum use of force and that taller officers had better capacities to observe field situations. They made no attempt to verify empirically the latter justification and the affidavits submitted in support of this theory were insufficient to warrant summary judgment on the issue. (See United States v. City of Buffalo, supra, 457 F. Supp. at 625–26; United States v. Virginia, supra, 454 F. Supp. at 1088 (opinion evidence that "height and weight are useful in police work" does not prove job relatedness, [**34] but rather only "a good faith belief of job-relatedness").)[8] To demonstrate business necessity under the former rationale, appellees would have to show: (1) that subduing suspects with a minimum use of force is an important element of job performance by police, and (2) that height is so significantly correlated with minimization of force in suspect control as to be necessary to safe and efficient job performance by police. Although the Police Department's job analysis indicated that control of resisting suspects occupies only a minor part of police duties, for present purposes we assume, Arguendo, that it is permissible to require all police to be capable of subduing suspects with a minimum use of force.[9] Even on [*1380] these

---

8 See the discussion of the availability of less discriminatory alternatives, Infra at 1381. The City's job analysis concluded that an officer had to wrestle with a suspect only once every 20 watches and that an officer was kicked or hit by a subject once every 33 watches.

9 **HN13** The EEOC guidelines recognize that validation studies should include persons who are excluded by the selection standards in question. (See 29 C.F.R. §1607.5)

Appendix

assumptions, appellees failed to demonstrate that the LAPD's height requirement is so significantly correlated with minimization of force as to make it a business necessity.

The City presented the results of two empirical studies in an effort to validate the height requirement. The first study attempted to correlate the height of police officers with resistance offered by suspects and force employed by officers. Based on questionnaires returned by arresting officers, the study concluded that while "(t)here is no relationship between officer height and suspect resistance, . . . (s)horter officers use strong force more often than do taller officers." The latter conclusion was based on the study's finding that "strong force" was used in 5 percent of all arrests by officers 5'8 and 5'9 in height, 4.5 percent of arrests by officers 6' and 6'1 in height, and 3.8 percent of arrests by police 6'2 and taller. The second study, based on simulations of police subduing suspects, concluded that taller [**36] officers generally perform the bar-arm control hold better than shorter officers. Appellees argued that shorter officers would be forced to resort to stronger force more frequently than taller officers who could better perform the bar-arm control hold.

Appellants vigorously disputed both the methodology and the findings of these studies. The studies failed to show that persons shorter than 5'6 (the level of the height requirement) would be more likely to use strong force than taller persons, because no data was reported for persons shorter than 5'6. Moreover, they noted that the studies failed to control for the effect of experience and job assignment. Appellants also argued that rater bias may have affected the results of the bar-arm control hold study and that neither study had attempted to differentially validate the effect of height by sex.

Appellants' attacks on the methodology of the studies

Appendix

are more than mere quibbles. Because neither of the studies included persons shorter than 5'6, the studies are of little value in determining whether the height requirement excludes individuals who would be more likely to resort to strong force.[10] This criticism is particularly [**37] telling in light of appellants' allegation that unreported data in one of the studies showed that persons 5'7 in height use strong force less frequently than persons between 5'8 and 5'11 in height. The lack of controls for experience may have systematically biased the studies' results because shorter officers may have been less experienced, given the previous reduction in the LAPD's height requirement.[11] The first study's ambiguous definition of "strong force" and the lack of controls for the level of suspect resistance, make it of little value in determining whether shorter officers use more force than would be necessary for taller officers to use.[12] The

---

10 The LAPD lowered its height requirement from 5'9 to 5'8 in 1954. Thus, all 20-year veterans on the force would be at least 5'9 in height. If the shorter officers in the study had less job experience, the study's results may be the product of job experience and not height. (See Boston Chapter, NAACP, Inc. v. Beecher (1st Cir. 1974) 504 F.2d 1017, 1025; League of United Latin American Citizens, supra, 410 F. Supp. at 904; Officers for Justice, supra, 395 F. Supp. at 380–81; 29 C.F.R. §1607.5(b)(4).

11 "Strong force" included everything from firing a weapon to use of a baton, sap or bar-arm control hold. The study failed to distinguish between these different levels of force when reporting the results, even though the premise of the second study was that shorter officers would use the bar-arm control hold less frequently than other forms of strong force. Although data on suspect resistance were reported, no controls were introduced in the study to determine if the force used was excessive in relation to the level of suspect resistance. Although defendants argued that the study showed that police 5'8 and 5'9 used strong force 31 percent more frequently than officers 6'2 and taller, in fact all the study showed was that there was a 95 percent chance that the level of force used by officers 6'2 and taller was different from the level of force used by officers 5'8 and 5'9. [**39]

12 See Albemarle, supra, 422 U.S. at 433 n.32, 95 S. Ct. at 2379 ("It cannot escape notice that Albemarle's study was conducted by plant officials, without neutral, on-the-scene oversight, at a time when this litigation was about to come to trial. Studies so closely controlled by an interested party in litigation must be examined with great care.") We express no opinion on the question whether appellees will be able to make a successful showing of business necessity at trial. We only hold that the evidence they presented in support of their motion for summary judgment was insufficient to meet their burden of demonstrating business necessity for the height requirement.

possibility [*1381] of rater bias in the second study is a potentially serious defect, particularly in light of appellants' allegations that the raters were interested in the litigation and aware of the purpose of the study.[13] Appellees' suggestion that methodological defects cannot controvert the probative force of their studies is amply refuted by existing case law. (Albemarle, supra, 422 U.S. at 425–35, 95 S. Ct. 2362; Boston Chapter, NAACP, Inc. v. Beecher (1st Cir. 1974) 504 F.2d 1017; [**38] League of United Latin American Citizens, supra, 410 F. Supp. 873; Officers for Justice, supra, 395 F. Supp. 378.)

Appellants did not confine their attack to methodological disputes; they also introduced evidence of contrary findings of other studies. They discovered that the City had been involved in four other studies that investigated the relationship of height to job performance by police. Each of these studies had concluded that height was not significantly related to police job performance. One of the studies, the "Drawn Weapon Frequency Survey," had found no correlation between police officer height and the frequency of drawing a weapon. This finding directly contradicted appellees' contention that shorter officers are more likely to use strong force, particularly force stronger than the bar-arm control hold. They also produced numerous [**40]

---

[13] The five events on the physical abilities test were: wall scale (running a total of 50 yards and scaling a smooth wall six feet high); hang (running a total of 50 yards and hanging from a chinning bar, using an overhand grip, for one minute); weight drag (running 50 feet and dragging a dead weight of 140 pounds for 50 feet); tremor (running 50 yards and holding a stylus steady for 17 seconds); endurance (running as many laps around a one-eighth mile track as possible in 12 minutes). The 11 measures of success in police academy training were: academy average (combination of academic performance, performance in physical training, marksmanship, and peer evaluations); target shooting III (score received on final test of target shooting performance given in the academy); combat shooting II and III (scores received on last two tests of combat shooting performance); physical training I, II, and III (scores received in the evaluations of performance in the academy physical training exercise program at three different points during training); self-defense (evaluation of self-defense skills at academy); peer evaluations (at 8 weeks and 16 weeks); graduation (whether the officer completed the police academy training course).

Appendix

depositions from police officials in other major American cities that have reduced or eliminated minimum height requirements for police. This testimony indicated that persons under 5'6 in height can, and are, safely and efficiently performing all aspects of police work.

Viewing all this evidence in the light most favorable to appellants, appellees failed to establish that the LAPD's height requirement was so manifestly job related as to be justified by business necessity.[14]

Appellees sought to demonstrate the job relatedness of the LAPD's physical abilities test through the results of two validation studies. The first study attempted to correlate performance on the five events [**41] used in the physical abilities test with 11 measures of success during police academy training.[15] The study found that four of the five events used in the physical abilities test had some significant correlation with at least seven of the 11 measures of training success. The second study concluded that performance on the physical abilities test had some significant correlation with performance of foot pursuit, field shooting, and emergency rescue simulations. Appellees also submitted affidavits detailing the procedures that were used to develop the physical abilities test.

---

14 See Officers for Justice, supra, 395 F. Supp. at 385; 29 C.F.R. §1607.11 ("no new test or other employee selection standard can be imposed upon a class of individuals protected by Title VII who, but for prior discrimination, would have been granted the opportunity to qualify under less stringent selection standards previously in force.")

15 Although appellees' claim that 4 of the 5 events used in the physical abilities test had some significant correlation with at least 7 of the 11 measures of training success sounds impressive, a closer analysis of the study reveals far less impressive results. The 11 measures of academy performance were based only on measures of shooting ability, physical ability, self-defense skills, and peer evaluations. The magnitude of the correlations for all but the 3 measures of physical training were always less than $r = .3$, indicating that less than 9 percent of the variance in the academy performance measures was explained by performance on the components of the physical abilities test. (See Johnston, Econometric Methods 35 (1972).) [**44]

Appendix

[**42] Appellants attacked both the methodology and conclusions of the validation studies, [*1382] contending that because the studies excluded persons who had failed the physical abilities test, they were of little value in demonstrating that the physical test excluded persons who would be unlikely to succeed as police officers. Moreover, appellants noted that the LAPD had not used a pre-employment physical test during the five years prior to the time when women were first permitted to apply for police officer positions. They questioned whether the physical test had been developed to test a representative sample of major or critical work behaviors as revealed by a careful job analysis. Extensive deposition testimony was presented indicating that police departments in other major American cities that do not use pre-employment physical abilities tests have experienced satisfactory job performance by police. Finally, they also questioned appellees' failure to differentially validate the physical abilities test by sex.

Viewing the record in the light most favorable to appellants, we cannot conclude that appellees met their burden of justifying use of the physical abilities test as [**43] a business necessity. The fact that the LAPD hired thousands of male police officers between 1968 and 1973 without using any pre-employment physical test suggests that the practice is not essential to safe and efficient job performance.[16] Moreover, the modest correlations between scores of successful candidates on the physical test and scores during academy training on peer evaluations, tests of physical ability and shooting skills, hardly establish that the physical test is

---

16 Appellees offered conclusory affidavits to the effect that the measures of academy performance were themselves significantly related to job performance. For example, a police academy instructor justified the peer evaluation measures on the grounds that "(t)he ability to establish a favorable rapport with peers and the public is an essential requirement for the professional Police Officer." While we do not question the desirability of having police officers with social skills, appellees cannot demonstrate that a physical test is job related because it measures the capacity of police to develop rapport with others in training.

Appendix

so intimately related to job performance as to be a business necessity.[17] Appellees had to demonstrate that their measures of training success are themselves significantly related to important aspects of job performance and they utterly failed to do so.[18] [**45] [*1383] Summary judgment on appellants' Title VII claims relating to appellees' post-1973 selection devices must be reversed.[19]

Availability of Less Discriminatory Alternatives

Even if an employer meets his burden of demonstrating business necessity, Title VII plaintiffs may prevail if they show that alternative selection devices are available that would serve the employer's legitimate interests without discriminatory effects. (Albemarle, supra, 422 U.S. at 425, 95 S. Ct. 2362.) Although the judgment must be reversed on the other grounds heretofore discussed, we nevertheless reach the alternative selection [**46]

---

17 We do not read Washington v. Davis, supra, 426 U.S. at 250–51, 96 S. Ct. 2040, as establishing that selection devices may be validated for Title VII purposes without reference to job performance. Washington v. Davis simply approved the use of a verbal abilities test to determine whether applicants had the capacity to understand a police training program. (See Washington v. Davis, supra, 426 U.S. at 255–56, 96 S. Ct. 2040 (Stevens, J., concurring); But see National Education Association v. South Carolina (1978) 434 U.S. 1026, 98 S. Ct. 756, 54 L. Ed. 2d 775 (White, J., dissenting from summary affirmance).) If employers were permitted to validate selection devices without reference to job performance, then non-job-related selection devices could always be validated through the simple expedient of employing them at both the pre-training and training stage. As the Second Circuit noted in Vulcan Society v. Civil Service Commission (2d Cir. 1973) 490 F.2d 387, 396 n.11: "The danger of distortion in this regard is particularly acute, since performance in the probationary school is also evaluated by means of a written examination. Thus, there is a distinct possibility that a claim that the qualifying examination tests for ability to learn in the probationary school is in fact no more than a claim that performance on the written qualifying examination predicts with reasonable accuracy performance on the written probationary examination. Without evidence that the second examination is job-related, such a demonstration is barren indeed."

18 Here, the strongest correlation shown by appellees' validation study was between performance on the pre-training physical abilities test and performance during training on physical abilities tests. This is not sufficient to validate the use of the physical abilities test without an independent demonstration of its relation to job performance.

19 Because the district court premised its rejection of appellants' challenges to other employment practices of the LAPD on its holding that the physical test and height requirement were appropriate selection devices as a matter of law, we need not discuss the other employment practices appellants challenge. We reverse the district court's award of summary judgment in its entirety.

Appendix

aspect of this Title VII action to avoid repetition of error that occurred in granting the motion for summary judgment.

The district court concluded that the LAPD "could be so structured as to permit the employment of an equal percentage of male and female applicants," (435 F. Supp. at 65.) However, the court held that the LAPD could not be required to adopt less discriminatory alternatives if they required modification of departmental policies. In support of this proposition, the district court cited Rizzo v. Goode (1976) 423 U.S. 362, 96 S. Ct. 598, 46 L. Ed. 2d 561. Compliance with the commands of Title VII may indeed require modification of departmental policies, and nothing in Rizzo v. Goode suggests that the contrary is true.

In Rizzo, the Supreme Court held that in absence of showing direct responsibility on the part of police officials for violations of rights by a small percentage of the police force, federal courts lacked power to require a local police department to adopt a new civilian complaint processing procedure. In our Title VII case, unlike the situation in Rizzo, the appellees here are themselves charged with violations of federal [**47] law. Acting pursuant to its constitutional authority, Congress has removed whatever latitude local police departments may ever have had to engage in sex discrimination. So long as non-discriminatory alternatives serve the legitimate interests of the police in safe and efficient job performance, police departments cannot pursue policies that require the use of selection standards that are themselves prima facie violations of Title VII.

III

EQUAL PROTECTION CLAIMS

The district court awarded summary judgment to appellees on the claims founded on the equal protection clause of the Fourteenth Amendment and the Civil Rights Act of 1871.

(42 U.S.C. 1983.) The district court held that neither the sex-segregated job classifications used by the LAPD before July 1, 1973, nor the selection devices used by the LAPD after that date, denied appellants equal protection. Because the statutory prohibition of sex discrimination embodied in Title VII is more comprehensive than the constitutional ban, it was unnecessary for the district court to reach the constitutional issue with respect to the selection devices used only after Title VII became applicable to the LAPD. Thus, [**48] we express no opinion about the district court's conclusion that no evidence of discriminatory intent supported appellants' constitutional attack on the employment practices used by the LAPD after July 1, 1973. Because the sex-segregated job classifications were used before Title VII became applicable to the LAPD, we review the district court's holding that this practice [*1384] did not contravene the equal protection clause.

As the district court recognized, undisputed evidence established that the LAPD used a gender-based system of job classifications during the period before Title VII became applicable to agencies of local government. Separate job classifications existed for men and women. Policewomen were not permitted to undertake regular patrol assignments, and they were barred from promotion above the level of sergeant.

In Craig v. Boren (1976) 429 U.S. 190, 97 S. Ct. 451, 50 L. Ed. 2d 397 the Supreme Court outlined the standard of review to be applied to gender-based classifications under the equal protection clause. The Court held that: *HN14* "classifications by gender must serve important governmental objectives and must be substantially related to the achievement [**49] of those objectives." (429 U.S. at 197, 97 S. Ct. at 457.) Among the objectives that have been held insufficient to justify gender-based classifications are "administrative ease and convenience," and

Appendix

"fostering 'old notions' of role typing." (Craig v. Boren, supra, 429 U.S. at 198, 97 S. Ct. at 457; Frontiero v. Richardson (1973) 411 U.S. 677, 93 S. Ct. 1764, 36 L. Ed. 2d 583; Stanton v. Stanton (1975) 421 U.S. 7, 95 S. Ct. 1373, 43 L. Ed. 2d 688.

The district court purported to apply the Craig v. Boren standard to determine that the LAPD's gender-based job classifications did not violate the equal protection clause. The district court first concluded "that the qualities of disposition, and physical size and strength are substantially related to the important governmental objective of providing an effective police force." (435 F. Supp. at 61.) The district court then considered whether gender was substantially related to the selection of police officers with these qualities. Citing Schlesinger v. Ballard (1975) 419 U.S. 498, 95 S. Ct. 572, 42 L. Ed. 2d 610, the district court said that "(t)he Supreme [**50] Court has at least implicitly approved the exclusive use of men in combat positions.... The same factors of size, strength, and disposition which make a man a more effective combatant than a woman in the event of war, also act to make a man a better Police Officer than a woman in those areas where physical tasks are involved." (435 F. Supp. at 60.) Thus, the district court concluded that the LAPD's job classifications did not violate the equal protection clause because "a classification based upon gender is substantially related to and serves (the) important governmental objective (of providing an effective police force)." (435 F. Supp. at 61.)

Even if we assume, Arguendo, that qualities of size, strength, and disposition are substantially related to the important objective of maintaining an effective police, it does not follow that women may constitutionally be excluded from serving as police officers. It must also be demonstrated that women lack the requisite size, strength, and disposition to be effective police. The Supreme Court's decision in Schlesinger v. Ballard provides no support for the proposition that women cannot be effective police [**51] or combatants. The issue in Schlesinger v. Ballard was not whether women could be excluded from combat duty, but whether the "disadvantageous conditions suffered by women" who were excluded from certain aspects of military service could be remedied by providing them more time before subjecting them to mandatory discharges. (Schlesinger v. Ballard, supra, 419 U.S. at 508, 95 S. Ct. at 577 ("Appellee has not challenged the current restrictions on women officers' participation in combat and in most sea duty."); Craig v. Boren, supra, 429 U.S. at 198 n.6, 97 S. Ct. at 457 ("Kahn v. Shevin, 416 U.S. 351, 94 S. Ct. 1734, 40 L. Ed. 2d 189 (1974) and Schlesinger v. Ballard, 419 U.S. 498, 95 S. Ct. 572, 42 L. Ed. 2d 610 (1975), upholding the use of gender-based classifications, rested upon the Court's perception of the laudatory purposes of those laws as remedying disadvantageous conditions suffered by women in economic and military life.").) The Supreme Court held that a gender-based classification could be used to remedy a disadvantage shared by all members of one sex to which it applied. (Schlesinger v. Ballard, supra, 419 U.S. at 508–10, 95 S. Ct. 572.) [**52] [*1385] Thus, Schlesinger v. Ballard provides no authority to support the exclusion of women from police patrol work, though it might support the constitutionality of actions to compensate women for that disadvantage.

It is undisputed that not all women lack the requisite traits to be effective police officers. The LAPD's experience since abolition of its gender-based job classifications amply demonstrates that women can be effective police. The district court did not dispute this. Instead, the court held that "(t)here has to be only a substantial relationship between the relevant traits and gender," in order to justify the exclusion of all persons of one gender from positions requiring the relevant traits. (435 F. Supp. at 60.)

Appendix

This conclusion is contrary to the clear teachings of a long line of Supreme Court decisions that [HN15] "archaic and overbroad generalizations" cannot justify "statutes employing gender as an inaccurate proxy for other, more germane bases of classification." (Craig v. Boren, supra, 429 U.S. at 198, 97 S. Ct. at 457; Weinberger v. Wiesenfield (1975) 420 U.S. 636, 95 S. Ct. 1225, 43 L. Ed. 2d 514 (financial position [**53] of working women); Frontiero v. Richardson (1973) 411 U.S. 677, 93 S. Ct. 1764, 36 L. Ed. 2d 583 (financial position of servicewomen); Reed v. Reed (1971) 404 U.S. 71, 92 S. Ct. 251, 30 L. Ed. 2d 225 (capabilities of women to be estate administrators). Cf. Schlesinger v. Ballard, supra, 419 U.S. at 508, 95 S. Ct. 572.) The fact that persons of one gender are less likely to possess certain traits than persons of the other gender cannot justify a gender-based classification unless the congruence between gender and possession of the traits is so great, and the prospects of developing more accurate proxies for the traits are so small, that the gender-based classification cannot be said to be based on administrative ease or convenience. (Craig v. Boren, supra, 429 U.S. at 198, 97 S. Ct. 451.)

We hold that undisputed facts before the district court established that the gender-based job classifications used before Title VII became applicable to the LAPD violated the equal protection clause of the Fourteenth Amendment. Exclusion of all women from regular police patrol duties and from promotions above the level of sergeant was not substantially [**54] related to the achievement of an important governmental objective. Because women could have served as effective police officers during this period, we can only conclude that the dual classification system was designed to serve administrative convenience and not to promote the maintenance of an effective police force. Thus, the gender-based classification

Appendix

system violated the equal protection clause, and appellees were not entitled to summary judgment on this portion of the constitutional claim.

IV
CROSS-APPEAL OF THE CLASS CERTIFICATION

The district court certified this action as a class action under Rules 23(b) (1) and 23(b)(2) of the Federal Rules of Civil Procedure on June 10, 1976.[20] On July 11, 1977, the district court entered summary judgment in favor of appellees. After appellants filed an appeal from the judgment, appellees filed a cross-appeal from the judgment "insofar as that judgment was based upon the Court's "Order Certifying Class." Appellees on cross-appeal ask this court, in the event any issue is remanded for further proceedings, to instruct the district court to re-examine the class certification order. They suggest that the named appellants [*1386] [**55] might not adequately represent the interests of the certified class, but they fail to specify any reasons for this fear.

HN16 Orders granting class certification normally are not appealable because they are not "final decisions" [**56] within the meaning of 28 U.S.C. §1291. (Blackie v. Barrack (9th Cir. 1975) 524 F.2d 891.) Appellees are able to bring their cross-appeal only because the district court's award of summary judgment to them constituted a final judgment. Because the district

---

20 The certified class was composed of "all women who are: a) Current and future applicants for all sworn positions at the Los Angeles Police Department, including, but not limited to, current and future applicants for the position of 'police officer'; b) All past applicants for sworn positions at the Los Angeles Police Department who applied within the applicable statute of limitations period, including, but not limited to, applicants for the position of 'police officer' (or pre-July 1973 equivalent); c) Current and future employees in sworn positions at the Los Angeles Police Department; d) Current and future retirees from such sworn positions at the Los Angeles Police Department who will be eligible for retirement payments or benefits within the applicable statute of limitations period."

court's judgment was in appellees' favor, their cross-appeal from the class certification order would have become moot if we had affirmed the district court's judgment. The only reason the class certification issue has not become moot is because we reverse the district court's summary judgment award and remand the case for further proceedings. Under these circumstances, it would not be appropriate for us to decide appellees' cross-appeal challenging the class certification order. The same considerations that normally bar interlocutory review of class certification orders (See Blackie v. Barrack, supra, 524 F.2d at 895; See also Coopers & Lybrand v. Livesay (1978) 437 U.S. 463, 473, 98 S. Ct. 2454, 2460, 57 L. Ed. 2d 351 ("The potential waste of judicial resources is plain.")), persuade us that we should not now review the class certification order merely because [**57] the district court erroneously entered summary judgment for appellees. Because we remand the case for further proceedings, the class certification order may be modified later. (Fed.R.Civ. Proc. 23(c)(1).) Nothing precludes appellees from obtaining review of the order after final judgment ultimately is entered. (Coopers & Lybrand v. Livesay, supra, 437 U.S. at 469, 98 S. Ct. 2454.)

The judgment is reversed and the cause is remanded to the district court for further proceedings consistent with the views herein expressed. Appellants are awarded their costs together with a reasonable attorney's fee as costs for the successful prosecution of this appeal. (42 U.S.C. §2000e-5(k).)

ACKNOWLEDGMENTS

By the time I met Fanchon Blake in 2010, she was 88 years old and had already been working on her manuscript for years. There wasn't just one draft, there were multiple drafts of multiple chapters, including a 25,000-word section about her involuntary recall by the Army to Japan and extensive personal material ranging from her romantic missteps to her battle with alcohol. Inherently she knew she needed someone to help her focus her book. That was not always the easiest task. Fanchon was feisty as hell, and nothing if not stubborn and determined to see things done her way. In the end, however, she realized that her determination to fight for equality was the focus of her memoir—indeed the focus of her life.

Fanchon knew this was an important story, so she wanted to find a publisher for her memoir. Even though that never worked out, she remained unwilling to self-publish. So the manuscript sat for years. Thankfully, she was able to hold in her hands a bound copy of her memoir before she passed in 2015 at the age of 93—at the time, I had an apparatus that allowed me to print and bind books at my home. But the fact that we had not managed to get Fanchon's story out into the world haunted me.

Acknowledgments

In the spring of 2020, Viet Trinh, a Yale doctoral candidate researching race and rebellion in Los Angeles, reached out saying he had been unable to find the memoir that Fanchon had talked about in so many articles. I had already been feeling like I needed to do something to bring Fanchon's book out of mothballs. It was time to pull the trigger and self-publish. And because November 20, 2020 marks the fortieth anniversary of the historic consent decree that would establish equitable hiring goals and standards for the LAPD, it had to happen fast.

After a renewed perspective that only years of distance can bring, it was clear that the manuscript needed further honing. So I dove back into the research files and wove in pertinent historical and legal facts. I compared the draft to Fanchon's original manuscript, as well as multiple drafts of chapters, and added material from those. And I pruned any content that wasn't relevant to Fanchon's experience at the LAPD or to the lawsuit she had filed.

Even after working so closely with her, I can't imagine how hard it must have been to sue a department she loved so much and so aspired to rise in. The fact that she did not pick the easy route changed the face of policing for minorities as well as women, not just in Los Angeles but across the country. We can all be grateful to her for that.

I wish Fanchon were alive to write her own acknowledgments. I know that despite the hardships, she would have thanked the LAPD. I know she was more than grateful to her attorneys Tom Hunt and Tim Flynn (now McFlynn), whom she adored. I know that attorney Barbara Schlei, Judge Jill Jakes, Communications Consultant Linda Douglass, Congresswoman Pat Schroeder, Los Angeles City Council member Pat Russell, Judge Joan Dempsey Klein, and the late Deputy Mayor Eleanor Chambers all had a special place in Fanchon's heart and that

Acknowledgments

she felt unending gratitude toward them. I fear that I'm leaving out a lot of people whom Fanchon would have acknowledged in these pages, but I do want to add that Joseph Wambaugh's support of this project, and of Fanchon, meant the world to her.

On my end, I would like to thank Fanchon's niece Shelley Maurice-Maier, who introduced me to her aunt after I had helped Shelley in a writing coach capacity with her first book, as well as historian Viet Trinh, who unwittingly prompted me to finally birth this memoir. Along the way, book designer Lieve Maas created a cover that does honor to Fanchon and to the book itself. Kelly Byrd's copyedit made me rest easy knowing that a skilled professional had my back. And Keri Barnum's input and help on the promotional front will hopefully give this memoir the wings it deserves.

Ironically, Fanchon's book could not have hit at a better time, for this is not just a book about overcoming sex discrimination. Her insights into the police status quo—including the propensity to violence—could have been written today and, along with her push to lift up female officers, provide answers to many current questions about potential police department restructuring. A recent CNN headline says it all: "Want to Reform the Police? Hire More Women."

Even more importantly, Fanchon's case reminds us that while legal recourse can often seem unbearably slow, changing laws changes society. May we all be brave enough to follow her example.

Linden Gross
July, 2020

Fanchon Blake joined the LAPD in 1948, determined to rise in the ranks despite rampant gender discrimination. Blake's persistence resulted in a promotion to sergeant after nearly two decades of service, but when official policy denied her any further advancement, she took the LAPD to court. Her resulting historic legal victory would affect police departments around the country.

Linden Gross is a two-time *New York Times*–bestselling writer who coaches both aspiring and bestselling authors. The ghostwriter for Julia "Butterfly" Hill's national bestseller *The Legacy of Luna*, Gross also authored *To Have or To Harm* (now *Surviving a Stalker*), the first book ever published about the stalking of ordinary people.

INTEGRATED MEDIA

Find a full list of our authors and
titles at www.openroadmedia.com

FOLLOW US
@OpenRoadMedia

EARLY BIRD BOOKS
FRESH DEALS, DELIVERED DAILY

Love to read?
Love great sales?

Get fantastic deals on bestselling ebooks delivered to your inbox every day!

Sign up today at
earlybirdbooks.com/book

www.ingramcontent.com/pod-product-compliance
Lightning Source LLC
Chambersburg PA
CBHW020358080526
44584CB00014B/1081